A LARGER MEMORY

Also by Ronald Takaki:

A
LARGER
MEMORY

*A History of Our Diversity,
with Voices*

Ronald Takaki

LITTLE, BROWN AND COMPANY
Boston   New York   Toronto   London

Copyright © 1998 by Ronald Takaki

Library of Congress Cataloging-in-Publication Data

Takaki, Ronald T.
A larger memory : a history of our diversity, with voices /
Ronald Takaki.
p. cm.
Includes bibliographical references.
ISBN 0-316-83169-7. — ISBN 0-316-31162-6 (pbk.)
1. Pluralism (Social sciences) — United States — History —
Sources. 2. Minorities — United States — Biography.
3. United States — Ethnic relations — Sources.
4. United States — Race relations — Sources. I. Title.
E184.A1T3375   1998
305.8'00973 — dc21   98-12931

MV-NY

Published simultaneously in Canada by
Little, Brown & Company (Canada) Limited

PRINTED IN THE UNITED STATES OF AMERICA

For Carol

Collaborator in challenging
the master narrative of
American history

In the sharing of our varied stories,
We create
Our community of a larger memory.

— RONALD TAKAKI

Contents

Contents

Part Four: A Multicultural Destiny

Contents

Contents

Epilogue

A Larger Memory

PROLOGUE

The "Varied Carols" of America: A Democratic History

———————▶ ◀———————

T WENTY YEARS AGO, my uncle Richard and I were "talking
story" in his backyard. We were enjoying a relaxed conversation in the warmth of the Hawaiian sunshine when I told him that
I was writing a book about the history of race relations, to be entitled *Iron Cages: Race and Culture in Nineteenth-Century America.* He listened
intently, proud of his nephew who had left the islands to attend
college and was now a university professor on sabbatical from
Berkeley. Suddenly, his eyes lit up, and he exclaimed in mellifluous
pidgin English: "Hey, Ronald, why you no go write a book about
us, huh? Why you only write about those folks on the mainland?
What about us in Hawaii? Your mother was born on the plantation.
And I was born on the plantation. What about us?"

My uncle Richard's request led me to undertake a study of the
immigrant laborers of Hawaii's sugar plantations. As I was working
on that book, I found myself rethinking the way I wrote history.
Until then, my scholarship had focused on elite policymakers like
Thomas Jefferson and Andrew Jackson, and had employed the the-
oretical language and complex concepts of intellectuals like Max
Weber and Antonio Gramsci. I was writing highly analytical work,
with my fellow academics in mind. For my uncle Richard, however, I wanted to write a democratic history — a history "of the
people, by the people, for the people."[1]

My aim this time was to offer a history that would still be scholarly but that my uncle and the people of Hawaii would find inter-

3

esting and readable. This desire opened the door for me to write narrative history, with the inclusion of stories and voices. Let the workers themselves give us their eye-level view of the cane fields. Let them tell, in their own words, what it was like to be rudely awakened by the shrieking five A.M. whistle, sweat as they cut the stalks towering over them, relax as they soaked in the steaming bath of a furo after work, raise children in crowded camps, and shout for higher wages in strike demonstrations. This would be history "by" the people.

My study of the past from "the bottom up" led to the writing of *Pau Hana: Plantation Life and Labor in Hawaii*, then *Strangers from a Different Shore: A History of Asian Americans*, and most recently, *A Different Mirror: A History of Multicultural America*.

A Larger Memory reflects my continued practice of presenting history through "voices." In the earlier studies, I wove pieces of recollections into my historical narrative; here the people become their own narrators. To connect their stories to our country's history and to place them within a conceptual chronology, I have written chapters that study the debate under way from the founding of Jamestown to the current "culture wars" over who is an American and what America stands for — a clash of different visions of our nation presented by John Winthrop and Mary Rowlandson, Thomas Jefferson and Abraham Lincoln, and Frederick Jackson Turner and Bill Clinton.

In their stories, the men and women of multicultural America convey a special expressiveness and elusive complexity as well as intonations and emotions that cannot be felicitously re-presented when paraphrased or quoted in fragments by scholars. The narrators also vividly describe the crisscrossings between their personal lives and the events of history. As I read and selected these documents, I often found myself stirred by the ways people responded to circumstances not of their choosing. Always, I was reminded that people are history: their experiences, feelings, adjustments, imaginings, hopes, uncertainties, dreams, fears, regrets, tragedies, and triumphs compose our past. Everywhere, I found their stories bursting in the telling.

This is a view of history I have been sharing with my students. Our parents and grandparents, I have been telling them, are worthy of scholarly attention: they have been actors in history, making choices as they left their homelands and settled in America. They helped to transform their adopted country, and, in turn, were themselves changed as they became Americans. The memories gathered in this study come from autobiographies, interviews, oral histories, letters, and solitary ruminations. Although the inclusion of all of our racial and ethnic diversity would be impossible in any single volume, I selected stories from a broad range of peoples with roots reaching to Europe, Africa, Asia, and the Americas. History is usually "his story," and I made certain to present also "her story."

The coming century will be a time when we will all be minorities in the United States. More than ever before, we find ourselves urged to reexamine our past and re-remember more inclusively who we have been as Americans. The "voices" of multicultural America represent what Walt Whitman called the "varied carols" of America. The people in this study challenge the master narrative of American history — the widely held but inaccurate view that Americans originally came just from Europe and that "American" means white or European in ancestry. They present discrete memories of individuals as members of different ethnic and racial communities, but together they carry a common message. They affirm what Herman Melville observed over a hundred years ago: "You cannot spill a drop of American blood, without spilling the blood of the whole world. We are not a narrow tribe." These tellers of memories also assure us that we have always been both culturally diverse and bound together in a nation dedicated to the "proposition" of equality. Finally, when broadly shared in the retelling, their varied stories enable us as Americans to create a community of a larger memory.[2]

PART ONE

A Larger Memory

The Ties That Bind

Roots: A Multicultural Memory

"THIS SECTION OF HOUSES was called 'lunas' row,'" my cousin Minoru Takaki remarked as he drove me down a tree-lined street on the Puunene Plantation. "Lunas" were foremen, and he was showing me the sugar plantation where my grandfather had worked decades before I was born. "Only the white lunas could live in these houses," my cousin noted. Next we drove to the camps where the workers were housed. The plantation had Japanese camps and Filipino camps as well as camps named "Young Hee Camp," "Ah Fong Camp," "Spanish A Camp," "Spanish B Camp." "There was," added Minoru, "one called 'Alabama Camp.'" Surprised, I asked: "Alabama?" "Yeah," he explained, "we used to have Negroes working on the plantation."[1]

As my cousin described the racial and ethnic diversity of the laborers in the camps, I remembered growing up in Palolo Valley on the island of Oahu, where my neighbors were Japanese, Korean, Chinese, Filipino, Hawaiian, and Portuguese. Ours was an ethnic diversity that had not been explained to me in school: why were there so many different peoples, speaking different languages and sharing different cultures, living together in Palolo?

Minoru's storytelling also led me to think about some documents I had come across in the archives. As the planters began to develop the sugar economy in the late nineteenth century, they pursued a plan: "Get labor first, and capital will follow." For supplies, they sent requisitions to the mercantile houses in Honolulu.

9

In a letter to a plantation manager, July 2, 1890, the Davies Company of Honolulu acknowledged receipt of a list of an order:

bonemeal
canvas
Japanese laborers
macaroni
Chinaman

A letter, May 5, 1908, from the vice president of H. Hackfield and Company to manager George Wilcox of the Grove Farm Plantation had itemized sections, listed alphabetically, for

Fertilizer
Filipinos[2]

Though they requisitioned workers along with supplies, planters were conscious of the nationalities of their laborers. They were systematically developing an ethnically diverse labor force in order to create divisions among their workers and reinforce management control. Plantation managers devised a policy: "Keep a variety of laborers, that is different nationalities, and thus prevent any concerted action in case of strikes, for there are few, if any, cases of Japs, Chinese, and Portuguese entering into a strike as a unit."[3]

These workers from many different countries found themselves in a world of regimented labor. Early in the morning, they were jarred from their sleep by the loud scream of the plantation siren. A work song captured the beginning of the workday:

"Awake! stir your bones! Rouse up!"
Shrieks the Five O'clock Whistle.
"Don't dream you can nestle
For one more sweet nap.
Or your ear-drums I'll rap
With my steam-hammer tap
Till they burst.
Br-r-row-aw-i-e-ur-ur-rup!
Wake up! wake up! wake up! w-a-k-e-u-u-u-up!

Filipino and Japanee;
Porto Rican and Portugee;
Korean, Kanaka and Chinese;
Everybody whoever you be
On the whole plantation —
Wake up! wake up! wake up! w-a-k-e-u-u-u-up!
Br-r-row-aw-i-e-ur-ur-rup!"[4]

"All the workers on a plantation in all their tongues and kindreds 'rolled out' sometime in the early morning, before the break of day," reported a visitor. In front of the mill, they lined up, shouldering their hoes, and were organized into gangs. Each of them was supervised by "a luna, or overseer, almost always a white man." The ethnicity of the gangs varied: some were composed of one nationality, while others reflected a mixture of Hawaiians, Filipinos, Puerto Ricans, Chinese, Japanese, Portuguese, and Koreans.[5]

For everyone, field work was punishing and brutal. "We worked like machines," a laborer complained. "For two hundred of us workers, there were seven or eight lunas and above them was a field boss on a horse. We were watched constantly." Harvesting the cane was dirty and exhausting work. The workers whispered to the wind, come, please come and cool our sweaty backs. But the breezes often could not reach them because they were surrounded by the green thicket. Twelve feet in height, the cane was like a formidable forest, and the workers were like miniature soldiers as they cut the stalks.[6]

Fighting back against the cane, workers also refused to be intimidated by management. Contrary to the stereotype of Asians as quiet and accommodating, these immigrants repeatedly engaged in strikes, inspired by fierce visions of what their labor and lives in Hawaii should be.

The first major strike was organized in 1909 by Japanese laborers who constituted 70 percent of the workforce. In their strike demands, the laborers called for equal pay for equal work: they wanted the same pay as workers from Puerto Rico and Portugal.

"It is not the color of his skin or hair, or the language he speaks, or manners and customs that grow cane in the field," the strikers declared. "It is labor that grows cane."

Their strike demands reflected the transformation of these sojourning laborers into settlers. "We have decided to permanently settle here [and] to unite our destiny with that of Hawaii, sharing the prosperity and adversity of Hawaii with other citizens of Hawaii." Significantly, these Japanese immigrants were framing their demands in "American" terms. They argued that the deplorable conditions on the plantations perpetuated an "undemocratic and un-American" society of "plutocrats and coolies." Fair wages would encourage laborers to work more industriously and productively and enable Hawaii to enjoy "perpetual peace and prosperity." Seeking to create "a thriving and contented middle class — the realization of the high ideal of Americanism," these strikers wanted to share in the American dream.[7]

But the planters were determined to make theirs a dream denied. They crushed the strike and then began importing Filipino laborers in a divide-and-rule strategy. By 1920, the Japanese workers represented only 44 percent of the labor force, and the Filipino workers constituted 30 percent. However, the laborers of both nationalities began to realize that the labor movement in Hawaii would have to be based on interethnic working-class unity.

In 1920, the Japanese and Filipino laborers went out on strike together. The Filipinos initiated the action when three thousand of them stopped working. Japanese newspapers urged the Japanese laborers to join the Filipino strikers: "Laborers from different countries" should take "action together." Between Filipinos and Japanese, there should be "no barriers of nationality, race, or color." At their strike rallies, Japanese and Filipinos waved American flags.[8]

Though the strikers held out for months, they were finally forced to return to work. But the strike had demonstrated the power of workers of different nationalities to struggle together for equality. Moreover, the strike represented the political expression of a cultural transformation. Coming from different countries, these immigrants had been transplanting customs and traditions to the islands.

The plantation camps had become places for ethnic holidays and celebrations. One of the most colorful and noisy festivals was Chinese New Year. During the midsummer, Japanese held their traditional "obon," or festival of souls. The most important celebration of Filipino laborers was Rizal Day — December 30, the anniversary of the Spanish execution of the famous revolutionary José Rizal in 1896.

In the camps, these immigrants from many countries enjoyed and shared their ethnic foods. The daughter of a Portuguese laborer remembered how her mother would make gifts of "little buns for the children in the camp. The Japanese families gave us sushis and the Hawaiians would give us fish." Everybody took their own lunches to school, Lucy Robello of the Waialua plantation said, and they would trade their foods with one another. Meanwhile, in the fields, their parents were also sharing their lunches. Together workers of different ethnicities would taste each other's foods and exclaim in Hawaiian: "Ono, ono!" "Tasty, tasty!"[9]

Initially, the laborers of each ethnic group spoke only their native tongue. But soon workers of different nationalities began to acquire a common language. Planters wanted the immigrant laborers to be taught a functional spoken English so they could give commands to their multilingual work force. "By this," explained a planter, "we do not mean the English of Shakespeare but the terms used in everyday plantation life. A great many of the small troubles arise from the imperfect understanding between overseers and laborers." Over the years, a plantation dialect developed called "pidgin English" — a basic English that incorporated Hawaiian, Japanese, Portuguese, and Chinese phrases as well as the rhythms and intonations of these languages. Though it had begun as "the language of command," this hybrid language with its luxuriant cadences, lyrical sounds, and expressive hand gestures soon became the language of the community. "The language we used had to be either pidgin English or broken English," explained a Filipino laborer. "And when we don't understand each other, we had to add some other words that would help to explain ourselves. That's how this pidgin English comes out beautiful."[10]

Gradually, over the years, the immigrants were planting roots in Hawaii through their children. In the schools, however, students were taught lessons that made them critical of the plantation system. From their teachers, many of whom were whites from the mainland, they learned about freedom and equality as they recited the Declaration of Independence. "Here the children learned about democracy or at least the theory of it," said a University of Hawaii student. They were taught that honest labor, fair play, and industriousness were virtues. But they "saw that it wasn't so on the plantation."[11]

However, their parents were determined to open equality of opportunity for their children. They had earned the right to claim America. After all, they had transformed the islands into a profitable sugar economy. "When we first came to Hawaii," the 1920 strikers proudly declared, "these islands were covered with ohia forests, guava fields and areas of wild grass. Day and night did we work, cutting trees and burning grass, clearing lands and cultivating fields until we made the plantations what they are today."[12]

"The Vast, Surging, Hopeful Army of Workers"

What happened in Hawaii was, in many significant ways, illustrative of a larger American narrative. The U.S. mainland in the nineteenth century also witnessed the making of a modern multicultural America. Workers of different ethnicities and races were laboring on the railroads in California and Utah, in the cotton fields of Georgia, the textile mills of Massachusetts, the garment factories of New York, the orchards of Washington, the steel mills of Pennsylvania, and the copper mines of Arizona.

Connecting the different regions of the nation and opening the way for the industrialization of America, the railroad system was the achievement of a diversity of workers. Hired out by their owners, twenty thousand slaves were used to build the rail lines of the

South — the Mississippi Railroad, the Georgia, the South Carolina, the Raleigh and Gaston, and others. Laying railroad ties, black laborers sang:

> Down the railroad, um-huh
> Well, raise the iron, um-huh
> Raise the iron, um-huh.[13]

Working on the rail lines for the Western and Atlantic Railroad from Atlanta to Chattanooga and the Union Pacific segment of the transcontinental railroad, Irish laborers heard their foremen yelling: "Now Mick do this, and Mick do that." And the Irish shouted back: "The divil take the railroad!" As they were laying the tracks, they tuned their bodies to the rhythms of a work song:

> Then drill, my Paddies, drill —
> Drill, my heroes, drill,
> Drill all day, no sugar in your tay
> Workin' on the U. P. railway.

While falling asleep at night, the Irish workers continued to feel the vibrations of the sledgehammers in their hands and to hear the pounding ringing in their heads. Then they felt the merciless biting of insects:

> When I lay me down to sleep,
> The ugly bugs around me creep;
> Bad luck to the wink that I can sleep,
> While workin' on the railroad.[14]

During the early twentieth century, ten thousand Japanese laborers worked in railroad construction, many of them for the Northern Pacific. Shuttled from one construction site to another, they lived in boxcars, sleeping in double-decked bunks. "We slept in the freight cars," one of them recalled, "suffering a lot from troops of bedbugs. In order to protect ourselves from these despicable insects we each made a big sleeping sack out of cotton cloth, crawled in with our comforter and blanket, and then pulled the string tight at the top to close up the sack." Japanese workers complained about the fickle and fierce weather in song:

A railroad worker —
That's me!
I am great.
Yes, I am a railroad worker.
Complaining:
"It is too hot!"
"It is too cold!"
"It rains too often!"
"It snows too much!"
They all ran off.
I alone remained.
I am a railroad worker![15]

Mexican laborers laid tracks in the Southwest and California. When they began working in Santa Barbara, a local newspaper reported that the "Chinamen section hands" of the Southern Pacific Railroad had been replaced by "a gang of Mexicans." By 1900, this company had forty-five hundred Mexican workers. A song in Spanish told what it was like to work on the railroad:

Some unloaded rails
Others unloaded ties . . .
Those who knew the work
Went repairing the jack
With sledge hammers and shovels,
Throwing earth up the track.
And others of my companions
Threw out thousands of curses.[16]

Brought together to build the industrial economy, workers of various ethnicities and races were often swept into antagonisms. Ethnic stereotypes and employment competition divided them by groups and drove them into conflicts. Even though they shared much in common in terms of class, they found themselves separated by languages, cultures, and identities based on their countries of origin.

Initially, many Irish saw parallels between themselves as an oppressed people and blacks in bondage. In Ireland, they saw themselves as the "slaves" of the British and supported the abolition of slavery in the United States. For example, in 1842, thousands of them signed a petition that declared: "Irishmen and Irishwomen! Treat the colored people as your equals, as brethren." But Irish sympathy for black slaves often turned to hostility in America. Frederick Douglass criticized the Irish immigrants for abandoning the idea of "liberty" they had nurtured in their homeland by becoming "the oppressors of another race" in this country. Irish freedom fighter Daniel O'Connell scolded the immigrants for their racism: "It was not in Ireland you learned this cruelty."[17]

What the Irish learned in America was a painful and complex lesson. Stereotyped as an ignorant and inferior people, they were forced to occupy the bottom rungs of employment. In the South, the Irish were even made to do the dirty and hazardous jobs that slaveowners would not assign to their slaves. A planter told a northern visitor that he had hired an Irish gang to drain a flooded area rather than use his own slaves. "It's dangerous work," he explained, "and a negro's life is too valuable to be risked at it. If a negro dies, it's a considerable loss, you know." In the North, the Irish competed with blacks for jobs as waiters and longshoremen. During the 1830s, a Philadelphia newspaper reported that these immigrants were displacing blacks as hackney coachmen, draymen, and stevedores.[18]

As they pushed blacks out of the labor market, many Irish promoted their whiteness. "In a country of the whites where [white workers] find it difficult to earn a subsistence," they asked, "what right has the negro either to preference or to equality, or to admission?" Targets of nativist resentment, the Irish sought to assimilate by attacking blacks. Complaining that blacks did not know their place, many Irish shouted: "Down with the Nagurs!" "Let them go back to Africa, where they belong."[19]

But blacks resented being told by immigrants to leave the country of their birth and "go back" to Africa. They complained that the Irish were taking jobs from them. "These impoverished and destitute beings, transported from the trans-Atlantic shores," a black observed, "are crowding themselves into every place of business and labor, and driving the poor colored American citizen out. Along the wharves, where the colored man once done the whole business of shipping and unshipping — in stores where his services were once rendered, and in families where the chief places were filled by him, in all these situations there are substituted foreigners."[20]

Irish laborers competed with not only blacks but also the Chinese. One instance of this occurred in New England in 1870. Irish workers in the shoemaking industry were struggling against low wages and the introduction of labor-eliminating machines; consequently, they organized the Secret Order of the Knights of St. Crispin. Demanding higher wages and an eight-hour day, the Crispins went out on strike at a shoe factory in North Adams, Massachusetts. The owner, Calvin T. Sampson, fired the disgruntled workers and pursued a strategy of divide-and-rule. He transported a contingent of seventy-five Chinese workers from San Francisco and used them as scabs to break the Irish strike. Sampson's bold action caught the attention of other employers as well as the national news media. Within three months after their arrival in North Adams, the Chinese workers were producing more shoes than the same number of white workers had been making before the strike. The success of Sampson's strategy was celebrated in the press. Writing for *Scribner's Monthly*, William Shanks contrasted the Chinese with the Irish workers. The Chinese "labored regularly and constantly, losing no blue Mondays on account of Sunday's dissipations nor wasting hours on idle holidays," he reported. "The quality of the work was found to be fully equal to that of the Crispins." The striking Crispins tried to promote working-class solidarity by organizing a Chinese lodge of St. Crispin. But their effort failed, and in the end, Sampson prevailed and broke the strike.[21]

Clearly, the expansive economy of the nineteenth century was the crucible for the making of America's modern multicultural society — what Walt Whitman saluted as the "vast, surging, hopeful army of workers." Irish immigrants worked in New England factories manufacturing textiles from cotton cultivated by enslaved blacks on lands taken from Indians and Mexicans, and settlers moved west on railroads built by the Irish and Chinese. The stories of all these groups were different, but they were not disconnected. Besides the economy and labor, however, there was something else, something deeply rooted in our very founding as a nation that tied us together as Americans.[22]

A Nation That Did "Not Perish from the Earth": A Legacy of Black Men in Blue

In his rough draft of the Declaration of Independence, Thomas Jefferson had included a paragraph on slavery in his long list of charges against the King — "facts" to be "submitted to a candid world":

> he has [violated] the most sacred rights of life & liberty in the persons of a distant people . . . captivating [sic] and carrying them into slavery in another hemisphere . . . he is now exciting those very people to rise in arms among us, and to purchase that liberty of which he has deprived them, by murdering the people upon whom he also obtruded them: thus paying off former crimes committed against the liberties of one people, with crimes which he urges them to commit against the lives of another.[23]

Jefferson was blaming the King for the fact that slaveholders like himself were violating the liberty of African Americans, and was denouncing the ruler for inciting slaves to seize their liberty by taking the lives of their masters. To include this paragraph in the Declaration would have been hypocritical. Many delegates to the Continental Congress quickly insisted that it be crossed out. In his notes on the revising of the draft, Jefferson explained the reason for the deletion: "The clause . . . reprobating the enslaving the inhabitants of Africa, was struck out in complaisance to South Carolina and Georgia, who had never attempted to restrain the importation of slaves, and who on the contrary still wished to continue it. Our Northern brethren also I believe felt a little tender under those censures; for tho' their people have very few slaves themselves yet they have been pretty considerable carriers of them to others."[24]

Jefferson and his fellow revolutionaries were unwilling to submit the "fact" of their slave trading and slaveholding to a "candid world." Instead, by deletion, they attempted to conceal the contradiction between the proclaimed ideals of liberty and equality and the practice of violating the "unalienable" rights of African Americans.

This contradiction, however, was unshrouded by the black poet Phillis Wheatly during the American Revolution. Born in Africa and transported as a slave to Boston, she had learned English and become a published poet. In one of her poems, Wheatly candidly submitted to the world the "fact" of Jefferson's deletions — "the iron chain," the "wanton tyranny" of slavery, how she had been "snatch'd from Afric's fancy'd happy seat" and forcibly separated from her parents, and how her song had sprung from her "love of Freedom."[25]

Many years later, during the Civil War, African Americans helped end the "tyrannic sway" of slavery by fighting in the Union army. Initially, concerned that the use of black soldiers would alienate the border states and also be resented by white soldiers, President Abraham Lincoln had refused to allow African Americans to serve in the military. In early 1863, however, the North was on the verge of losing the war. "Manpower now posed a real problem," observed historian David Donald. "There had been severe losses in a contest that had now lasted nearly two years. The terms for which many regiments had enlisted were about to expire, and soldiers wanted to go home. . . . There were almost no new volunteers. It would be months before a new conscription act could bring in recruits." At this moment of military crisis, Lincoln announced that African Americans would be received into the armed services. He wrote to the military governor of Tennessee, Andrew

Johnson: "The colored population is the great *available* and yet *un-available* of, force for restoring the Union." By the end of the year, General Lorenzo Thomas, commander in the Mississippi Valley, had enrolled twenty regiments of African Americans.

Lincoln decided he would free all of the slaves in order to save the Union and made emancipation a war aim. Without "the physical force which the colored people now give," Lincoln thought, "and promise us . . . neither the present, nor any coming administration, *can* save the Union." Noting that there were nearly 200,000 blacks in the Union army, Lincoln explained that without them "we would be compelled to abandon the war in 3 weeks." In other words, black men in blue made the difference in determining that this "government of the people, by the people, for the people," did "not perish from the earth."[26]

The military sacrifices of African Americans were particularly horrendous: one-third of the 186,000 black soldiers were listed as missing or dead. In an editorial, "Men of Color, To Arms!" Frederick Douglass had explained the reason for their willingness to fight and to die for the Union: "From East to West, from North to South, the sky is written all over: 'Now or never.' 'Liberty won by white men would lose half its luster.' 'Who would be free themselves must strike the blow.'. . . The chance is now given you to end in a day the bondage of centuries, and to rise in one bound from social degradation to the plane of common equality with all other varieties of men." Black men, Douglass pointed out, were "on the battlefield mingling their blood with that of white men in one common effort to save the country." Declaring that the nation belonged to all Americans regardless of race, the black leader forcefully noted that the Constitution stated, "We, the People," not "We, the white people."[27]

Black and white Union soldiers together had brought to an end what Lincoln called "this mighty scourge of war" as well as "the bondsman's two hundred and fifty years of unrequited toil."[28] But liberation from slavery did not lead to freedom from serfdom. After the failed Reconstruction, blacks found themselves in the de facto bondage of the exploitative system of sharecropping.

By then, the migration of "strangers from a different shore" had begun. The Chinese initially rushed to the gold fields of California in the 1850s, followed by tens of thousands as agricultural and industrial workers. In 1882, however, Congress passed the Chinese Exclusion Act. An immigrant angrily protested against what he saw as an unfaithfulness to America's founding principles. "No nation can afford to let go its high ideals," Yan Phou Lee wrote in the *North American Review*. "The founders of the American Republic asserted the principle that all men are created equal, and made this fair land a refuge for the world. Its manifest destiny, therefore, is to be the teacher and leader of nations in liberty. Its supremacy should be maintained by good faith and righteous dealing, and not by the display of selfishness and greed. But now, looking at the actions of this generation of Americans in their treatment of other races, who can get rid of the idea that that Nation, which Abraham Lincoln said was conceived in liberty, waxed great through oppression, and was really dedicated to the proposition that all men are created to prey on one another? How far this Republic has departed from its high ideal and reversed its traditional policy may be seen in the laws passed against the Chinese."[29]

Lee's protest was undoubtedly dismissed by most Americans, but the struggle to make this republic adhere to its ideals sometimes surfaced at the workplace. Though laborers of different races and ethnicities were forced to compete against each other, they demonstrated a capacity for intergroup cooperation. In 1903, for example, Mexican and Japanese farm laborers went on strike together in Oxnard, California. They organized the Japanese-Mexican Labor Association, and conducted strike meetings in Japanese and Spanish. The Japanese branch was led by Y. Yamaguchi and the Mexican branch by J. M. Lizarras. In a joint statement, the leaders declared: "Many of us have family, were born in the country, and are lawfully seeking to protect the only property that we have — our labor. It is just as necessary for the welfare of the valley that we get a decent living wage, as it is that the machines in the great sugar factory be properly oiled — if the machines stop, the wealth of the valley stops, and likewise if the laborers are not given a decent wage, they too, must stop work and the whole people of this country suffer with them."

The Japanese and Mexican workers won their strike. Lizarras then requested a charter for their labor association from the American Federation of Labor. Samuel Gompers, the president of the federation, agreed to issue a charter but on one condition: "Your union will under no circumstances accept membership of any . . . Japanese." This requirement contradicted the strikers' spirit of brotherhood as well as the nation's founding principle of equality. Refusing the charter, Lizarras protested:

> We beg to say in reply that our Japanese brothers here were the first to recognize the importance of cooperating and uniting in demanding a fair wage scale. . . . In the past we have counseled, fought and lived on very short rations with our Japanese brothers, and toiled with them in the fields, and they have been uniformly kind and considerate. We would be false to them and to ourselves and to the cause of unionism if we now accepted privileges for ourselves which are not accorded to them. . . . We will refuse any other kind of charter, except one which will wipe out race prejudice and recognize our fellow workers as being as good as ourselves. I am ordered by the Mexican union to write this letter to you and they fully approve its words.[30]

Without the AFL charter and the general support of organized labor, the Japanese and Mexican union passed out of existence within a few years. But they had passionately affirmed the American principle of equality. Three decades later, during the Great Depression, the poet Langston Hughes echoed their message when he urged his fellow citizens to "let America be America again," to let us breathe the equality in our air.[31]

Our commitment to the nation's founding principles was tested again during World War II. Should minorities fight for a democracy that did not include them? Malcolm Little, later known as Malcolm X, recalled how one of his friends refused to serve. Trying to fail the physical examination, he took a drug to make his heart sound defective. "Shorty felt about the war the same way I and most ghetto Negroes did: 'Whitey owns everything. He wants us to go and bleed for him? Let him fight.' "[32]

However, most young Americans, regardless of racial and ethnic backgrounds, chose to defend democracy. In a letter found on his body after he was killed on the battlefield, a Jewish soldier explained to his parents the reasons why he was fighting for America:

> Mom, I want you to know that I asked for a combat assignment. I did so for several reasons. One is that I had certain ideals within my own mind, for which I had often argued verbally. I didn't feel right to sit safe, far behind the lines, while men were risking their lives for principles which I would fight for only with my lips. I felt that I also must be willing to risk my life in the fight for freedom of speech and thought I was using and hoped to use in the future.
>
> Another reason . . . is the fact that I am Jewish. I felt, again, it wasn't right for me to be safe behind the lines, while others were risking their lives, with one of their goals the principles of no race prejudice. I knew this meant fighting for me and my family because if Hitler won, my family — you, Rolly and Pop — would certainly suffer more than the families of other soldiers who died in the fight.
>
> I felt that I must risk my life, on that point, so that I could earn the right of my family to live in peace and free from race prejudice.[33]

African Americans, too, understood what it meant to risk their lives for the principle of "no race prejudice." For them, World War II was a campaign for "double victory" — a fight against fascism abroad and racism at home. "There should be no illusions about the nature of this struggle," declared black scholar Ralph Bunche. "The fight now is not to save democracy, for that which does not exist cannot be saved. But the fight is to maintain those conditions under which people may continue to strive for the realization of democratic ideals. This is the inexorable logic of the nation's position dictated by the world anti-democratic revolution and Hitler's projected new world order."[34]

"We are also children of the United States," Mexican Americans declared. "We will defend her." On his way to the European front, a Mexican-American soldier reflected on the possibility of dying and the meaning of such a sacrifice: "What if I were killed? What would happen to my wife, my three children? My mother? All the horrible thoughts imaginable would grip me, and before I could find the answers, other thoughts would begin to swirl in. I remembered about us, the Mexican-Americans . . . how the Anglo had pushed and held back our people in the Southwest. Why fight for America when you have not been treated as an American?" But he was overwhelmed by "the feeling" he had for his "home" in America. "All we wanted," he decided, "was a chance to prove how loyal and American we were."[35]

A year after the attack on Pearl Harbor, the *New York Times* reported that 8,800 of the 60,000 Native American males between the ages of twenty-one and forty-four were in military uniform, a higher rate than for the general population. A Native American soldier wrote home from the battlefield: "I don't know anything about the white man's way. I never went outside the reservation. . . . I am proud to be in a [military] suit like this now. It is to protect my country, my people. . . ."[36]

World War II was particularly stressful for Americans of Japanese ancestry. Though they had been herded into internment camps and though they were angry over the denial of their constitutional rights, tens of thousands of Japanese Americans served in the U.S. armed forces. In a letter to his family written from the battlefront, one of them explained why he was ready to die for this country: "By virtue of the Japanese attack on our nation, we as American citizens of Japanese ancestry have been mercilessly flogged with criticism and accusations. But I'm not going to take it sitting down! I may not be able to come back. But that matters little. My family and friends — they are the ones who will be able to back their arguments with facts. . . . In fact, it is better that we are sent to the front and that a few of us do not return, for the testimony will be stronger in favor of the folks back home."[37]

Altogether, thirty-three thousand Japanese Americans served in the military. As soldiers in the all Japanese-American 442nd Regimental Combat Team, they fought heroically in Italy and France, earning over eighteen thousand individual military decorations. At a White House ceremony in 1946, they received the Presidential Unit Citation from Harry Truman. "You fought for the free nations of the world . . ." the president declared. "You fought not only the enemy, you fought prejudice — and you won. Keep up that fight . . . continue to win — make this great Republic stand for what the Constitution says it stands for: 'the welfare of all the people, all the time.' "[38]

This war for "double victory" defeated fascism abroad but not at home. Nevertheless, it opened the way for the civil rights movement. Jailed in Alabama for protesting against segregation, Martin Luther King identified our country's true manifest destiny. "We will reach the goal of freedom in Birmingham and all over the nation," he wrote in a letter to his fellow Americans on April 16, 1963, "because the goal of America is freedom. Abused and scorned though we may be, our destiny is tied up with America's destiny." Then on August 28, at the March on Washington, as he stood before the Lincoln Memorial a century after the Gettysburg Address, King shared his vision: "I say to you today, my friends, that in spite of the difficulties and frustrations of the moment I still have a dream. It is a dream deeply rooted in the American dream. I have a dream that one day this nation will rise up and live out the true meaning of its creed: 'We hold these truths to be self-evident; that all men are created equal.' "[39]

This creed was still a dream deferred. Excluded from equality, Americans from minority communities felt a special reason to pur-

sue our nation's "proposition" and a particularly passionate commitment to carry forward our "unfinished work."

Breaking Silences: Brushing Against the Grain

Our stories "aren't just entertainment," Leslie Marmon Silko cau-
tioned. "Don't be fooled." But, then, what are they?[40]
"I hope this survey do a lot of good for Chinese people," a Chinese immigrant told an interviewer from Stanford University in
the 1920s. "Make American people realize that Chinese people are
humans. I think very few American people really know anything
about Chinese." After Harriet Jacobs escaped from slavery in the
South, she wrote in her autobiography: "[My purpose] is not to
tell you what I have heard but what I have seen — and what I
have suffered." "Our stories should be listened to by many young
people," said a ninety-one-year-old retired Japanese plantation laborer. "It's for their sake. We really had a hard time, you know."
In her autobiography, Jewish immigrant Minnie Miller wrote:
"This story is dedicated to the descendants of Lazar and Goldie
Glauberman. My history is bound up in their history and the generations that follow should know where they come from to know
better who they are."[41]
Most important, in the telling and retelling of what happened,
the people of multicultural America brush against the grain of the
master narrative of American history, the ethnocentric story told
from the perspective of the English colonists and their descendants.
They break a silence imposed on them. "It is very natural that the
history written by the victim," explained a Mexican in 1874, "does
not altogether chime with the story of the victor." In giving their
own accounts, people reveal themselves not merely as "victims"
but as actors in history, making decisions and taking actions in
order to change the circumstances that surrounded their lives.[42]
Finally, our stories tell about the making of Americans. "We got
such good, fantastic stories to tell," seventy-five-year-old Tomo
Shoji explained. "All our stories are different." Indeed, our narra-
tives reveal the diversity of experiences and reflections among vari-

ous ethnic groups as well as within a group — differences of class, gender, national origins, generations, times, and places. These memories resist the essentialisms and the ethnocentricisms that seek to entrap the human spirit. Our recounted experiences show that ethnic identity is not something pure, static, primordial, natural, or eternal. Rather, as Lisa Lowe insightfully observes, who we are is only partly inherited. Our identities are fluid, negotiated, socially constructed, "imagined," and "invented."[43]

America turned out to be an ideal site for such transitions and transformations due to its liminality — the nation's ambiguous geographical and cultural location "betwixt and between all fixed points of classification." Here the "cake of custom" of the Old Worlds was broken. To be sure, as various peoples encountered each other here, they were often pulled into antagonisms, driven by narrow definitions of the "we" and "them." But diversity did not necessarily mean division. For example, groups like the Japanese and Filipino laborers in Hawaii or the Japanese and Mexican laborers in California discovered that ethnic boundaries were mutable and porous. Forging new associations and forming new identities, the people of multicultural America were able to unknot traditional ties that had bound them and to pursue possibilities for reinventing themselves. As they socially constructed their identity in different circumstances, they expanded the already extraordinary range of their identities as Americans. Ethnicity became a field for the making of "imagined communities." Swept into the "play" of history with all of its rushing events and forces, they made choices that revised and reformulated notions of themselves and also America itself.[44]

As Americans, we have been, all along, more complex and multidimensional than many of us may think we are. Our ethnic identity does have inherited parts — family, national origins, gender, and race. But what is ascriptive and what is achieved blur into one another in the dynamic and interactive process of becoming American. In the recovering and sharing of our "varied carols," we have been creating a community of "a larger memory."

28

PART TWO

A City upon a Hill

Introduction

——————▶ ◀——————

A S JOHN WINTHROP and his fellow English colonizers sailed across the Atlantic on the *Arbella* in 1630, he presented a vision for their mission. "For wee must Consider that wee shall be as a Citty upon a Hill, the eies of all people are uppon us." Their purpose was to found a "new" England.[1]

Their "errand into the wilderness" was a continuation of an English westward expansion that had been under way for over two centuries, beginning with the conquest of Ireland. What happened to the native people in Ireland was a preview for what would happen to the Indians in New England. Stereotyping the Irish as "savages," English colonizers burned their villages and crops, took their land, and relocated them on reservations. Bloody battles ensued. In a letter to John Winthrop, Jr., Samuel Gorton compared the violence of the two English frontiers: "I remember the time of the wars in Ireland (when I was young, in Queen Elizabeth's days of famous memory) where much English blood was spilt by a people much like unto these [Indians]. . . . And after these Irish were subdued by force, what treacherous and bloody massacres have they attempted is well known."[2]

Even before his departure for the new world, Winthrop had formulated a justification for taking lands from the "savages" of Massachusetts. "The whole earth is the Lord's garden and he hath given it to the sons of men [to] increase and multiply and replenish the earth and subdue it," he explained in 1629. "Why then should we stand starving here for the places of habitation . . . and in the mean-

31

time suffer a whole Continent as fruitful and convenient for the use of man to lie waste without any improvement."[3]

Actually, Indians had been farming the land for a long time and had already been transforming the wilderness into cultivated fields. This reality led to competition between the original inhabitants and the English intruders over resources. Within ten years after the arrival of Winthrop's group, twenty thousand additional colonists had come to New England. This growing English population had to be squeezed into a limited area of arable land. Less than 20 percent of the region was useful for agriculture, and the Indians had already established themselves on the prime lands. Consequently, the colonists often settled on or directly next to Indian communities. In the Connecticut Valley, for example, they erected towns like Springfield (1636), Northampton (1654), Hadley (1661), Deerfield (1673), and Northfield (1673) adjacent to Indian agricultural clearings at Agawam, Norwottuck, Pocumtuck, and Squakheag.

Over the years, the expansion of English settlement led to wars against the native peoples. During the Pequot War of 1637, 700 Pequots were killed by the colonists and their Indian allies. Describing the massacre at Fort Mystic, an English officer wrote: "Many were burnt in the fort, both men, women, and children. . . . There were about four hundred souls in this fort, and not above five of them escaped out of our hands. Great and doleful was the bloody sight." To justify this atrocity, Commander John Mason explained that God had pushed the devilish Pequots into a "fiery oven," "filling the place with dead bodies." Forty years later, during King Philip's War, over six thousand Indians, or half their population in southern New England, died from combat and disease. Again, the colonists justified their violence by demonizing their enemies. The Indians, Increase Mather declared, were "so Devil driven as to begin an unjust and bloody war upon the English, which issued in their speedy and utter extirpation from the face of God's earth." Cotton Mather depicted the conflict as a manifestation of a great metaphysical battle: "The Devil decoyed those miserable savages [to New England] in hopes that the Gospel of the Lord Jesus Christ would never come here to destroy or disturb His *absolute empire* over them."[4]

The triumph of the English over the Indians was trumpeted by Edward Johnson in his *Wonder-Working Providence*. Where there had originally been "hideous Thickets" inhabited by wolves, bears, and Indians, he proudly exclaimed in 1654, there were now streets "full of Girls and Boys sporting up and down, with a continued concourse of people." Initially, the colonists themselves had lived in "wigwams" like Indians, he explained, but now they had "orderly, fair, and well-built houses . . . together with Orchards filled with goodly fruit trees, and gardens with variety of flowers." The settlers had fought against the Devil who had inhabited the bodies of the Indians. Victorious over what they rationalized as the devil in disguise, the English had made New England a thriving center of production and trade. "This Wilderness" had been transformed into a prosperous "mart." "Thus," proclaimed Johnson, "hath the Lord been pleased to turn one of the most hideous, boundless, and unknown Wildernesses in the world in an instant . . . to a well-ordered Commonwealth."[5]

Within the English settlements, however, there were some uncertainties about what Johnson and his fellow colonizers celebrated as progress resulting from Indian destruction. Such doubting surfaced, inadvertently, in a bestselling book — *A True History of the Captivity and Restoration of Mrs. Mary Rowlandson*, published in 1682. Retaliating for English attacks on their villages during King Philip's War, a band of Narragansetts raided a small town, capturing several settlers, including Rowlandson. In her captivity story, she described living with the Indians for eleven weeks. Her account reflected and reinforced English stereotypes of Indians as "barbarous creatures," "merciless and cruel heathens," and "hellhounds," deserving the punishment they had received at the hands of the colonizers.

But Rowlandson's narrative also contained a subversive subtext. As one of my students, David Ford, so perceptively noted in a paper, Rowlandson also told stories that suggested an understanding of the Indians' suffering as well as a recognition of their humanity. She related, for example, how some of the Indians had noticed that she lacked the strength to carry her wounded six-year-old daughter, so they put her on a horse with the child on her lap. One cold day, an Indian woman welcomed Rowlandson into her wigwam to give her warmth and some ground nuts. Afterward, she told the Englishwoman to come back again sometime. Commenting on this hospitality, Rowlandson wrote: "Yet these were strangers to me that I never saw before." On one occasion, King Philip asked her to knit a shirt for his son and paid her a shilling for it; on another occasion, she knitted a cap for the boy, and King Philip invited her to eat dinner with his family. Rowlandson contrasted the Indians in retreat with the English in pursuit. In the dead of winter, the Indians were able to survive by eating nuts, roots, and weeds as well as wild animals; whereas the English soldiers ran out of provisions and were forced to return to the settlements. Indian resourcefulness impressed Rowlandson: "I did not see (all the time I was among them) one man, woman, or child, dy with hunger." These observations, complimentary of the Indians, offered possibilities for friendlier English relations with the hosts of their adopted land. But Rowlandson's favorable descriptions of the Indians were probably overlooked by her readers, and if noticed, rejected.[6]

Meanwhile, in the colony of Virginia, the English had also been making choices that would have consequences for race in America. In 1619, eleven years before the *Arbella* arrived on the Massachusetts shore, a Dutch ship landed at Jamestown. "About the last of August," wrote John Rolfe in his diary, "came in a dutch man of warre that sold us twenty Negars." Since slavery had not yet been instituted, these first Africans became indentured servants. But many of them, as well as others brought later from Africa, were soon reduced to de facto slaves. Although their legal status was one of indentured servitude, their required years of labor had, in fact, been extended indefinitely. In 1663, the Virginia Assembly made slavery de jure: a law specified that Africans were to serve "Durante Vita," or for life.[7]

However, despite the fact that a labor supply from Africa was available, the black population in Virginia remained small. The planters saw their colony as an English society, and to meet their labor needs for tobacco production, they preferred to rely on white indentured servants. In 1650, Africans constituted 300 of Virginia's 15,000 inhabitants, or only 2 percent. By 1675, there were 1,600 Africans, or just 5 percent.

Then a year later, Bacon's Rebellion exploded. A planter from upcountry Virginia, Nathaniel Bacon, raised a militia to attack the Indians who were threatening the settlers. But his followers had their own goals — free land and greater opportunity to become farmers. They wanted to share the profits of the booming production of tobacco and to pursue what would later be called the American Dream. Most of the rebels were white indentured servants and landless workers. Many blacks joined the movement: for them revolution was the path to freedom from slavery. Together, white and black, the rebels belonged to a working class described by the elite as the "giddy multitude."

Bacon's insurrection alarmed the planters. Governor William Berkeley charged him with treason, an act punishable by death. Bacon retaliated by marching five hundred armed men against the governor's troops and burned Jamestown to the ground. Shortly afterward, Bacon died, probably from dysentery. The rebels were described by the fleeing Governor Berkeley as "Poor Indebted Discontented and Armed."[8]

"Armed" was what really frightened the planter class. Governor Berkeley returned with troop reinforcements. At one of the rebel fortifications, Captain Thomas Grantham encountered four hundred "English and Negroes in Armes." Lying to them, Grantham said they had been "pardoned and freed from their Slavery." Most of them accepted his offer, but eighty black and twenty white rebels refused to surrender. Promised safe passage across the York River, the holdouts were captured when Grantham threatened to blow them out of the water. All of the captured "Negroes & Servants," Grantham reported, were returned "to their Masters."[9]

After quelling the insurrection, the planters wanted to make certain such an uprising would never happen again. The overwhelming majority of the laborers in Virginia were white, but the planters could not deny whites the right to bear arms. However, they could drive a wedge between white and black laborers. The planter elite enacted legislation to disarm Africans based on the color of their skin. Other laws singled out Africans for subjugation. Slaves were denied freedom of assembly and movement. The manumission, or formal emancipation, of slaves was prohibited unless the master paid for transporting them out of the colony. The "abominable mixture" of interracial unions was banned, and white violators of this law were subject to banishment. The white mother of a racially mixed illegitimate child would be fined fifteen pounds, and the child would be enslaved for thirty years. "Black" had been made to signify "slave" and hence stigmatized as inferior and degraded.

Within this context of racial repression, planters began shifting from armed and free white indentured labor to unarmed and unfree black labor. Importations of Africans increased steeply: by 1700, blacks represented 20,000 of Virginia's population of 63,000, or 33 percent. The colony was being transformed into a biracial society tiered into "white over black." A rush to purchase slaves from Africa was under way. In a letter to Ralph Wormely in 1681, William Fitzhugh noted that there were "some Negro Ships expected into York now every day." "If you intend to buy any for yours self, and it be not too much trouble . . . secure me five or six." Observing this clamor for enslaved laborers from Africa, Francis Nicholson commented: "There were as many buyers as negroes, and I think that, if 2000 were imported, there would be substantial buyers for them." "The negroes are brought annually in large numbers," a visitor to Virginia reported. "They can be selected according to pleasure, young and old, men and women. They are entirely naked when they arrive, having only corals of different colors around their neck and arms."[10]

In massive numbers, Africans were being forcibly transported to America, changing the original intent of the colonizers to establish a new English society in America. The planter elite were making decisions that reflected their selfish and short-term needs. They were using race to divide and control the working class. In the crucible of white-white class conflict emerged the racially based system of slave labor that buttressed the hegemony of the planter elite over blacks as well as over poor and laboring whites.

Decades later, after slavery had been established and expanded in the colonies, a clerk in Mount Holly, New Jersey, was directed by his employer to draw up a bill of sale for a slave. The transaction pricked John Woolman's conscience and led him to write a pamphlet, published in 1754, entitled: *Considerations on the Keeping of Negroes: Recommended to the Professors of Christianity of every Denomination.* Distributed widely by the Philadelphia Quakers, Woolman's protest against slavery inspired an uncompromising moral resolve that would eventually lead to the abolition of slavery.

Woolman urged his fellow Christians to remember that "all Nations are of one Blood, *Gen.* iii. 20." "To consider Mankind otherwise than Brethren, to think Favours are peculiar to one Nation, and exclude others, plainly supposes a Darkness in Understanding: For as God's Love is universal, so where the Mind is sufficiently influenced by it, it begets a Likeness of itself, and the Heart is enlarged towards all Men." The terrible conditions of slavery, Woolman explained, had made blacks disrespectful and contemptible. "Placing on men the ignominious Title SLAVE, dressing them in uncomely Garments, keeping them to servile Labour, in which they are often dirty, tends gradually to fix a Notion in the Mind, that they are a Sort of People below us in Nature, and leads us to consider them as such in all our Conclusions about them." What Woolman was saying was sociologically insightful: reduced by slavery to be objects of disdain, blacks were then being blamed for their own degradation.[11]

A destiny of the new society had begun to manifest itself: America had become a "city upon a hill." The pursuit of progress and profits had triumphed in New England as well as Virginia. Within this context, Indian lands had been appropriated, black labor exploited, and a white laboring population disciplined. Shortsighted and self-interested choices had been made by the governing elites with tragic and far-reaching consequences that would ricochet down the corridors of what would become the United States of America.

A Horror Remembered: Olaudah
Equiano's Passage to America

The movement of Africans as slaves to the New World was massive. During the ten years from 1783 to 1793 alone, Liverpool slave traders transported 303,737 Africans across the Atlantic. The total numbers for all European slave traders was enormous: 2.75 million in the seventeenth century and 7 million in the eighteenth. These figures may not be "accurate," historian John Hope Franklin notes, but they are "among the most conservative."[1]

One of the Africans forcibly brought to America was Olaudah Equiano. Born in 1745 in what is now Nigeria, he was only ten years old when he was kidnapped by raiders from another tribe and sold to English slave traders who transported him to America. He was bought by a planter in Virginia, and then resold to a British naval officer who took him to London. Equiano was eventually able to purchase his own freedom in 1766. In his autobiography, published thirteen years later, he vividly describes his traumatic experience. The following excerpt begins after Equiano has been forcibly marched to the sea and put on a slave ship. On board, he faces horrors, imagined and real.

THE FIRST OBJECT which saluted my eyes when I arrived on the coast was the sea, and a slave-ship, which was then riding at anchor, and waiting for its cargo. These filled me with astonishment, which was soon converted into terror, which I am yet at a loss to describe, nor the then feelings of my mind. When I was carried on board I was immediately handled, and tossed up, to see if I were sound, by some of the crew; and I was now persuaded that I had gotten into a world of bad spirits, and that they were going to kill me. Their complexions too differing so much from ours, their long hair, and the language they spoke, which was very different from any I had ever heard, united to confirm me in this belief. Indeed, such were the horrors of my views and fears at the moment, that, if ten thousand worlds had been my own, I would have freely parted with them all to have exchanged my condition with that of the meanest slave in my own country. When I looked round the ship too, and saw a large furnace of copper boiling, and a multitude of black people of every description chained together, every one of their countenances expressing dejection and sorrow, I no longer doubted of my fate, and, quite overpowered with horror and anguish, I fell motionless on the deck and fainted. When I recovered a little, I found some black people about me, who I believed were some of those who brought me on board, and had been receiving their pay; they talked to me in order to cheer me, but all in vain. I asked them if we were not to be eaten by those white men with horrible looks, red faces, and long hair? They told me I was not; and one of the crew brought me a small portion of spirituous liquor in a wine glass; but, being afraid of him, I would not take it out of his hand. One of the blacks therefore took it from him and gave it to me, and I took a little down my palate, which, instead of reviving me, as they thought it would, threw me into the greatest consternation at the strange feeling it produced, having never tasted any such liquor before. Soon after this, the blacks who brought me on board went off, and left me abandoned to despair. I now saw myself deprived of all chance of returning to my native country, or even the least glimpse of hope of gaining the shore, which I now considered as friendly: and I even wished for my former slavery in preference to my present situation, which was filled with horrors of every kind, still heightened by my ignorance of what I was to undergo. I was not long suffered to indulge my grief; I was soon put down under the decks, and there I received such a salutation in my nostrils as I had never experienced in my life; so that with the loathsomeness of the stench, and crying together, I became so sick and low that I was not able to eat, nor had I the least desire to taste any thing. I now wished for the last friend, Death, to relieve me; but soon, to my grief, two of the white men offered me eatables; and, on my refusing to eat, one of them held me fast by the hands, and laid me across, I think, the windlass, and tied my feet, while the other flogged me severely.

A LARGER MEMORY

I had never experienced any thing of this kind before; and although, not being used to the water, I naturally feared that element the first time I saw it; yet, nevertheless, could I have got over the nettings, I would have jumped over the side, but I could not; and, besides, the crew used to watch us very closely who were not chained down to the decks, lest we should leap into the water; and I have seen some of these poor African prisoners most severely cut for attempting to do so, and hourly whipped for not eating. This indeed was often the case with myself. In a little time after, amongst the poor chained men, I found some of my own nation, which in a small degree gave ease to my mind. I inquired of these what was to be done with us? they gave me to understand we were to be carried to these white people's country to work for them. I then was a little revived, and thought, if it were no worse than working, my situation was not so desperate: but still I feared I should be put to death, the white people looked and acted, as I thought, in so savage a manner; for I had never seen among any people such instances of brutal cruelty; and this not only shewn towards us blacks, but also to some of the whites themselves. One white man in particular I saw, when we were permitted to be on deck, flogged so unmercifully with a large rope near the foremast, that he died in consequence of it; and they tossed him over the side as they would have done a brute. This made me fear these people the more; and I expected nothing less than to be treated in the same manner. I could not help expressing my fears and apprehensions to some of my countrymen: I asked them if these people had no country, but lived in this hollow place the ship? they told me they did not, but came from a distant one. "Then," said I, "how comes it in all our country we never heard of them?" They told me, because they lived so very far off. I then asked where were their women? had they any like themselves! I was told they had: "And why," said I, "do we not see them?" they answered, because they were left behind. I asked how the vessel could go? they told me they could not tell; but that there were cloths put upon the masts by the help of the ropes I saw, and then the vessel went on; and the white men had some spell or magic they put in

40

the water when they liked in order to stop the vessel. I was exceedingly amazed at this account, and really thought they were spirits.
I therefore wished much to be from amongst them, for I expected
they would sacrifice me: but my wishes were vain; for we were
so quartered that it was impossible for any of us to make our escape. While we staid on the coast I was mostly on deck; and one
day, to my great astonishment, I saw one of these vessels coming
in with the sails up. As soon as the whites saw it, they gave a great
shout, at which we were amazed; and the more so as the vessel
appeared larger by approaching nearer. At last she came to an anchor in my sight, and when the anchor was let go, I and my countrymen who saw it were lost in astonishment to observe the vessel
stop; and were now convinced it was done by magic. Soon after
this the other ship got her boats out, and they came on board of
us, and the people of both ships seemed very glad to see each other.
Several of the strangers also shook hands with us black people, and
made motions with their hands, signifying, I suppose, we were to
go to their country; but we did not understand them. At last, when
the ship we were in had got in all her cargo, they made ready with
many fearful noises, and we were all put under deck, so that we
could not see how they managed the vessel. But this disappointment was the least of my sorrow. The stench of the hold while
we were on the coast was so intolerably loathsome, that it was
dangerous to remain there for any time, and some of us had been
permitted to stay on the deck for the fresh air; but now that the
whole ship's cargo were confined together, it became absolutely
pestilential. The closeness of the place, and the heat of the climate,
added to the number in the ship, which was so crowded that each
had scarcely room to turn himself, almost suffocated us. This produced copious perspirations, so that the air soon became unfit for
respiration, from a variety of loathsome smells, and brought on a
sickness among the slaves, of which many died, thus falling victims
to the improvident avarice, as I may call it, of their purchasers.
This wretched situation was again aggravated by the galling of the
chains, now become insupportable; and the filth of the necessary
tubs, into which the children often fell, and were almost suffo-

cated. The shrieks of the women, and the groans of the dying, rendered the whole a scene of horror almost inconceivable. Happily perhaps for myself I was soon reduced so low here that it was thought necessary to keep me almost always on deck; and from my extreme youth I was not put in fetters. In this situation I expected every hour to share the fate of my companions, some of whom were almost daily brought upon deck at the point of death, which I began to hope would soon put an end to my miseries. Often did I think many of the inhabitants of the deep much more happy than myself; I envied them the freedom they enjoyed, and as often wished I could change my condition for theirs. Every circumstance I met with served only to render my state more painful, and heighten my apprehensions, and my opinion of the cruelty of the whites. One day they had taken a number of fishes; and when they had killed and satisfied themselves with as many as they thought fit, to our astonishment who were on the deck, rather than give any of them to us to eat, as we expected, they tossed the remaining fish into the sea again, although we begged and prayed for some as well as we could, but in vain; and some of my countrymen, being pressed by hunger, took an opportunity, when they thought no one saw them, of trying to get a little privately; but they were discovered, and the attempt procured them some very severe floggings.

One day, when we had a smooth sea, and moderate wind, two of my wearied countrymen, who were chained together (I was near them at the time), preferring death to such a life of misery, somehow made through the nettings, and jumped into the sea: immediately another quite dejected fellow, who, on account of his illness, was suffered to be out of irons, also followed their example; and I believe many more would very soon have done the same, if they had not been prevented by the ship's crew, who were instantly alarmed. Those of us that were the most active were, in a moment, put down under the deck; and there was such a noise and confusion amongst the people of the ship as I never heard before, to stop her, and get the boat out to go after the slaves. However, two of the wretches were drowned, but they got the other, and afterwards flogged him unmercifully, for thus attempting to prefer death to slavery. In this manner we continued to undergo more hardships than I can now relate; hardships which are inseparable from this accursed trade. — Many a time we were near suffocation, from the want of fresh air, which we were often without for whole days together. This, and the stench of the necessary tubs, carried off many. During our passage I first saw flying fishes, which surprised me very much: they used frequently to fly across the ship, and many of them fell on the deck. I also now first saw the use of the quadrant. I had often with astonishment seen the mariners make observations with it, and I could not think what it meant. They at last took notice of my surprise; and one of them, willing to increase it, as well as to gratify my curiosity, made me one day look through it. The clouds appeared to me to be land, which disappeared as they passed along. This heightened my wonder: and I was now more persuaded than ever that I was in another world, and that every thing about me was magic. At last we came in sight of the island of Barbadoes, at which the whites on board gave a great shout, and made many signs of joy to us. We did not know what to think of this; but as the vessel drew nearer we plainly saw the harbour, and other ships of different kinds and sizes: and we soon anchored amongst them off Bridge Town. Many merchants and planters now came on board, though it was in the evening. They put us in separate parcels, and examined us attentively. They also made us jump, and pointed to the land, signifying we were to go there. We thought by this we should be eaten by these ugly men, as they appeared to us; and, when soon after we were all put down under the deck again, there was much dread and trembling among us, and nothing but bitter cries to be heard all the night from these apprehensions, insomuch that at last the white people got some old slaves from the land to pacify us. They told us we were not to be eaten, but to work, and were soon to go on land, where we should see many of our country people. This report eased us much; and sure enough, soon after we were landed, there came to us Africans of all languages. We were conducted immediately to the merchant's yard, where we were all pent up together like so many sheep in a fold, without regard to sex or age. As every object was new to me, every thing I saw filled me with surprise. What struck me first was, that the houses were built with bricks, in stories, and in every other respect different from those I have seen in Africa: but I was still more astonished on seeing people on horseback. I did not know what this could mean; and indeed I thought these people were full of nothing but magical arts. . . . We were not many days in the merchant's custody before we were sold after their usual manner, which is this: — On a signal given (as the beat of a drum), the buyers rush at once into the yard where the slaves are confined, and make choice of that parcel they like best. The noise and clamour with which this is attended, and the eagerness visible in the countenances of the buyers, serve not a little to increase the apprehensions of the terrified Africans, who may well be supposed to consider them as the ministers of that destruction to which they think themselves devoted. In this manner, without scruple, are relations and friends separated, most of them never to see each other again. I remember in the vessel in which I was brought over, in the men's apartment, there were several brothers, who, in the sale, were sold in different lots; and it was very moving on this occasion to see and hear their cries at parting. O, ye nominal Christians! might not an African ask you, learned you this from your God? who says unto you, Do unto all men as you would men should do unto you? Is it not enough that we are torn from our country and friends to toil for your luxury and lust of gain? Must every tender feeling be likewise sacrificed to your avarice? Are the dearest friends and relations, now rendered more dear by their separation from their kindred, still to be parted from each other, and thus prevented from cheering the gloom of slavery with the small comfort of being together and mingling their sufferings and sorrows? Why are parents to lose their children, brothers their sisters, or husbands their wives? Surely this is a new refinement in cruelty, which, while it has no advantage to atone for it, thus aggravates distress, and adds fresh horrors even to the wretchedness of slavery.

PART THREE

A Manifest Destiny

Introduction

————◆——

FROM THE VERY BEGINNING of settlement, one of the purposes of English colonization was economic. In New England
and Virginia, the clearing of the wilderness involved the conversion
of America's resources into lumber, pelts, tobacco, and other exports. By the second half of the eighteenth century, many colonists
resented British economic restrictions. The Proclamation of 1763,
which prohibited settlement west of the Appalachian Mountains,
restricted the advancement of settlement. British regulations limited manufacturing in order to keep the colonies dependent on
industrial goods imported from England, and British merchants
used this advantage to flood the colonial market. The War for Independence secured economic freedom for America: freedom to con-
vert Indian lands west of the Appalachians into private property,
trade whenever and with whomever they wished, import products
like tea and molasses without paying taxes to an external authority,
issue their own currency, develop domestic manufacturing, and in
general, expand the market.

Visiting the United States in the 1830s, Alexis de Tocqueville
noticed "an inordinate love of material gratification" among
Americans. Democracy itself seemed to be its source. "When the
reverence that belonged to what is old has vanished," he explained,
"birth, condition, and profession no longer distinguish men . . .
hardly anything but money remains to create strongly marked differences between them and to raise some of them above the common level." Money had become the nexus of social relations.
"When all the members of the community are independent of or

indifferent to each other, the co-operation of each of them can be obtained only by paying for it: This infinitely multiplies the purposes to which wealth may be applied and increases its value." No longer restrained by laws made in England, Americans ushered the new nation into the era of the Market Revolution — the "take-off" years that transformed America into a highly complex industrial nation.[1]

In 1800, the U.S. economy was predominantly agricultural. Most people were engaged in subsistence farming, growing food crops mainly for their own needs. Living in the interior regions, many of these farmers found that the transportation of surplus crops to the market was too expensive. The cost of carrying a ton of goods only thirty miles overland was as much as shipping it three thousand miles from America to Europe. Thus commercial activity was limited to the areas near the seaboard and navigable waterways.

By 1860, this static economy had been transformed. Advances in transportation such as the steamboat and the railroad now linked the three major regions — the East, West, and South. Each region represented a division of production. New England and the Middle Atlantic states concentrated on manufacturing. The Western states of Ohio, Indiana, and Illinois became the food-producing sector. The Southern states of Georgia, South Carolina, Alabama, Mississippi, and Louisiana produced cotton — the country's leading export. Cotton constituted 39 percent of the total value of exports from 1816 to 1820, 63 percent from 1836 to 1840, and over fifty percent from 1840 to 1860.

The causes of this tremendous economic transformation were multiple. The shipping boom of the early 1800s had enabled merchants like Francis Lowell to accumulate capital to invest in manufacturing ventures. The proliferation of banks and the expansion of the credit system made it possible for farmers to borrow money and buy land for commercial agriculture. Technological progress introduced new machinery and paved the way for factory production. Government intervention in the form of protective tariffs and the development of transportation also contributed to the advancement of the market. The transportation revolution laid vast networks of turnpikes, canals, and railroads across the country: between 1815 and 1860, freight charges for shipments overland had been reduced by 95 percent.

The most "decisive" impetus for the Market Revolution, however, was cotton. "Cotton was strategic," observed economist Douglas C. North, "because it was the major independent variable in the interdependent structure of internal and international trade. The demands for western foodstuffs and northeastern services and manufactures were basically dependent upon the income received from the cotton trade." Dominant in the export trade, cotton was crucial in the development of inter-regional specialization. The income derived from the export of this product helped to finance enterprises throughout the American economy.[2]

The rise of the cotton kingdom depended on the appropriation of Indian lands and the expansion of slavery. The major cotton-producing states — Alabama, Mississippi, and Louisiana — had been carved out of Indian territory. Tribe after tribe in the South had been forced to cede their lands to the federal government and move west of the Mississippi River. Eleven treaties of cession were negotiated with these tribes between 1814 and 1824; from these agreements the United States acquired millions of acres of lands, including one-fifth of Mississippi and three-quarters of Alabama. Sales of Indian lands were followed by increases in the slave population: between 1820 and 1850, the number of slaves jumped from 42,000 to 343,000 in Alabama, 33,000 to 310,000 in Mississippi, and 69,000 to 245,000 in Louisiana. Cotton production in Alabama, Arkansas, Florida, Louisiana, and Mississippi nearly doubled from 559,000 bales in 1833 to 1,160,000 ten years later.

The Market Revolution opened the way to the making of an even more multicultural America, for it led to the massive influx of laborers from Ireland, the war against Mexico with its annexation of the Southwest territories, and eventually to American expansion into Asia and Chinese immigration east across the Pacific. The economy fastened these different peoples to each other, their histories woven into the tapestry of a greater diversity. Working in the textile mills of New England, Irish immigrant women manufactured fabric made from cotton grown on former Indian land and picked by enslaved African Americans; meanwhile, Irish immigrant men labored in New England shoe factories, making shoes from hides shipped by Mexican workers in California. Chinese and Irish railroad workers laid the transcontinental tracks that closed the frontier and changed forever the lives of Indians in the West.

As the Market Revolution expanded the institution of slavery and propelled the westward movement into Indian territory, the increasing racial and ethnic diversity challenged the idea of America as a homogeneous white nation.

In a letter to James Monroe written shortly before he negotiated the Louisiana Purchase, Thomas Jefferson offered his vision of America's manifest destiny. The president stated that he looked forward to distant times when this continent would be covered with "a people speaking the same language, governed in similar forms, and by similar laws." Believing that the "people" should be racially homogeneous, Jefferson recoiled with horror from the possibility of "either blot or mixture on that surface."[3]

Slavery was a most perplexing problem for Jefferson. "How is it," asked Dr. Samuel Johnson, "that the loudest yelps for liberty come from the drivers of slaves?" As the owner of two hundred slaves and the author of the Declaration of Independence, Jefferson was conscious of the contradiction. "The love of justice and the love of country plead equally the cause of these people [slaves]," he confessed, "and it is a moral reproach to us that they should have pleaded it so long in vain." In a letter to his brother-in-law Francis Eppes on July 30, 1787, Jefferson made a revealing slip. Once "my debts" have been cleared, he promised, "I shall try some plan of making their [his slaves'] situation happier, determined to content myself with a small portion of their liberty labour." Jefferson had first written "liberty"; then realizing that he was depriving them of an "unalienable right," he crossed it out, rationalizing his ownership of human beings as just an appropriation of their "labour." Dependent on the labor of his slaves to pay off his debts,

Jefferson hoped he would be able to free them and "put them ultimately on an easier footing," which he promised to do the moment "they" had paid off his financial obligations, two-thirds of which had been "contracted by purchasing them." In effect, Jefferson was requiring his slaves to reimburse him for the debt he had incurred by buying them! Unfortunately, he died insolvent, and his slaves were never freed.[4]

But, for Jefferson, the slaves should not be freed unless they were also removed from the country. Contrasting Roman slavery to American slavery, he wrote: "Among the Romans emancipation required but one effort. The slave, when made free, might mix with, without staining the blood of his master. But with us a second is necessary, unknown to history. When freed, he is to be removed beyond the reach of mixture."[5]

Jefferson insisted that he would be willing to make the sacrifice and free all of his slaves, but only if they could be removed to the West Indies or Africa. "I can say," he asserted, "with conscious truth, that there is not a man on earth who would sacrifice more than I would to relieve us from this heavy reproach, in any practicable way. The cession of that kind of property . . . is a bagatelle which would not cost me a second thought, if, in that way, a general emancipation and expatriation could be effected."

A pragmatic philosopher inordinately attentive to details, Jefferson had a plan for the expatriation of the slaves. To deport all of them at once, he admitted, would not be "practicable." Such a removal would take twenty-five years, and the slave population would have doubled during that time. Furthermore, the value of the slaves would amount to $600 million, and the cost of transportation and provisions would be an additional $300 million. "It cannot be done in this way," Jefferson decided. The only "practicable" plan, he decided, would be to deport the future generation of blacks. Infants would be taken from their mothers and placed in orphanages. Since a newborn child was worth only $25.50, Jefferson calculated, the estimated loss of slave property would be reduced to $37.5 million. When these children had reached a proper age, they would be transported to Santo Domingo. "Suppose," Jefferson calculated, "the whole annual increase to be sixty thousand effective births, fifty vessels, of four hundred tons burthen each, constantly employed in that short run, would carry off the increase of every year, and the old stock would die off in the disappearance." Jefferson was confident the effects of his plan would be "blessed." He brushed off any moral squeamishness about taking children from their mothers. "The separation of infants from their mothers . . . would produce some scruples of humanity," he argued. "But this would be straining at a gnat, and swallowing a camel."[6]

Clearly, when he penned those powerful words, "all men are created equal," Jefferson was envisioning a new nation only for people like himself.

Decades later, Jefferson's view became explicitly embedded in law when the U.S. Supreme Court declared in the 1857 Dred Scott decision that Scott, a slave, was not entitled to sue for his freedom. As a Negro, Chief Justice Roger B. Taney argued, he was not a citizen. When the nation was founded, Taney continued, blacks were considered "so far inferior, that they had no rights which the white man was bound to respect." The Founding Fathers, he insisted, had not included blacks in the Declaration of Independence.[7]

An emerging leader of an anti-slavery party strongly disagreed with the Supreme Court, however. In Abraham Lincoln's judgment, Taney had done "obvious violence to the plain unmistakable language of the Declaration." The meaning of the Declaration became the heated focus of the debates between Lincoln and Stephen A. Douglas. Trumpeting Taney's pronouncements on blacks, Douglas declared that blacks belonged to "an inferior race, who in all ages, and in every part of the globe, . . . had shown themselves incapable of self-government." In rebuttal, Lincoln argued that the authors of the Declaration of Independence had never intended "to say all were equal in color, size, intellect, moral developments, or social capacity," but that they "did consider all men created equal — equal in 'certain inalienable rights, among which are life, liberty, and the pursuit of happiness.' "[8]

Introduction

In an earlier exchange with Douglas over whether or not slavery could be excluded from the territories, Lincoln had delineated even more sharply his disagreement with Douglas. Whether slavery could be prohibited in the territories, Lincoln declared, depended upon "whether a negro is *not* or *is* a man." He explained that Douglas had "no very vivid impression that the negro [was] human; and consequently [had] no idea that there [could] be any moral question in legislating about him." But the Declaration of Independence had taught him that all men are created equal, Lincoln insisted, and hence there could be no moral right to slavery because the Negro was a man. In a letter to his old friend Joshua F. Speed, Lincoln wrote that the United States began with the declaration that all men were created equal, but now it was practically read as "all men are created equal, *except negroes.*" If the Know Nothings gained control, he added, it would read "all men are created equal, except negroes, *and foreigners and catholics.*" When these things came to pass, Lincoln continued, "I should prefer emigrating to some country where they make no pretense of loving liberty — to Russia, for instance, where despotism can be taken pure, and without the base alloy of hypocrisy."[9]

But Lincoln was not so certain about how the country should handle the race problem. Like Jefferson, Lincoln considered the idea of colonization for blacks. But where Jefferson wanted to remove a "blot" in order to make the republic racially homogeneous, Lincoln was worried about the welfare of free blacks in a society dominated by prejudice. He thought they might be happier and have more opportunities elsewhere. Moreover, Lincoln regarded colonization as impractical. He said that he would like "to free all slaves, and send them to Liberia — to their own native land. But a moment's reflection would convince me, that whatever of high hope (as I think there is) there may be in this, in the long run, its sudden execution is impossible. If they were all landed there in a day, they would all perish in the next ten days; and there are not surplus shipping and surplus money enough in the world to carry them there in many times ten days." As president, however, Lincoln continued to show some interest in plans for voluntary

53

black emigration. But his considerations were mainly strategic: he thought that these proposals might help to reinforce the support of the border states by offering the reassurance that emancipation would not burden them with free blacks.[10]

But Lincoln never pursued colonization seriously, and military needs and the prospect of losing the war quickly led Lincoln to reject colonization. In the Emancipation Proclamation, effective January 1, 1863, Lincoln declared that former slaves would be received into the armed forces. "An unstated corollary of the President's new position," observed historian David Donald, "was that plans to colonize blacks outside the United States were abandoned. Henceforth Lincoln recognized that blacks were to make their future as citizens of the United States."[11]

During the next few months of the war, the shocking violence, the immense cost in lives, and the critical contribution of black soldiers moved Lincoln to reflect deeply on the nation's destiny that was being manifested on the battlefields. What he had called "the mystic chords of memory" stretching from battlefields to patriot graves had bonded whites and blacks in a common struggle to save the Union. On August 26, 1863, Lincoln wrote to James C. Conkling: "There will be some black men, who can remember that with silent tongue, and clenched teeth, and steady eye, and well-poised bayonet, they have helped mankind on to this great consummation."[12]

On November 9, with nearly 200,000 black men in the Union army, Lincoln gave his Gettysburg Address. At that bloody three-day battle, the casualty rate had been horrific: 3,155 killed and 20,000 wounded and missing for the Union army, and 3,903 killed and 24,000 wounded and missing for the Confederate army. Lincoln had come to help consecrate the cemetery for the dead soldiers. The president declared that "our fathers" had brought forth on this continent, "a new nation, conceived in Liberty, and dedicated to the proposition that all men are created equal." The war was "testing" whether this country so conceived and so dedicated could long endure. Men had given their lives to preserve the Union. "It is for us the living . . . ," Lincoln solemnly told his twenty thousand listeners and all Americans, "to be dedicated here to the unfinished work which they who fought here have thus far so nobly advanced."

A "re-founding father," Lincoln had redefined Jefferson's idea of equality. He had transformed equality into a "self-evident truth" for "all men," regardless of race. In a speech that was just 272 words long, Lincoln gave us what scholar Gary Wills describes as "the words that remade America."[13]

Meanwhile, in communities across the country, the voices of multicultural America were also remaking America. They were not as eloquent as Lincoln, but they, too, were challenging Jefferson's view of a white manifest destiny for the expanding country. Urging us to realize our nation's "unfinished work," they were affirming Walt Whitman's vision for an America where "all races and cultures" would be "accepted" and "saluted," not "controlled or placed in hierarchy," and where all would be welcomed — "Chinese, Irish, German, pauper or not, criminal or not — all, all, without exceptions." Ours was not destined to be a society for "special types" but for the "great mass of people — the vast, surging, hopeful army of workers."[14]

The Significance of the
Frontier in American History:
An Indian Perspective

————————▶ ◀————————

WITHIN ONLY A FEW decades of the arrival of the English colonizers, the original peoples of what would be named New England could see that the new settlers constituted a serious threat to them and their way of life. In 1642 the Narragansett leader Miantonomo urged his people to resist the English intruders. "You know our fathers had plenty of deer and skins, our plains were full of deer, as also our woods, and of turkies, and our coves full of fish and fowl. But these English having gotten our land, they with scythes cut down the grass, and with axes fell the trees; their cows and horses eat the grass, and their hogs spoil our clam banks, and we shall all be starved." Miantonomo called for pan-Indian unity: Indians from all tribes must be "brother to one another," or else all of them will be "gone shortly." Indians should ambush the colonizers, and "kill men, women, and children, but no cows." The cows should be used for food "till our deer be increased again."[1]

The English expansion continued, however, and led to the establishment of a new nation. What would be the future of the original peoples in the republic? On February 16, 1803, President Thomas Jefferson wrote a letter to a political leader in Tennessee regarding federal policies toward Indians. The government, he informed Andrew Jackson, must advise the Indians to sell their "useless" forests and become farmers. Jefferson had also considered what to do if

Indians refused: they should be removed toward what he called the "Stony mountains." Thirty years later, the Cherokees of Georgia had become farmers, but they were still removed because their cultivated lands were coveted by whites.[2]

In 1829, the state legislature passed a law extending its authority over the territory of the Cherokee Nation. The Cherokees were given a choice — leave the state or be subjugated by white rule.

In a message to the General Council of the Cherokee Nation in July 1830, Chief John Ross protested the new policy. He criticized President Andrew Jackson for refusing to protect the Cherokees against Georgia's illegal and unfair actions. The federal government, he insisted, was obligated to honor the treaties guaranteeing the sovereignty of the Cherokee Nation and the integrity of their territory. In 1834, Chief Ross wrote to President Jackson: "The relations of peace and friendship so happily and so long established between the white and the red man . . . induces us, as representatives of the Cherokee nation, to address you [as] Father. The appellation in its original sense carries with it simplicity, and the force of filial regard." By treaty, the Cherokee people had placed themselves under the protection of the federal government, which in turn had given "*assurances* of protection, good neighborhood and the solemn guarantee" for the territorial integrity of the Cherokee Nation.[3]

But Jackson pushed for their removal. Most of the Cherokees refused to migrate. In the spring of 1838, General Winfield Scott carried out the order to remove them by force. He warned the Cherokees that they had to cooperate: "My troops already occupy many positions . . . and thousands and thousands are approaching from every quarter to render assistance and escape alike hopeless. Will you, then by resistance compel us to resort to arms . . . or will you by flight seek to hide yourself in mountains and forests and thus oblige us to hunt you down?" The soldiers first erected internment camps and then rounded up the Cherokees. "Families at dinner were startled by the sudden gleam of bayonets in the doorway and rose up to be driven with blows and oaths along the weary miles of trail that led to the stockade. Men were seized in their fields . . . women were taken from their wheels and children from their play." The process of dispossession was violent and cruel. "The Cherokees are nearly all prisoners," the Reverend Evan Jones protested. "They had been dragged from their houses . . . allowed no time to take any thing with them, except the clothes they had on. Well-furnished houses were left prey to plunderers, who, like hungry wolves, follow in the train of the captors. . . . The property of many have been taken, and sold before their eyes for almost nothing — the sellers and buyers, in many cases having combined to cheat the poor Indians."[4]

From the internment camps, the Cherokees were marched westward. "We are now about to take our final leave and kind farewell to our native land the country that the Great Spirit gave our Fathers," a Cherokee informed Chief Ross. "We are on the eve of leaving that Country that gave us birth. . . . [I]t is with [sorrow] that we are forced by the authority of the white man to quit the scenes of our childhood."[5]

The march took place in the dead of winter. "We are still nearly three hundred miles short of our destination," wrote the Reverend Evan Jones in Little Prairie, Missouri. "It has been exceedingly cold . . . those thinly clad very uncomfortable . . . we have, since the cold set in so severely, sent on a company every morning, to make fires along the road, at short intervals. . . . At the Mississippi river, we were stopped from crossing, by the ice running so that boats could not pass. . . ." The exiles were defenseless against the weather and disease. "Among the recent immigrants," wrote a witness near Little Rock, "there has been much sickness, and in some neighborhoods the mortality has been great. . . . Since last October about 2,000 immigrants have come. Twenty-five hundred more are on their way . . . much sickness and mortality among them." Quatie Ross, the wife of the chief, died of pneumonia at Little Rock. "Long time we travel on way to new land," one of the exiles recalled bitterly. "People feel bad when they leave Old Nation. Women cry and make sad wails. Children cry and many men cry, and all look sad when friends die, but they say nothing and just put heads down and keep on going towards West."[6]

Removal meant separation from a special and sacred place —

their homeland created by the Great Buzzard. A Cherokee song acquired new and deeper meaning from the horror of removal:

> Toward the black coffin of the upland in the Darken-
> ing Land
> your paths shall stretch out.
> So shall it be for you. . . .
> Now your soul has faded away.
> It has become blue.
> When darkness comes your spirit shall grow less and
> dwindle away, never to reappear.

A Cherokee recalled how there were so many bodies to bury: "Looks like maybe all be dead before we get to new Indian country, but always we keep marching on." By the time they reached the new land west of the Mississippi, more than four thousand Cherokees — nearly one-fourth of this exiled Indian nation — died on what they have bitterly remembered as the "Trail of Tears."[7]

Indian removal helped to open the way for westward expansion, and Jefferson's vision of a republic stretching from the Atlantic to the Pacific was fulfilled in the nineteenth century. In 1890, the year the Census Bureau announced the end of the frontier, a Paiute leader of Nevada named Wovoka called upon all Indians to join the Ghost Dance. Wear the muslim "ghost shirts," he told them, and they would be protected against bullets. Wovoka's message promised the restoration of Indian lands and the buffalo: "All Indians must dance, everywhere, keep on dancing. Pretty soon in next spring Big Man [Great Spirit] come. He bring back all game of every kind. . . . When Old Man [God] comes this way, then all the Indians go to mountains, high up away from whites. Whites can't hurt Indians then. Then while Indians way up high, big flood comes like water and all white people die, get drowned. After that water go away and then nobody but Indians everywhere and game all kinds thick."[8]

Wovoka's vision swept across Indian country and was embraced by many Sioux on the Pine Ridge Reservation in South Dakota. The federal government decided to repress the Ghost Dance. Troops surrounded a group of families led by Big Foot, encamped at a creek called Wounded Knee, and ordered the Indians to turn over their guns. The soldiers received the arms, but then began searching the tepees for arms that might have been hidden. Suddenly, shots rang out. The soldiers quickly retreated, and then, firing Hotchkiss guns from the hills above, rained down death on the Indian camp.

"The white man," Luther Standing Bear of the Sioux explained, "does not understand the Indian for the reason that he does not understand America." Continuing to be "troubled with primitive fears," the intruder has "in his consciousness the perils of this frontier continent. . . . The man from Europe is still a foreigner and an alien. And he still hates the man who questioned his path across the continent." Indians questioned what Frederick Jackson Turner trumpeted as "progress." For them, the frontier had a different "significance": their history was how the West was lost.[9]

The Coming of the Wasichus:
Black Elk's Boyhood Memories

In 1930, writer John G. Neihardt visited the Pine Ridge Reservation in South Dakota, where he met a Sioux named Black Elk. Two years later, he published Black Elk Speaks, based on a series of conversations with the holy man and his friends, Fire Thunder and Standing Bear. By then, Black Elk was an old man, and he shared memories of his long life, including growing up on the plains as the civilization of the "Wasichus" (whites) expanded westward. Here he tells us about a "bad dream" becoming real.

———————————▶ ◀———————————

I AM A LAKOTA of the Ogalala band. My father's name was Black Elk, and his father before him bore the name, and the father of his father, so that I am the fourth to bear it. He was a medicine man and so were several of his brothers. Also, he and the great Crazy Horse's father were cousins, having the same grandfather. My mother's name was White Cow Sees; her father was called Refuse-to-Go, and her mother, Plenty Eagle Feathers. I can remember my mother's mother and her father. My father's father was killed by the Pawnees when I was too little to know, and his mother, Red Eagle Woman, died soon after.

I was born in the Moon of the Popping Trees (December) on the Little Powder River in the Winter When the Four Crows Were Killed (1863), and I was three years old when my father's right leg was broken in the Battle of the Hundred Slain. From that wound he limped until the day he died, which was about the time when Big Foot's band was butchered on Wounded Knee (1890). He is buried here in these hills.

I can remember that Winter of the Hundred Slain as a man may remember some bad dream he dreamed when he was little, but I can not tell just how much I heard when I was bigger and how much I understood when I was little. It is like some fearful thing in a fog, for it was a time when everything seemed troubled and afraid.

I had never seen a Wasichu [white man] then, and did not know what one looked like; but every one was saying that the Wasichus were coming and that they were going to take our country and rub us all out and that we should all have to die fighting. It was the Wasichus who got rubbed out in that battle, and all the people were talking about it for a long while; but a hundred Wasichus was not much if there were others and others without number where those came from.

I remember once that I asked my grandfather about this. I said: "When the scouts come back from seeing the prairie full of bison somewhere, the people say the Wasichus are coming; and when strange men are coming to kill us all, they say the Wasichus are coming. What does it mean?" And he said, "That they are many."

When I was older, I learned what the fighting was about that winter and the next summer. Up on the Madison Fork the Wasichus had found much of the yellow metal that they worship and that makes them crazy, and they wanted to have a road up through our country to the place where the yellow metal was; but my people did not want the road. It would scare the bison and make them go away, and also it would let the other Wasichus come in like a river. They told us that they wanted only to use a little land, as much as a wagon would take between the wheels; but our people knew better. And when you look about you now, you can see what it was they wanted.

Once we were happy in our own country and we were seldom hungry, for then the two-leggeds and the four-leggeds lived together like relatives, and there was plenty for them and for us. But the Wasichus came, and they have made little islands for us and other little islands for the four-leggeds, and always these islands are becoming smaller, for around them surges the gnawing flood of the Wasichu; and it is dirty with lies and greed.

A long time ago my father told me what his father told him,
that there was once a Lakota holy man, called Drinks Water, who
dreamed what was to be; and this was long before the coming of
the Wasichus. He dreamed that the four-leggeds were going back
into the earth and that a strange race had woven a spider's web
all around the Lakotas. And he said: "When this happens, you shall
live in square gray houses, in a barren land, and beside those square
gray houses you shall starve." They say he went back to Mother
Earth soon after he saw this vision, and it was sorrow that killed
him. You can look about you now and see that he meant these
dirt-roofed houses we are living in, and that all the rest was true.
Sometimes dreams are wiser than waking.

And so when the soldiers came and built themselves a town of
logs there on the Piney Fork of the Powder, my people knew they
meant to have their road and take our country and maybe kill us
all when they were strong enough. Crazy Horse was only about
19 years old then, and Red Cloud was still our great chief. In the
Moon of the Changing Season (October) he called together all the
scattered bands of the Lakota for a big council on the Powder River,
and when we went on the warpath against the soldiers, a horseback
could ride through our villages from sunrise until the day was
above his head, so far did our camp stretch along the valley of the
river; for many of our friends, the Shyela [Cheyennes] and the Blue
Clouds [Arapahoes], had come to help us fight.

And it was about when the bitten moon was delayed (last quarter) in the Time of the Popping Trees when the hundred were
rubbed out. My friend, Fire Thunder here, who is older than I,
was in that fight and he can tell you how it was.

Fire Thunder Speaks:

I was 16 years old when this happened, and after the big council
on the Powder we had moved over to the Tongue River where we
were camping at the mouth of Peno Creek. There were many of
us there. Red Cloud was over all of us, but the chief of our band
was Big Road. We started out on horseback just about sunrise,
riding up the creek toward the soldiers' town on the Piney, for

we were going to attack it. The sun was about half way up when we stopped at the place where the Wasichu's road came down a steep, narrow ridge and crossed the creek. It was a good place to fight, so we sent some men ahead to coax the soldiers out. While they were gone, we divided into two parts and hid in the gullies on both sides of the ridge and waited. After a long while we heard a shot up over the hill, and we knew the soldiers were coming. So we held the noses of our ponies that they might not whinny at the soldiers' horses. Soon we saw our men coming back, and some of them were walking and leading their horses, so that the soldiers would think they were worn out. Then the men we had sent ahead came running down the road between us, and the soldiers on horseback followed, shooting. When they came to the flat at the bottom of the hill, the fighting began all at once. I had a sorrel horse, and just as I was going to get on him, the soldiers turned around and began to fight their way back up the hill. I had a six-shooter that I had traded for, and also a bow and arrows. When the soldiers started back, I held my sorrel with one hand and began killing them with the six-shooter, for they came close to me. There were so many bullets, but there were more arrows — so many that it was like a cloud of grasshoppers all above and around the soldiers; and our people, shooting across, hit each other. The soldiers were falling all the while they were fighting back up the hill, and their horses got loose. Many of our people chased the horses, but I was not after horses; I was after Wasichus. When the soldiers got on top, there were not many of them left and they had no place to hide. They were fighting hard. We were told to crawl up on them, and we did. When we were close, some-one yelled: "Let us go! This is a good day to die. Think of the helpless ones at home!" Then we all cried, "Hoka hey!" and rushed at them. I was young then and quick on my feet, and I was one of the first to get in among the soldiers. They got up and fought very hard until not one of them was alive. They had a dog with them, and he started back up the road for the soldiers' town, howl-ing as he ran. He was the only one left. I did not shoot at him because he looked too sweet; but many did shoot, and he died full of arrows. So there was nobody left of the soldiers. Dead men and horses and wounded Indians were scattered all the way up the hill, and their blood was frozen, for a storm had come up and it was very cold and getting colder all the time. We left all the dead lying there, for the ground was solid, and we picked up our wounded and started back; but we lost most of them before we reached our camp at the mouth of the Peno. There was a big blizzard that night; and some of the wounded who did not die on the way, died after we got home. This was the time when Black Elk's father had his leg broken.

Black Elk Continues:

I am quite sure that I remember the time when my father came home with a broken leg that he got from killing so many Wasichus, and it seems that I can remember all about the battle too, but I think I could not. It must be the fear that I remember most. All this time I was not allowed to play very far away from our tepee, and my mother would say, "If you are not good the Wasichus will get you."

We must have broken camp at the mouth of the Peno soon after the battle, for I can remember my father lying on a pony drag with bison robes all around him, like a baby, and my mother riding the pony. The snow was deep and it was very cold, and I remember sitting in another pony drag beside my father and mother, all wrapped up in fur. We were going away from where the soldiers were, and I do not know where we went, but it was west.

It was a hungry winter, for the deep snow made it hard to find the elk; and also many of the people went snowblind. We wandered a long time, and some of the bands got lost from each other. Then at last we were camping in the woods beside a creek somewhere, and the hunters came back with meat.

I think it was this same winter when a medicine man, by the name of Creeping, went around among the people curing snowblinds. He would put snow upon their eyes, and after he had sung a certain sacred song that he had heard in a dream, he would blow on the backs of their heads and they would see again, so I have heard. It was about the dragonfly that he sang, for that was where he got his power, they say.

When it was summer again we were camping on the Rosebud, and I did not feel so much afraid, because the Wasichus seemed farther away and there was peace there in the valley and there was plenty of meat. But all the boys from five or six years up were playing war. The little boys would gather together from the different bands of the tribe and fight each other with mud balls that they threw with willow sticks. And the big boys played the game called Throwing-Them-Off-Their-Horses, which is a battle all but the killing; and sometimes they got hurt. The horsebacks from the different bands would line up and charge upon each other, yelling; and when the ponies came together on the run, they would rear and flounder and scream in a big dust, and the riders would seize each other, wrestling until one side had lost all its men, for those who fell upon the ground were counted dead.

When I was older, I, too, often played this game. We were always naked when we played it, just as warriors are when they go into battle if it is not too cold, because they are swifter without clothes. Once I fell off on my back right in the middle of a bed of prickly pears, and it took my mother a long while to pick all the stickers out of me. I was still too little to play war that summer, but I can remember watching the other boys, and I thought that when we all grew up and were big together, maybe we could kill all the Wasichus or drive them far away from our country.

It was in the Moon When the Cherries Turn Black (August) that all the people were talking again about a battle, and our warriors came back with many wounded. It was The Attacking of the Wagons, and it made me afraid again, for we did not win that battle as we did the other one, and there was much mourning for the dead. Fire Thunder was in that fight too, and he can tell you how it was that day.

Fire Thunder Speaks:

It was very bad. There is a wide flat prairie with hills around it, and in the middle of this the Wasichus had put the boxes of their wagons in a circle, so that they could keep their mules there at night. There were not many Wasichus, but they were lying behind the boxes and they shot faster than they ever shot at us before. We thought it was some new medicine of great power that they had, for they shot so fast that it was like tearing a blanket. Afterwards I learned that it was because they had new guns that they loaded from behind, and this was the first time they used these guns. We came on after sunrise. There were many, many of us, and we meant to ride right over them and rub them out. But our ponies were afraid of the ring of fire the guns of the Wasichus made, and would not go over. Our women were watching us from the hills and we could hear them singing and mourning whenever the shooting stopped. We tried hard, but we could not do it, and there were dead warriors and horses piled all around the boxes and scattered over the plain. Then we left our horses in a gulch and charged on foot, but it was like green grass withering in a fire. So we picked up our wounded and went away. I do not know how many of our people were killed, but there were very many. It was bad.

Black Elk Continues:

I do not remember where we camped that winter but it must have been a time of peace and of plenty to eat.

Standing Bear Speaks:

I am four years older than Black Elk, and he and I have been good friends since boyhood. I know it was on the Powder that we camped where there were many cottonwood trees. Ponies like to eat the bark of these trees and it is good for them. That was the winter when High Shirt's mother was killed by a big tree that fell on her tepee. It was a very windy night and there were noises that 'woke me, and then I heard that an old woman had been killed, and it was High Shirt's mother.

Black Elk Continues:

I was four years old then, and I think it must have been the next summer that I first heard the voices. It was a happy summer and nothing was afraid, because in the Moon When the Ponies Shed (May) word came from the Wasichus that there would be peace and that they would not use the road any more and that all the soldiers would go away. The soldiers did go away and their towns were torn down; and in the Moon of Falling Leaves (November), they made a treaty with Red Cloud that said our country would be ours as long as grass should grow and water flow. You can see that it is not the grass and the water that have forgotten. . . .

The End of the Frontier
for a Winnebago

In 1920, ethnologist Paul Radin published "The Autobiography of a Winnebago Indian" in the University of California Publications in American Archaeology and Ethnology. The life story of this Indian born in the nineteenth century was written in a syllabic form of the Winnebago language and then translated by Radin. Here he gives us a different view of the end of the frontier than the one presented by Frederick Jackson Turner. For this Winnebago, the triumph of "civilization" over "savagery" meant performing as an "Indian" in a Wild West show.

Early Childhood

FATHER AND MOTHER had four children and after that I was born, it is said. An uncle of mother's who was named White-Cloud, said to her, "You are to give birth to a child who will not be an ordinary person." Thus he spoke to her. It was then my mother gave birth to me. As soon as I was born and was being washed — as my neck was being washed — I laughed out loudly.

I was a good-tempered boy, it is said. At boyhood my father told me to fast and I obeyed. In the winter every morning I would crush charcoal and blacken my face with it. I would arise very early and do it. As soon as the sun rose I would go outside and sit looking at the sun and I would cry to the spirits.

Thus I acted until I became conscious.

Then there were not as many white people around as there are now. My father always hunted. Our lodge was covered with rush mattings and we had reed mattings spread over the floor. After my father had hunted for a considerable time in one place we would move away. My father, mother, older sisters, and older brothers

69

all carried packs on their backs, in which they carried many things. Thus we would pass the time until the spring of the year, and then in the spring we used to move away to live near some stream where father could hunt muskrats, mink, otter, and beaver.

In the summer we would go back to Black River Falls, Wisconsin.

The Indians all returned to that place after they had given their feasts. We then picked berries. When we picked berries my father used to buy me gum, so that I would not eat many berries when I was picking. However, I soon managed to eat berries and chew gum at the same time. After a while I learned to chew tobacco and then I did not eat any berries (while picking them). Later on I got to like tobacco very much and I probably used up more value (in tobacco) than I would have done had I eaten the berries.

In the fall of the year we would pick cranberries and after that, when the hunting season was open, I would begin to fast again.

I did this every year for a number of years.

After a while we got a pony on which we used to pack all our belongings when we moved camp. And in addition about three of us would ride on top of the pack. Sometimes my mother rode and father drove the pony when we moved from one place to another. . . .

In those days we used to travel in canoes. My father used to spear fish and would always take me along with him, and I enjoyed it very much. He kept a club in the canoe and after he had speared a fish, I would kill it with the club as it was jumping around in the canoe. Sometimes my mother accompanied us as a third person. She would sit at the rear end and row while father, standing in the prow, speared the fish. I killed all those that were thrown into the canoe with my club.

Sometimes my parents started out without me but I would then cry so bitterly that I always induced them to take me along. Sometimes they would whip me and tell me to go home but I used to follow them so far that they were afraid to let me go back alone and they would let me ride along with them. Indeed I exerted myself greatly in crying for them, and as I cried and ran after them and followed them very far, I was in the end always taken along.

In those days we always lived in the old-fashioned Indian lodges. In winter our fire was placed in the center of the lodge and my father used to keep it burning all night. When he placed a large log in the fire it would burn a long time. This is what we used to do in the winter.

We were three boys, of whom I was the youngest, and at night we used to sleep together. In cold weather we used to fight as to who was to sleep in the middle for whoever got that place was warm, for while those at either end used to pull the cover from each other, the one in the middle was always covered. Even after I grew up I always took the covering away from whomsoever I was sleeping with. I would always fold it under me, for it had become a habit with me to take the cover away from the other person (whenever I slept on the outside).

We always ate out of one dish. Sometimes we did not have enough food on hand and then I would always try to get enough by eating very fast. In this way I always succeeded in depriving the others of their proper portion. Sometimes, on the other hand, I would purposely eat slowly, and then when the others were finished, I would say that I had not been given enough and so I would get some of their food. In this way I developed a habit (that I still have), for I am a fast eater. Even after I grew up, whenever I ate with other people, I always finished sooner than they. (Another habit that I acquired then) was the ability to go without food for a whole day while traveling. I did not mind this in the least for (during my fasting) I had grown accustomed to going without food for long periods of time.

In the summer, at the season when people pick berries, I used to go around visiting, sometimes for a day, sometimes for longer. I would often receive nothing to eat, but I did not mind that. In the summer, when people pick berries, they generally go out in bands and settle here and there. Some were far away from others. . . .

Courting

It was at this time that I desired to court women and I tried it. However, I did not know the proper thing to say. The young men always went around at night courting. I used to mix with the women in the daytime but when I went to them at night I did not know what to say. A brother of mine, the oldest, seemed to know how to do it. He was a handsome man and he offered to show me how. Then I went with him at night. We went to a girl who was having her menses at that time. She was a young girl. When girls get their menses they always have to live apart. It was to such a one that we went. We were very cautious about the matter for the girls were always carefully watched as their relatives knew that it was customary to court them at such a time. (One of the precautions they used) was to pile sticks and branches about the lodge so that it would be difficult to enter. If a person tried to enter he was likely to make a noise moving the branches and this would awaken the people living in the larger lodge nearby and they might run out to see what was the matter.

It was to such a place that we went. After working at the obstacles placed near the entrance for some time, my brother entered the lodge. I went as close as possible and lay down to listen. He spoke in an audible whisper so that I might hear him. Sure enough I heard him. However after lying there for some time I fell asleep. When I snored my brother would wake me up. Afterwards the girl found out and she sent us both away. Thus we acted every now and then.

After a while I entered the lodges myself. We always had blankets wrapped around us and we took care to have our heads well covered (on such occasions).

Sometimes a girl was acquainted with quite a large number of men and then these would gather around her lodge at night and annoy her parents a good deal. We would keep them awake all night. Some of these people owned vicious dogs.

There was one old woman who had a daughter and when this daughter had her menses, she stayed in an oblong lodge with just room enough for two persons. She watched her daughter very carefully. Finally she slept with her. We nevertheless bothered her all the time just out of meanness. One night we went there and kept her awake almost all night. However, just about dawn she fell asleep, so we — there were several of us — pulled up the whole lodge, poles and everything, and threw the poles in the thicket. The next morning the two were found sleeping in the open, it was rumored, and the mother was criticised for being over careful.

The reason why some of the (older) people were so careful at that time was because it had been reported that some young men had forced themselves into lodges where they had not been received willingly.

Once I went to see a young girl and arrived there before the people had retired, so I waited near the lodge until they would go to sleep. As I lay there waiting, listening to them, I fell asleep. When I woke up it was morning and as the people got up they found me sleeping there. I felt very ashamed of myself and they laughed at me. I was not long in getting away.

We always did these things secretly for it was considered a disgrace to be caught or discovered.

On another occasion, in another place, I was crawling into a lodge when someone woke up as I was about halfway in. I immediately stopped and remained quiet and waited for the people to fall asleep again. However in waiting I, myself, fell asleep. When they woke me up in the morning I was lying halfway inside the lodge, asleep. After waking me up they asked me whether I would not stay for breakfast, but I immediately ran away.

After a while I began going around with some particular girl and I liked it so much that I would never go to sleep at night. My older brothers were very much the same. We used to sleep during the day. . . .

Wandering and Hunting

After a while I used to get in the habit of going to town. When I got there, I would look into all the barrels to see if there was any food in them, and if there was I would fill my pockets (with whatever I found). My pockets would be full. I used to steal a great deal.

About springtime we always moved away (from town). We would move to whatever place my father intended to trap in, generally to some farming community where there were few Indians. There my mother used to make baskets and sell them to the farmers. We would also circulate a written petition (asking) for any help people cared to give us. Whenever they went on this kind of a (begging) trip, I always went along with them, for sometimes people would take pity on us and at such times they often gave me old clothes. Sometimes we would even get a good meal at some farmer's house. For these reasons, I was always envious of those who went along on such trips.

Occasionally when we got a lot of provisions I had to carry some of them, but I never minded that. In the spring of the year we would begin to shoot with bows and arrows. When the birds returned north, father used to make us bows and arrows and we would shoot birds and sometimes kill many of them. We also used to kill squirrels and my grandmother would roast them for us. My older brother used to be a good shot. I was greatly inferior to him. He often killed pheasants.

Whenever (the older people) went to a large town circulating petitions for help, we youngsters always went along with them. We always took our bows and arrows along with us, for the whites wanted to see how well we could shoot and often placed five-cent pieces on some object at a considerable distance and had us shoot at them. We generally hit a number. I would also let my brother shoot at twenty-five-cent pieces that I would hold between my fingers and he never hit my fingers. We would often make as much as five dollars in this manner and we always gave this money to our parents.

In summer the Indians were accustomed to return from the various places (where they had been camping) to Black River Falls. Therefore we also returned to Black River Falls. In summer we would go out shooting with our bows and arrows and we generally stayed away all day. At evening when we got home, of course we always expected to get a scolding so we always had some excuse made up for the occasion. It really would have been better had we returned earlier in the day, but we always enjoyed (the hunting) so much that night would overtake us when we were still a long distance from home. Often we would not eat anything all day, but we were quite accustomed to that. Sometimes we would go fishing down a stream that runs nearby and again we would forget (the time) and not return home until it was very late. We would then get a scolding even if we gave some sort of an excuse. . . .

Marriage

One fall I stayed with my grandfather. He told me to get married. I was about twenty-three years old then. I had courted women ever since I was old enough. Every time I did anything I always thought of women in connection with it. I tried to court as many women as I could. I wanted badly to be a beau for I considered it a great thing. I wanted to be a ladies' man.

My grandfather had asked me to marry a certain girl, so I went over to the place where she was staying. When I arrived there I tried to meet the girl secretly, which I succeeded in doing. I told her of my intention and asked her to go home with me. Then she went home for I had met her some distance from her home.

After a while she came back all dressed up and ready. She had on a waist covered with silver buckles and a beautifully colored hair ornament and she wore many strings of beads around her neck, and bracelets around her wrists. Her fingers were covered with rings and she wore a pair of ornamented leggings. She wore a wide-flap ornamented moccasin and in each ear she had about half a dozen ear holes and they were full of small silver pieces made into ear ornaments. She was painted also. She had painted her cheeks red and the parting of her hair red. She was all dressed up.

I went there on horseback. We rode the horse together. We were not going that night to the place from which I had come, because

I had previously been asked to sing at a medicine feast by my band (at a place) which was on our way home. I would therefore not go home until the next morning. So on my way there I had the girl hide near the place where we were to have the feast, for we were eloping and that was the custom.

The girl had a red blanket which she was wearing so I had her hide under a small oak bush. It rained all night and the next day. When we were through in the morning, I went to the place (where I had put her) and she was still there, but she was soaked through and through from the rain and her paint was smeared over her face in such a way that one could hardly recognize her. Then we went home. When we arrived home, my grandfather's wife came out to meet us and she helped the girl down from the horse and led her into the lodge. Then we ate. When we were through, the girl took off her clothing and gave it to them and they gave her other clothing to wear. After the girl had stayed there three nights, she had her menses, so she had to camp by herself, and there she had to sleep at night. Then a horse was given to this girl that I had married.

After a while my grandfather had a private talk with me, and he said: "Grandson, it is said that this girl you have married is not a maiden but really a widow, and I am not pleased with it, as this is your first marriage and you are a young man. I suppose you know whether it is true or not, whether she is a maiden or not?" "Yes," I answered. "You can stop living with her, if you wish," he said. So I went away on a visit and from there I went away for good. After some time I learned that the woman had gone home. Then I went home. He (my grandfather) was glad that I had not stayed with her. "You can marry another and a better one," said he to me, "one that I shall choose for you, you shall marry." Thus he spoke to me. However I said to him, "Grandfather, you have begged women for me often enough. Don't ever ask for anyone for me again, as I do not care to marry a woman that is begged for." Thus I spoke to him. He was not at all pleased at this for he said I was not allowing him to command me. . . .

Drinking

About this time I got in the habit of giving women whiskey and getting them drunk, and when I drank and got a woman drunk, then I would steal anything of value she had (on her person). I used to abuse people a great deal. At one time I got to be very handy with boxing gloves. I was never defeated, and that is why I always acted meanly to people. They were always afraid of me for they knew (of my skill). My father was a strong man and had never been defeated at wrestling and my older brothers likewise had never been defeated. For these reasons I was very arrogant. Besides this, I was very big. I am six feet and two inches tall and I weighed two hundred and fifty-five pounds. As a matter of fact I was not strong but merely acted as though I were, for every time I got drunk, I always found myself bound when I got sober. I never stayed with any woman long. All I did was to wander around visiting and doing nothing but drink.

I had four sisters and it was from them and my parents that I received everything I ever possessed, yet I claimed to be a great man. I then had two women staying with me as my wives, and, at one time I had as many as four, two at my parents' house and two staying with other relatives of mine. I wasn't serious with any of them. I lied all the time and I knew how to tell falsehoods. On one occasion four children were born to me and each one had a different mother. Nevertheless even after that I still courted women and kept on drinking. . . .

With a Circus

Once we went out hunting in the fall of the year. We killed some game. We used to sell the hind quarters of the deer we killed. Sometimes we would ship them away to Chicago. We were, of course, only permitted to hunt for thirty days. If anyone hunted longer than that, he would (of course) be arrested (if caught). Such was the law. But in spite of the law we hunted beyond the prescribed time on the theory that the law was only meant for the whites. We shipped some more (deer) away and were detected. We had shipped deer and as a result my elder brother and myself were arrested and taken to court, where we were told that we would have to spend sixty days in jail. We were then put in jail. There we stayed. During our imprisonment I never had my hair cut and from that time on I wore my hair long. I told people that he whom we call Trickster had instructed me to do this and that he had blessed me, and I told my elder brother to do the same thing (i.e., to let his hair grow) and (Trickster) would bless him with (long) life. From that time on I wore long hair.

After a while my hair grew very long. Then I went out among the whites with a show. They (the people) liked me very much because I had long hair and I was well paid. During all that time I drank. After a while I learned to ride a bicycle and I also learned to ride wild horses. I always used to say that I was a cowboy, because I wore my hair long. I used to ride many vicious horses and many times I was thrown off. I did all this because I was wild, not because I (really) was an expert. (At one time) I took part in a bicycle race on a race track. I was in full Indian costume and wore long hair.

This (show) played at St. Paul, Minn. I took part in it every summer. Soon I became acquainted with many people and they always asked me to come again. Finally I would not even return to the Indians in winter.

From Sunup to Sundown:
Laboring in the Cotton Fields

---------→ ◄---------

IN THE SOUTH, 4 million blacks were slaves, representing 35 percent of the total population in 1860. They constituted the essential labor force in Southern agriculture for tobacco, hemp, rice, sugar, and especially cotton cultivation.

Work on the plantations began early in the morning when a horn awakened the slaves an hour before daylight. "All work-hands are [then] required to rise and prepare their cooking, etc. for the day," a plantation manual stated. "The second horn is blown just at good day-light, when it is the duty of the driver to visit every house and see that all have left for the field." Work was highly regimented. A glimpse of plantation labor was captured by a traveler in Mississippi: "First came, led by an old driver carrying a whip, forty of the largest and strongest women I ever saw together; they were all in a simple uniform dress of a bluish check stuff, the skirts reaching little below the knee; their legs and feet were bare; they carried themselves loftily, each having a hoe over the shoulder, and walking with a free, powerful swing, like *chasseurs* on the march. Behind came the cavalry, thirty strong, mostly men, but a few of them women, two of whom rode astride on the plow mules. A lean and vigilant white overseer, on a brisk pony, brought up the rear."[1]

A slave described the routine of a workday: "The hands are required to be in the cotton field as soon as it is light in the morning, and, with the exception of ten or fifteen minutes, which is given to them at noon to swallow their allowance of cold bacon, they

79

are not permitted to be a moment idle until it is too dark to see, and when the moon is full, they often times labor till the middle of the night." After they left the fields, they had more work to do. "Each one must attend to his respective chores. One feeds the mules, another the swine — another cuts the wood, and so forth; besides the packing [of cotton] is all done by candle light. Finally, at a late hour, they reach the quarters, sleepy and overcome with the long day's toil."[2]

Slavemasters often characterized their slaves as Sambos, docile and happy. Asked about whether he desired freedom, a slave replied to a curious visitor: "No, massa, me no want to be free, have good massa, take care of me when I sick, never 'buse nigger; no, me no want to be free." In a letter to his master, who was away on a trip, a slave ended his report on plantation operations: "The respects of your affec. Svt. unto D[eath] in hopes ever to merit your esteem. Your most dutiful servant. Harford."[3]

But slaves who behaved like Sambos might not have actually been Sambos: they might have been playing the role of loyal and congenial slaves in order to get favors or to survive, while keeping their inner selves hidden. "The only weapon of self defence that I could use successfuly, was that of deception," explained fugitive slave Henry Bibb. Another former slave explained that one had to "know the *heart* of the poor slave — learn his secret thoughts — thoughts he dare not utter in the hearing of the white man."[4]

Indeed, many slaves wore masks of docility and deference in order to shroud subversive plans. Every year thousands of slaves became fugitives, making their way North to freedom, and many of these runaways had seemed passive and cheerful before they escaped. After his flight north, fugitive J. W. Loguen received a letter from his former slave mistress. "You know that we reared you as we reared our own children," wrote Mrs. Sarah Logue, "that you was never abused, and that shortly before you ran away, when your master asked you if you would like to be sold, you said you would not leave him to go with any body." In his reply, Loguen caustically remarked: "Woman, did you raise your *own children* for the market? Did you raise them for the whipping-post?" The ex-slave boldly proclaimed his love for liberty: "Wretched woman! Be it known to you that I value my freedom . . . more, indeed, than my own life; more than all the lives of all the slaveholders and tyrants under heaven."[5]

Sometimes a slave would play the role of Sambo and then strike directly at his tyrant. Slavemaster William Pearce told one of his erring slaves that he would be whipped after supper. When the slave was called out, he approached Pearce submissively. As soon as he was within striking distance, the slave pulled out a concealed axe and split his master's head. Nat Turner, according to historian Kenneth Stampp, was "apparently as humble and docile as a slave was expected to be." In Virginia on August 22, 1831, he led seventy fellow slaves in a violent insurrection that lasted two days and left nearly sixty whites dead. After his arrest, Turner made a statement to the authorities. His master, he acknowledged, was "kind": "in fact, I had no cause to complain of his treatment to me." But Turner had had a religious experience: "I had a vision — and I saw white spirits and black spirits engaged in battle . . . and blood flowed in streams. . . ." A voice told him to wait for a sign from heaven: "And on the appearance of the sign, (the eclipse of the sun last February) I should arise and prepare myself, and slay my enemies with their own weapons." Turner carried out his mission, and a white Virginian nervously observed: "It will long be remembered in the annals of our country, and many a mother as she presses her infant darling to her bosom, will shudder at the recollection of Nat Turner."[6]

The reality for many slaves may have been even more complex and subtle than a duality of roles. Some Sambo-like behavior may have been not so much a veil to hide inner emotions of rage and discontent as a means of expressing them. Lying, stealing, laziness, immaturity, and ignorance all contained within them an aggressive quality: they constituted, in effect, resistance to efficiency, discipline, work, and productivity.

"Hands won't work unless I am in sight," a Virginia planter scribbled angrily in his diary. "I left the Field at 12 [with] all going on well, but very little done after [that]." Slaves occasionally de-

A LARGER MEMORY

stroyed tools and machinery and treated farm work animals so brutally that they frequently crippled them. "They can neither hoe,
nor ditch, chop wood, nor perform any kind of labor with a white
man's skill," complained a master. "They break and destroy more
farming utensils, ruin more carts, break more gates, spoil more
cattle and horses, and commit more waste than five times the number of white laborers do." A continual problem for masters was
the stealing of chickens and pigs. But slaves often viewed the matter
differently: they were simply "taking" property (pigs) for use by
other property (themselves). In other words, the master's "meat"
was taken out of "one tub" and put in "another." "When I tuk
the turkey and eat it," a slave said, "it got to be a part of me."
This appropriation seemed justified because their weekly food allowance was so meager, and their masters were profiting from
their labor.[7]

During the Civil War, information about the conflict circulated
through slave quarters. Pretending indifference, house servants listened intently as their masters talked among themselves about the
military and political events of the conflict. "We'se can't read, but
we'se can listen," a South Carolina slave told Union soldiers. What
was most striking was the way the presence of federal troops in
an area stimulated noticeable changes in slave behavior. A few days
after Union soldiers camped near her plantation, a slaveholder
wrote in her diary: "The Negroes are going off in great numbers
and are beginning to be very independent and impudent."[8]

Slaves were impatient, ready to break for freedom. During the
war, some half a million slaves ran off to the federal lines. In 1863,
a Northern clergyman asked a Virginia slave whether she had heard
of the Emancipation Proclamation. "Oh, yes, massa!" she responded, "we all knows about it; only we darsn't let on. We pre-
tends not to know. I said to my ole massa, 'What's this Massa
Lincoln is going to do to the poor nigger? I hear he is going to
cut 'em up awful bad. How is it, massa?' I just pretended foolish,
sort of." Shortly after this conversation, she ran off to the Union
lines.[9]

Another slave remembered the day the Union troops arrived at his master's plantation located on the coast of South Carolina: "De people was all a hoein'. . . . Dey was a hoein' in de rice-field, when de gunboats come. Den ebry man drap dem hoe, and leff de rice. De mas'r he stand and call, 'Run to de wood for hide. Yankee come, sell you to Cuba! run for hide!' Ebry man he run, and my God! run all toder way! Mas'r stand in de wood. . . . He say 'Run to de wood!' an ebry man run by him, straight to de boat."[10]

"Don't Give a Nigger an Inch":
Frederick Douglass Learns to Read

Frederick Douglass was born a slave on the Eastern Shore of Maryland in 1817. He was raised by his grandparents during his early years. "My only recollections of my own mother," he recalled, "are of a few hasty visits made in the night on foot, after the daily tasks were over, and when she was under the necessity of returning in time to respond to the driver's call to the field in the early morning. . . . Of my father I know nothing." Douglass came to believe that his father was his master. "I was given away by my father [Thomas Auld], or the man who was called my father," he later wrote, "to his own brother [Hugh]." At the age of nine, Douglass was taken to Baltimore, where he lived in the home of Hugh Auld and his wife, Sophia. There he had an experience that changed his life: he was taught to read. His teacher, Sophia, had given the young slave an "inch" of an awareness of his own humanity, and he took not an "ell" (forty-five inches) but a mile. Douglass would later escape from slavery to become a leading abolitionist and would help to free America from the national curse of slavery.[1]

E STABLISHED IN MY new home in Baltimore, I was not very long in perceiving that in picturing to myself what was to be my life there, my imagination had painted only the bright side, and that the reality had its dark shades as well as its light ones. The open country which had been so much to me was all shut out. Walled in on every side by towering brick buildings, the heat of the summer was intolerable to me, and the hard brick pavements almost blistered my feet. If I ventured out on to the streets, new and strange objects glared upon me at every step, and startling sounds greeted my ears from all directions. My country eyes and ears were confused and bewildered. Troops of hostile boys pounced upon me at every corner. They chased me, and called me "eastern-shore man," till really I almost wished myself back on the Eastern Shore. My new mistress happily proved to be all she had seemed, and in her presence I easily forgot all outside annoyances. Mrs. Sophia was naturally of an excellent disposition — kind, gentle, and cheerful. The supercilious contempt for the rights and feelings of others, and the petulance and bad humor which generally characterized slaveholding ladies, were all quite absent from her manner and bearing toward me.

She had never been a slaveholder — a thing then quite unusual at the South — but had depended almost entirely upon her own industry for a living. To this fact the dear lady no doubt owed the excellent preservation of her natural goodness of heart, for slavery could change a saint into a sinner, and an angel into a demon. I hardly knew how to behave towards "Miss Sopha," as I used to call Mrs. Hugh Auld. I could not approach her even as I had formerly approached Mrs. Thomas Auld. Why should I hang down my head, and speak with bated breath, when there was no pride to scorn me, no coldness to repel me, and no hatred to inspire me with fear? I therefore soon came to regard her as something more akin to a mother than a slaveholding mistress. So far from deeming it impudent in a slave to look her straight in the face, she seemed ever to say, "Look up, child; don't be afraid." The sailors belonging to the sloop esteemed it a great privilege to be the bearers of parcels or messages for her, for whenever they came, they were sure of a most kind and pleasant reception. If little Thomas was her son, and her most dearly loved child, she made me something like his half-brother in her affections. If dear Tommy was exalted to a place on his mother's knee, "Freddy" was honored by a place at the mother's side. Nor did the slave-boy lack the caressing strokes of her gentle hand, soothing him into the consciousness that, though motherless, he was not friendless. Mrs. Auld was not only kind-hearted, but remarkably pious, frequent in her attendance at public worship and much given to reading the Bible and to chanting hymns of praise when alone.

Mr. Hugh was altogether a different character. He cared very little about religion, knew more of the world and was more a part

of the world, than his wife. He doubtless set out to be, as the world
goes, a respectable man and to get on by becoming a successful
ship-builder, in that city of shipbuilding. This was his ambition,
and it fully occupied him. I was of course of very little consequence
to him, and when he smiled upon me, as he sometimes did, the
smile was borrowed from his lovely wife, and like borrowed light,
was transient, and vanished with the source whence it was derived.
Though I must in truth characterize Master Hugh as a sour man
of forbidding appearance, it is due to him to acknowledge that he
was never cruel to me, according to the notion of cruelty in Maryland. During the first year or two, he left me almost exclusively
to the management of his wife. She was my lawgiver. In hands so
tender as hers, and in the absence of the cruelties of the plantation,
I became both physically and mentally much more sensitive, and
a frown from my mistress caused me far more suffering than had
Aunt Katy's hardest cuffs. Instead of the cold, damp floor of my
old master's kitchen, I was on carpets; for the corn bag in winter,
I had a good straw bed, well furnished with covers; for the coarse
corn meal in the morning, I had good bread and mush occasionally; for my old tow-linen shirt, I had good clean clothes. I was
really well off. My employment was to run of errands, and to take
care of Tommy, to prevent his getting in the way of carriages, and
to keep him out of harm's way generally.

So for a time everything went well. I say for a time, because the
fatal poison of irresponsible power, and the natural influence of
slave customs, were not very long in making their impression on
the gentle and loving disposition of my excellent mistress. She at
first regarded me as a child, like any other. This was the natural
and spontaneous thought; afterwards, when she came to consider
me as property, our relations to each other were changed, but a
nature so noble as hers could not instantly become perverted, and
it took several years before the sweetness of her temper was wholly
lost.

The frequent hearing of my mistress reading the Bible aloud,
for she often read aloud when her husband was absent, awakened
my curiosity in respect to this mystery of reading, and roused in me

the desire to learn. Up to this time I had known nothing whatever of this wonderful art, and my ignorance and inexperience of what it could do for me, as well as my confidence in my mistress, emboldened me to ask her to teach me to read. With an unconscious and inexperience equal to my own, she readily consented, and in an incredibly short time, by her kind assistance, I had mastered the alphabet and could spell words of three or four letters. My mistress seemed almost as proud of my progress as if I had been her own child, and supposing that her husband would be as well pleased, she made no secret of what she was doing for me. Indeed, she exultingly told him of the aptness of her pupil and of her intention to persevere, as she felt it her duty to do, in teaching me, at least, to read the Bible. And here arose the first dark cloud over my Baltimore prospects, the precursor of chilling blasts and drenching storms. Master Hugh was astounded beyond measure and, probably for the first time, proceeded to unfold to his wife the true philosophy of the slave system, and the peculiar rules necessary in the nature of the case to be observed in the management of human chattels. Of course he forbade her to give me any further instruction, telling her in the first place that to do so was unlawful, as it was also unsafe, "for," said he, "if you give a nigger an inch he will take an ell. Learning will spoil the best nigger in the world. If he learns to read the Bible it will forever unfit him to be a slave. He should know nothing but the will of his master, and learn to obey it. As to himself, learning will do him no good, but a great deal of harm, making him disconsolate and unhappy. If you teach him how to read, he'll want to know how to write, and this accomplished, he'll be running away with himself." Such was the tenor of Master Hugh's oracular exposition, and it must be confessed that he very clearly comprehended the nature and the requirements of the relation of master and slave. His discourse was the first decidely anti-slavery lecture to which it had been my lot to listen. Mrs. Auld evidently felt the force of what he said, and, like an obedient wife, began to shape her course in the direction indicated by him. The effect of his words on me was neither slight nor transitory. His iron sentences, cold and harsh, sunk like heavy weights deep into my heart, and stirred up within me a rebellion not soon to be allayed.

This was a new and special revelation, dispelling a painful mystery against which my youthful understanding had struggled, and struggled in vain, to wit, the white man's power to perpetuate the enslavement of the black man. "Very well," thought I. "Knowledge unfits a child to be a slave." I instinctively assented to the proposition, and from that moment I understood the direct pathway from slavery to freedom. It was just what I needed, and it came to me at a time and from a source whence I least expected it. Of course I was greatly saddened at the thought of losing the assistance of my kind mistress, but the information so instantly derived, to some extent compensated me for the loss I had sustained in this direction. Wise as Mr. Auld was, he underrated my comprehension, and had little idea of the use to which I was capable of putting the impressive lesson he was giving to his wife. He wanted me to be a slave; I had already voted against that on the home plantation of Col. Lloyd. That which he most loved I most hated, and the very determination which he expressed to keep me in ignorance only rendered me the more resolute to seek intelligence. In learning to read, therefore, I am not sure that I do not owe quite as much to the opposition of my master as to the kindly assistance of my amiable mistress. I acknowledge the benefit rendered me by the one, and by the other, believing that but for my mistress I might have grown up in ignorance.

"The Best Mistress and Master in the World": Millie Evans

This life story of Millie Evans is based on an oral history done by the Federal Writers' Project during the 1930s. It was included in Lay My Burden Down: A Folk History of Slavery, *edited by B. A. Botkin and published by the University of Chicago Press in 1945. In general, slavery meant the harsh and brutal exploitation of black human beings. There were, however, instances of bonds of affection between slaves and their masters.*

W AS BORN IN 1849, but I don't know just when. My birthday comes in fodder-pulling time 'cause my ma said she was pulling up till 'bout a hour 'fore I was born. Was born in North Carolina and was a young lady at the time of surrender.

I don't 'member Old Master's name; all I 'member is that we call 'em Old Master and Old Mistress. They had 'bout a hundred niggers, and they was rich. Master always tended the men, and Mistress tended to us.

Every morning 'bout four 'clock Old Master would ring the bell for us to git up by, and you could hear that bell ringing all over the plantation. I can hear it now. It would go ting-a-ling, ting-a-ling, and I can see 'em now stirring in Carolina. I git so lonesome when I think 'bout times we used to have. 'Twas better living back yonder than now.

I stayed with my ma every night, but my mistress raised me. My ma had to work hard, so every time Old Mistress thought we little black children was hungry 'tween meals she would call us up to the house to eat. Sometimes she would give us johnnycake and plenty of buttermilk to drink with it. They had a long trough for us that they would keep so clean. They would fill this trough

89

with buttermilk, and all us children would git round the trough and drink with our mouths and hold our johnnycake with our hands. I can just see myself drinking now. It was so good. There was so many black folks to cook for that the cooking was done outdoors. Greens was cooked in a big black washpot just like you boils clothes in now. And sometime they would crumble bread in the potlicker and give us spoons, and we would stand round the pot and eat. When we et our regular meals, the table was set under a chinaberry tree with a oilcloth tablecloth, and when they called us to the table they would ring the bell. But we didn't eat out of plates. We et out of gourds and had homemade wood spoons. And we had plenty to eat. Whooo-eee! Just plenty to eat. Old Master's folks raised plenty of meat, and they raise their sugar, rice, peas, chickens, eggs, cows, and just everything good to eat.

Every evening at three 'clock Old Mistress would call all us litsy bitsy children in, and we would lay down on pallets and have to go to sleep. I can hear her now singing to us pickaninnies. . . .

When I got big 'nough I nursed my mistress' baby. When the baby go to sleep in the evening, I would put it in the cradle and lay down by the cradle and go to sleep. I played a heap when I was little. We played Susanna Gal, jump rope, calling cows, running, jumping, skipping, and just everything we could think of. When I got big 'nough to cook, I cooked then.

The kitchen of the big house was built 'way off from the house, and we cooked on a great big old fireplace. We had swing pots and would swing 'em over the fire and cook and had a big old skillet with legs on it. We call it a oven and cooked bread and cakes in it.

We had the best mistress and master in the world, and they was Christian folks, and they taught us to be Christian-like too. Every Sunday morning Old Master would have all us niggers to the house while he would sing and pray and read the Bible to us all. Old Master taught us not to be bad; he taught us to be good; he told us to never steal nor to tell false tales and not to do anything that was bad. He said: "You will reap what you sow, that you sow it single and reap double." I learnt that when I was a little child, and

I ain't forgot it yet. When I got grown I went the Baptist way. God called my pa to preach and Old Master let him preach in the kitchen and in the back yard under the trees. On preaching day Old Master took his whole family and all the slaves to church with him.

We had log schoolhouses in them days, and folks learnt more than they does in the bricks today.

Down in the quarters every black family had a one- or two-room log cabin. We didn't have no floors in them cabins. Nice dirt floors was the style then, and we used sage brooms. Took a string and tied the sage together and had a nice broom outen that. We would gather broom sage for our winter brooms just like we gathered our other winter stuff. We kept our dirt floors swept as clean and white. And our bed was big and tall and had little beds to push under there. They was all little enough to go under the other and in the daytime we would push 'em all under the big one and make heaps of room. Our beds was stuffed with hay and straw and shucks, and, believe me, child, they sure slept good.

When the boys would start to the quarters from the field, they would get a turn of lider [lightwood] knots. I 'specks you knows 'em as pine knots. That was what we use for light. When our fire went out, we had no fire. Didn't know nothing 'bout no matches. To start a fire we would take a skillet lid and a piece of cotton and a flint rock. Lay the cotton on the skillet lid and take a piece of iron and beat the flint rock till the fire would come. Sometime we would beat for thirty minutes before the fire would come and start the cotton, then we would light our pine.

Up at the big house we didn't use lider knots but used tallow candles for lights. We made the candles from tallow that we took from cows. We had molds and would put string in there and leave the end sticking out to light and melt the tallow and pour it down around the string in the mold.

We use to play at night by moonlight, and I can recollect singing with the fiddle. Oh, Lord, that fiddle could almost talk, and I can hear it ringing now. Sometime we would dance in the moonlight too.

Old Master raised lots of cotton, and the womenfolks carded

and spun and wove cloth, then they dyed it and made clothes. And we knit all the stockings we wore. They made their dye too, from different kinds of bark and leaves and things. They would take the bark and boil it and strain it up and let it stand a day, then wet the 'terial in cold water and shake it out and drop in the boiling dye and let it set 'bout twenty minutes, then take it out and hang it up and let it dry right out of that dye. Then rinse it in cold water and let it dry, then it would be ready to make.

I'll tell you how to dye. A little beech bark dyes slate color, set with copperas. Hickory bark and bay leaves dye yellow, set with chamber lye; bamboo dyes turkey red, set color with copperas. Pine straw dyes purple, set color with chamber lye. To dye cloth brown we would take the cloth and put it in the water where leather had been tanned and let it soak, then set the color with apple vinegar. And we dyed blue with indigo and set the color with alum.

We wore drawers made out of domestic that come down longer than our dresses, and we wore seven petticoats with sleeves in them petticoats in the winter, and the boys wore big old long shirts. They didn't know nothing 'bout no britches till they was great big, just went round in they shirttails. And we all wore shoes 'cause my pa made shoes.

Master taught Pa to make shoes, and the way he done, they killed a cow and took the hide and tanned it. The way they tanned it was to take red oak bark and put in vats made something like troughs that held water. First he would put in a layer of leather and a layer of oak ashes and a layer of leather and a layer of oak ashes till he got it all in and cover with water. After that he let it soak till the hair come off the hide. Then he would take the hide out, and it was ready for tanning. Then the hide was put to soak in with the red oak bark. It stayed in the water till the hide turned tan, then Pa took the hide out of the red oak dye, and it was a pretty tan. It didn't have to soak long. Then he would get his pattern and cut and make tan shoes outen the tanned hides. We called 'em brogans.

They planted indigo, and it growed just like wheat. When it got ripe, they gathered it, and we would put it in a barrel and let it soak 'bout a week, then we would take the indigo stems out and squeeze all the juice out of 'em and put the juice back in the barrel and let it stand 'bout 'nother week, then we just stirred and stirred one whole day. We let it set three or four days, then drained the water off and left the settlings, and the settlings was blueing just like we have these days. We cut ours in little blocks, and we dyed clothes with it too.

We made vinegar out of apples. Took overripe apples and ground 'em up and put 'em in a sack and let drip. Didn't add no water, and when it got through dripping we let it sour and strained and let it stand for six months and had some of the best vinegar ever made.

We had homemade tubs and didn't have no washboards. We had a block and battling stick. We put our clothes in soak, then took 'em out of soak and lay them on the block and take the battling stick and battle the dirt out of 'em. We mostly used rattan vines for clotheslines, and they made the best clotheslines they was.

Old Master raised big patches of t'baccy, and when they gather it they let it dry and then put it in 'lasses. After the 'lasses dripped off, then they roll it up and twisted it and let it dry in the sun ten or twelve days. It sure was ready for some grand chewing and it was sweet and stuck together so you could chew and spit and 'joy it.

The way we got our perfume we took rose leaves, Cape jasmines, and sweet basil and laid 'em with our clothes and let 'em stay three or four days, then we had good-smelling clothes that would last too.

When there was distressful news Master would ring the bell. When the niggers in the field would hear the bell, everyone would listen and wonder what the trouble was. You'd see 'em stirring too. They would always ring the bell at twelve 'clock. Sometimes then they would think it was something serious and they would stand up straight, but if they could see they shadow right under 'em they would know it was time for dinner.

The reason so many white folks was rich was they made money

and didn't have nothing to do but save it. They made money and raised everything they used, and just didn't have no use for money. Didn't have no banks in them days, and Master buried his money.

The floors in the big house was so pretty and white. We always kept them scoured good. We didn't know what it was to use soap. We just took oak ashes out of the fireplace and sprinkled them on the floor and scoured with a corn-shuck mop. Then we would sweep the ashes off and rinse two times and let it dry. When it dried it was the cleanest floor they was. To make it white, clean sand was sprinkled on the floor, and we let it stay a couple of days, then the floor would be too clean to walk on. The way we dried the floor was with a sack and a rag. We would get down on our knees and dry it so dry.

I 'member one night one of Old Master's girls was going to get married. That was after I was big 'nough to cook, and we was sure doing some cooking. Some of the niggers of the place just naturally would steal, so we cook a big cake of corn bread and iced it all pretty and put it out to cool, and some of 'em stole it. This way Old Master found out who was doing the stealing 'cause it was such a joke on 'em they had to tell.

All Old Master's niggers was married by the white preacher, but he had a neighbor who would marry his niggers hisself. He would say to the man: "Do you want this woman?" and to the girl, "Do you want this boy?" Then he would call the Old Mistress to fetch the broom, and Old Master would hold one end and Old Mistress the other and tell the boy and girl to jump this broom, and he would say: "That's your wife." They called marrying like that jumping the broom.

Now, child, I can't 'member everything I done in them days, but we didn't have to worry 'bout nothing. Old Mistress was the one to worry. 'Twasn't then like it is now, no 'twasn't. We had such a good time, and everybody cried when the Yankees cried out: "Free." T'other niggers say they had a hard time 'fore they was free, but 'twas then like 'tis now. If you had a hard time, we done it ourselves.

Old Master didn't want to part with his niggers, and the niggers

didn't want to part with Old Master, so they thought by coming
to Arkansas they would have a chance to keep 'em. So they got on
their way. We loaded up our wagons and put up our wagon sheet,
and we had plenty to eat and plenty of horse feed. We traveled
'bout fifteen or twenty miles a day and would stop and camp at
night. We would cook enough in the morning to last all day. The
cows was drove together. Some was gentle and some was not, and
did they have a time. I mean, they had a time. While we was on
our way, Old Master died, and three of the slaves died too. We
buried the slaves there, but we camped while Old Master was carried back to North Carolina. When Old Mistress come back, we
started on to Arkansas and reached here safe, but when we got
here we found freedom here too. Old Mistress begged us to stay
with her, and we stayed till she died, then they took her back to
Carolina. There wasn't nobody left but Miss Nancy, and she soon
married and left, and I lost track of her and Mr. Tom.

"Git This Nigger to the Cotton Patch":
Jenny Proctor's Complaint

Like Millie Evans's story, Jenny Proctor's personal account of slavery is based on an oral history done by the Federal Writers' Project during the 1930s and was included in Lay My Burden Down: A Folk History of Slavery. *Unlike Evans, Proctor says she "ain't never seen no good times" during the days of slavery.*

———————————▶ ◀———————————

I'S HEAR TELL of them good slave days, but I ain't never seen no good times then. My mother's name was Lisa, and when I was a very small child I hear that driver going from cabin to cabin as early as 3 o'clock in the morning, and when he comes to our cabin he say, "Lisa, Lisa, git up from there and git that breakfast." My mother, she was cook, and I don't recollect nothing 'bout my father. If I had any brothers and sisters I didn't know it. We had old ragged huts made out of poles and some of the cracks chinked up with mud and moss and some of them wasn't. We didn't have no good beds, just scaffolds nailed up to the wall out of poles and the old ragged bedding throwed on them. That sure was hard sleeping, but even that feel good to our weary bones after them long hard days' work in the field. I 'tended to the children when I was a little gal and tried to clean the house just like Old Miss tells me to. Then soon as I was ten years old, Old Master, he say, "Git this here nigger to that cotton patch."

I recollects once when I was trying to clean the house like Old Miss tell me, I finds a biscuit, and I's so hungry I et it, 'cause we never see such a thing as a biscuit only sometimes on Sunday morning. We just have corn bread and syrup and sometimes fat bacon, but when I et that biscuit and she comes in and say, "Where that biscuit?" I say, "Miss, I et it 'cause I's so hungry." Then she grab that broom and start to beating me over the head with it and calling me low-down nigger, and I guess I just clean lost my head 'cause I knowed better than to fight her if I knowed anything 't all, but I start to fight her, and the driver, he comes in and he grabs me and starts beating me with that cat-o'-nine-tails, and he beats me till I fall to the floor nearly dead. He cut my back all to pieces, then they rubs salt in the cuts for more punishment. Lord, Lord, honey! Them was awful days. When Old Master come to the house, he say, "What you beat that nigger like that for?" And the driver tells him why, and he say, "She can't work now for a week. She pay for several biscuits in that time." He sure was mad, and he tell Old Miss she start the whole mess. I still got them scars on my old back right now, just like my grandmother have when she die, and I's a-carrying mine right on to the grave just like she did.

Our master, he wouldn't 'low us to go fishing — he say that too easy on a nigger and wouldn't 'low us to hunt none either — but sometime we slips off at night and catch possums. And when Old Master smells them possums cooking 'way in the night, he wraps up in a white sheet and gits in the chimney corner and scratch on the wall, and when the man in the cabin goes to the door and say, "Who's that?" he say, "It's me, what's ye cooking in there?" and the man say, "I's cooking possum." He say, "Cook him and bring me the hindquarters and you and the wife and the children eat the rest." We never had no chance to git any rabbits 'cept when we was a-clearing and grubbing the new ground. Then we catch some rabbits, and if they looks good to the white folks they takes them and if they no good the niggers git them. We never had no gardens. Sometimes the slaves git vegetables from the white folks' garden and sometimes they didn't.

Money? Uh-uh! We never seen no money. Guess we'd-a bought something to eat with it if we ever seen any. Fact is, we wouldn't-a knowed hardly how to bought anything, 'cause we didn't know nothing 'bout going to town.

They spinned the cloth what our clothes was made of, and we had straight dresses or slips made of lowell. Sometimes they dye 'em with sumac berries or sweet-gum bark, and sometimes they didn't. On Sunday they make all the children change, and what we wears till we gits our clothes washed was gunny sacks with holes cut for our head and arms. We didn't have no shoes 'cepting some homemade moccasins, and we didn't have them till we was big children. The little children they goes naked till they was big enough to work. They was soon big enough though, 'cording to our master. We had red flannel for winter underclothes. Old Miss she say a sick nigger cost more than the flannel.

Weddings? Uh-uh! We just steps over the broom and we's married. Ha! Ha! Ha!

Old Master he had a good house. The logs was all hewed off smooth-like, and the cracks all fixed with nice chinking, plumb 'spectable-looking even to the plank floors. That was something. He didn't have no big plantation, but he keeps 'bout three hundred slaves in them little huts with dirt floors. I thinks he calls it four farms what he had.

Sometimes he would sell some of the slaves off of that big auction block to the highest bidder when he could git enough for one.

When he go to sell a slave, he feed that one good for a few days, then when he goes to put 'em up on the auction block he takes a meat skin and greases all round that nigger's mouth and makes 'em look like they been eating plenty meat and such like and was good and strong and able to work. Sometimes he sell the babes from the breast, and then again he sell the mothers from the babes and the husbands and the wives, and so on. He wouldn't let 'em holler much when the folks be sold away. He say, "I have you whupped if you don't hush." They sure loved their six children though. They wouldn't want nobody buying them.

We might-a done very well if the old driver hadn't been so mean, but the least little thing we do he beat us for it and put big chains round our ankles and make us work with them on till the blood be cut out all around our ankles. Some of the masters have what they call stockades and puts their heads and feet and arms through holes in a big board out in the hot sun, but our old driver he had a bull pen. That's only thing like a jail he had. When a slave do anything he didn't like, he takes 'em in that bull pen and chains 'em down, face up to the sun, and leaves 'em there till they nearly dies.

None of us was 'lowed to see a book or try to learn. They say we git smarter than they was if we learn anything, but we slips around and gits hold of that Webster's old blue-back speller and we hides it till 'way in the night and then we lights a little pine torch, and studies that spelling book. We learn it too. I can read some now and write a little too.

They wasn't no church for the slaves, but we goes to the white folks' arbor on Sunday evening, and a white man he gits up there to preach to the niggers. He say, "Now I takes my text, which is, Nigger obey your master and your mistress, 'cause what you git from them here in this world am all you ever going to git, 'cause you just like the hogs and the other animals — when you dies you ain't no more, after you been throwed in that hole." I guess we believed that for a while 'cause we didn't have no way finding out different. We didn't see no Bibles.

Sometimes a slave would run away and just live wild in the woods, but most times they catch 'em and beats 'em, then chains 'em down in the sun till they nearly die. The only way any slaves on our farm ever goes anywhere was when the boss sends him to carry some news to another plantation or when we slips off way in the night. Sometimes after all the work was done a bunch would have it made up to slip out down to the creek and dance. We sure have fun when we do that, most times on Saturday night.

All the Christmas we had was Old Master would kill a hog and give us a piece of pork. We thought that was something, and the way Christmas lasted was 'cording to the big sweet-gum backlog what the slaves would cut and put in the fireplace. When that burned out, the Christmas was over. So you know we all keeps a-looking the whole year round for the biggest sweet gum we could find. When we just couldn't find the sweet gum, we git oak, but it wouldn't last long enough, 'bout three days on average, when we didn't have to work. Old Master he sure pile on them pine knots, gitting that Christmas over so we could git back to work.

We had a few little games we play, like Peep Squirrel Peep, You Can't Catch Me, and such like. We didn't know nothing 'bout no New Year's Day or holidays 'cept Christmas.

We had some corn-shucking sometimes, but the white folks gits the fun and the nigger gits the work. We didn't have no kind of cotton-pickings 'cept just pick our own cotton. I's can hear them darkies now, going to the cotton patch 'way 'fore day a-singing "Peggy, does you love me now?"

One old man he sing:

> Saturday night and Sunday too
> Young gals on my mind.
> Monday morning 'way 'fore day
> Old Master got me gwine.
> Peggy, does you love me now?

Then he whoops a sort of nigger holler, what nobody can do just like them old-time darkies, then on he goes:

> Possum up a 'simmon tree,
> Rabbit on the ground.
> Lord, Lord, possum,
> Shake them 'simmons down.
> Peggy, does you love me now?

> Rabbit up a gum stump,
> Possum up a holler.
> Git him out, little boy
> And I gives you half a dollar.
> Peggy, does you love me now?

We didn't have much looking after when we git sick. We had to take the worst stuff in the world for medicine, just so it was cheap. That old blue mass and bitter apple would keep us out all night. Sometimes he have the doctor when he thinks we going to die, 'cause he say he ain't got anyone to lose, then that calomel what that doctor would give us would pretty nigh kill us. Then they keeps all kinds of lead bullets and asafetida balls round our necks, and some carried a rabbit foot with them all the time to keep off evil of any kind.

Lord, Lord, honey! It seems impossible that any of us ever lived to see that day of freedom, but thank God we did.

When Old Master comes down in the cotton patch to tell us 'bout being free, he say, "I hates to tell you, but I knows I's got to — you is free, just as free as me or anybody else what's white." We didn't hardly know what he means. We just sort of huddle round together like scared rabbits, but after we knowed what he mean, didn't many of us go, 'cause we didn't know where to of went. Old Master he say he give us the woods land and half of what we make on it, and we could clear it and work it or starve. Well, we didn't know hardly what to do 'cause he just gives us some old dull hoes and axes to work with; but we all went to work, and as we cut down the trees and the poles he tells us to build the fence round the field and we did, and when we plants the corn and the cotton we just plant all the fence corners full too, and I never seen so much stuff grow in all my born days. Several ears of corn to the stalk, and them big cotton stalks was a-laying over on the ground. Some of the old slaves they say they believe the Lord knew something 'bout niggers after all. He lets us put corn in his crib, and then we builds cribs and didn't take long 'fore we could buy some hosses and some mules and some good hogs. Them mangy hogs what our master give us the first year was plumb good hogs after we grease them and scrub them with lye soap. He just give us the ones he thought was sure to die, but we was a-gitting going now, and 'fore long we was a-building better houses and feeling kind of happy-like. After Old Master dies, we keeps hearing talk of Texas, and me and my old man — I's done been married several years then and had one little boy — well, we gits in our covered wagon with our little mules hitched to it, and we comes to Texas. We worked as sharecroppers around Buffalo, Texas, till my old man he died. My boy was nearly grown then, so he wants to come to San Angelo and work, so here we is. He done been married long time now and git six children. Some of them work at hotels and cafés and filling stations and in homes.

After Slavery: A Personal Account of the New Bondage

What happened to blacks after freedom is told in this powerful personal story. It was based on an interview published as a "lifelet" in the Independent *magazine in the early twentieth century. For many African Americans, emancipation turned out to be de facto slavery.*

I AM A NEGRO and was born some time during the war in Elbert County, Ga., and I reckon by this time I must be a little over forty years old. My mother was not married when I was born, and I never knew who my father was or anything about him. Shortly after the war my mother died, and I was left to the care of my uncle. All this happened before I was eight years old, and so I can't remember very much about it. When I was about ten years old my uncle hired me out to Captain ____. . . . I was told that the Captain wanted me for his house-boy, and that later on he was going to train me to be his coachman. To be a coachman in those days was considered a post of honor, and young as I was, I was glad of the chance.

But I had not been at the Captain's a month before I was put to work on the farm, with some twenty or thirty other Negroes — men, women and children. From the beginning the boys had the same tasks as the men and women. There was no difference. We all worked hard during the week, and would frolic on Saturday nights and often on Sundays. And everybody was happy. The men got $3 a week and the women $2. I don't know what the children got. Every week my uncle collected my money for me, but it was very little of it that I ever saw. My uncle fed and clothed me, gave me a place to sleep, and allowed me ten or fifteen cents a week for "spending change," as he called it.

I must have been seventeen or eighteen years old before I got tired of that arrangement, and felt that I was man enough to be working for myself and handling my own wages. . . . Unknown to my uncle or the Captain I went off to a neighboring plantation and hired myself out to another man. The new landlord agreed to give me forty cents a day and furnish me one meal. I thought that I was doing fine. Bright and early one Monday morning I started for work, still not letting the others know anything about it. But they found it out before sundown. The Captain came over to the new place and brought some kind of officer of the law. The officer pulled out a long piece of paper from his pocket and read it to my new employer. When this was done I heard my new boss say:

"I beg your pardon, Captain. I didn't know this nigger was bound out to you, or I wouldn't have hired him."

"He certainly is bound out to me," said the Captain. "He belongs to me until he is twenty-one, and I'm going to make him know his place."

So I was carried back to the Captain's. That night he made me strip off my clothing down to my waist, had me tied to a tree in his backyard, ordered his foreman to give me thirty lashes with a buggy whip across my bare back, and stood by until it was done. After that experience the Captain made me stay on his place night and day, — but my uncle still continued to "draw" my money.

I was a man nearly grown before I knew how to count from one to one hundred. I was a man nearly grown before I ever saw a colored school teacher. I never went to school a day in my life. To-day I can't write my own name, though I can read a little. I was a man nearly grown before I ever rode on a railroad train, and then I went on an excursion from Elberton to Athens. What was true of me was true of hundreds of other Negroes around me — 'way off there in the country, fifteen or twenty miles from the nearest town.

When I reached twenty-one the Captain told me I was a free man, but he urged me to stay with him. He said he would treat me right, and pay me as much as anybody else would. The Captain's son and I were about the same age, and the Captain said that, as he had owned my mother and uncle during slavery, and as his son didn't want me to leave them (since I had been with them so long), he wanted me to stay with the old family. And I stayed. I signed a contract — that is, I made my mark — for one year. The captain was to give me $3.50 a week, and furnish me a little house on the plantation — a one-room log cabin similar to those used by his other laborers.

During that year I married Mandy. For several years Mandy had been the house-servant for the Captain, his wife, his son and his three daughters, and they all seemed to think a good deal of her. As an evidence of their regard they gave us [some] furniture, which cost about $25, and we set up housekeeping in one of the Captain's two-room shanties. I thought I was the biggest man in Georgia. Mandy still kept her place in the "Big House" after our marriage. We did so well for the first year that I renewed my contract for the second year, and the third, fourth and fifth year I did the same thing.

Before the end of the fifth year the Captain had died, and his son, who had married some two or three years before, took charge of the plantation. Also, for two or three years, this son had been serving at Atlanta in some big office to which he had been elected. I think it was in the Legislature or something of that sort — anyhow, all the people called him Senator. At the end of the fifth year the Senator suggested that I sign up a contract for ten years; then, he said, we wouldn't have to fix up papers every year. I asked my wife about it; she consented; and so I made a ten-year contract.

Not long afterward the Senator had a long, low shanty built on his place. A great big chimney, with a wide, open fireplace, was built at one end of it, and on each side of the house, running lengthwise, there was a row of frames or stalls just large enough to hold a single mattress. . . . They looked for all the world like stalls for horses. . . . Nobody seemed to know what the Senator was fixing for.

All doubts were put aside one bright day in April when about forty able-bodied Negroes, bound in iron chains, and some of them handcuffed, were brought out to the Senator's farm in three big wagons. They were quartered in the long, low shanty, and it was afterward called the stockade. This was the beginning of the Senator's convict camp. These men were prisoners who had been leased by the Senator from the State of Georgia at about $200 each per year, the State agreeing to pay for guards and physicians, for necessary inspection, for inquests, all rewards for escaped convicts, the cost of litigation and all other incidental camp expenses. When I saw these men in shackles, and the guards with their guns, I was scared nearly to death. I felt like running away, but I didn't know where to go. And if there had been any place to go to, I would have had to leave my wife and child behind.

We free laborers held a meeting. We all wanted to quit. We sent a man to tell the Senator about it. Word came back that we were all under contract for ten years and that the Senator would hold us to the letter of the contract, or put us in chains and lock us up — the same as the other prisoners. It was made plain to us by some white people we talked to that in the contracts we had signed we had all agreed to be locked up in a stockade at night or at any other time that our employer saw fit; further, we learned that we could not lawfully break our contract for any reason and go and hire ourselves to somebody else without the consent of our employer; and, more than that, if we got mad and ran away, we could be run down by bloodhounds, arrested without process of law, and be returned to our employers, who, according to the contract, might beat us brutally or administer any other kind of punishment that he thought proper.

In other words, we had sold ourselves into slavery — and what could we do about it? The white folks had all the courts, all the guns, all the hounds, all the railroads, all the telegraph wires, all the newspapers, all the money, and nearly all the land — and we had only our ignorance, our poverty and our empty hands. We decided that the best thing to do was to shut our mouths, say nothing, and go back to work. And most of us worked side by side with those convicts during the remainder of the ten years.

But this first batch of convicts was only the beginning. Within six months another stockade was built, and twenty or thirty other convicts were brought to the plantation, among them six or eight women! The Senator had bought an additional thousand acres of land, and to his already large cotton plantation he added two great big saw-mills and went into the lumber business. Within two years the Senator had in all nearly 200 Negroes working on his plantation — about half of them free laborers, so called, and about half of them convicts. The only difference between the free laborers and the others was that the free laborers could come and go as they pleased, at night — that is, they were not locked up at night, and were not, as a general thing, whipped for slight offenses.

The troubles of the free laborers began at the close of the ten-year period. To a man, they all wanted to quit when the time was up. To a man, they all refused to sign new contracts — even for one year, not to say anything of ten years. And just when we thought that our bondage was at an end we found that it had really just begun. Two or three years before, or about a year and a half after the Senator had started his camp, he had established a large store, which was called the commissary. All of us free laborers were compelled to buy our supplies — food, clothing, etc. — from the store. We never used any money in our dealings at the commissary, only tickets or orders, and we had a general settlement once each year, in October. In this store we were charged all sorts of high prices for goods, because every year we would come out in debt to our employer. If not that, we seldom had more than $5 or $10 coming to us — and that for a whole year's work. Well, at the close of the tenth year, when we kicked and meant to leave the Senator, he said to some of us with a smile (and I never will forget that smile — I can see it now):

"Boys, I'm sorry you're going to leave me. I hope you will do well in your new places — so well that you will be able to pay me the little balances which most of you owe me."

Word was sent out for all of us to meet him at the commissary at 2 o'clock. There he told us that, after we had signed what he called a written acknowledgment of our debts, we might go and look for new places. The store-keeper took us one by one and read to us statements of our accounts. According to the books there was no man of us who owed the Senator less than $100; some of us were put down for as much as $200. I owed $165, according to the bookkeeper. These debts were not accumulated during one year, but ran back for three and four years, so we were told — in spite of the fact that we understood that we had had a full settlement at the end of each year. But no one of us would have dared to dispute a white man's word — on, no; not in those days. Besides, we fellows didn't care anything about the amounts — we were after getting away; and we had been told that we might go, if we signed the acknowledgments. We would have signed anything, just to get away. So we stepped up, we did, and made our marks.

That same night we were rounded up by a constable and ten or twelve white men, who aided him, and we were locked up, every one of us, in the Senator's stockades. The next morning it was explained to us by the two guards appointed to watch us that, in the papers we had signed the day before, we had not only made acknowledgment of our indebtedness, but that we had also agreed to work for the Senator until the debts were paid by hard labor. And from that day forward we were treated just like convicts. Really we had made ourselves lifetime slaves, or peons, as the laws called us. But, call it slavery, peonage, or what not, the truth is we lived in a hell on earth what time we spent in the Senator's peon camp.

I lived in that camp, as a peon, for nearly three years. My wife fared better than I did, as did the wives of some of the other Negroes, because the white men about the camp used these unfortunate creatures as their mistresses. When I was first put in the stockade, my wife was still kept for a while in the "Big House," but my little boy, who was only nine years old, was given away to a Negro family across the river in South Carolina, and I never saw or heard of him after that. When I left the camp, my wife had had two children by some one of the white bosses, and she was living in fairly good shape in a little house off to herself.

But the poor Negro women who were not in the class with my wife fared about as bad as the helpless Negro men. Most of the time the women who were peons or convicts were compelled to wear men's clothes. Sometimes, when I have seen them dressed like men, and plowing or hoeing or hauling logs or working at the blacksmith's trade, just the same as men, my heart would bleed and my blood would boil, but I was powerless to raise a hand. It would have meant death on the spot to have said a word. Of the first six women brought to the camp, two of them gave birth to children after they had been there more than twelve months — and the babies had white men for their fathers!

The stockades in which we slept were, I believe, the filthiest places in the world. They were cesspools of nastiness. During the three years that I was there I am willing to swear that a mattress was never moved after it had been brought there, except to turn it over once or twice a month. No sheets were used, only dark-colored blankets. Most of the men slept every night in the clothing that they had worked in all day. Some of the worst characters were made to sleep in chains. The doors were locked and barred each night, and tallow candles were the only lights allowed. Really the stockades were but little more than cow sheds, horse stables or hog pens.

Strange to say, not a great number of these people died while I was there, though a great many came away maimed and bruised and, in some cases, disabled for life. As far as I remember only about ten died during the last ten years that I was there, two of these being killed outright by the guards for trivial offenses. . . .

The working day on a peon farm begins with sunrise and ends when the sun goes down; or, in other words, the average peon works from ten to twelve hours each day, with one hour (from 12 o'clock to 1 o'clock) for dinner. Hot or cold, sun or rain, this is the rule. As to their meals, the laborers are divided up into squads of companies, just the same as soldiers in a great military camp would be. Two or three men in each stockade are appointed as cooks. From thirty to forty men report to each cook. In the warm months (or eight or nine months out of the year) the cooking is done on the outside, just behind the stockades; in the cold months the cooking is done inside the stockades.

Each peon is provided with a great big tin cup, a flat tin pan and two big tin spoons. No knives or forks are ever seen, except those used by the cooks. At the meal time the peons pass in single file before the cooks, and hold out their pans and cups to receive their allowances. Cow peas (red or white, which when boiled turn black), fat bacon and old-fashioned Georgia corn bread, baked in pones from one to two and three inches thick, make up the chief articles of food. Black coffee, black molasses and brown sugar are also used abundantly. Once in a great while, on Sundays, biscuits would be made, but they would always be made from the kind of flour called "shorts." As a rule, breakfast consisted of coffee, fried bacon, corn bread, and sometimes molasses — and one "helping" of each was all that was allowed. Peas, boiled with huge hunks of fat bacon, and a hoe-cake, as big as a man's hand, usually answered for dinner. Sometimes this dinner bill of fare gave place to bacon and greens (collard or turnip) and pot liquor. Though we raised corn, potatoes and other vegetables, we never got a chance at such things unless we would steal them and cook them secretly. Supper consisted of coffee, fried bacon and molasses. But, although the food was limited to certain things, I am sure we all got a plenty of the things allowed. As coarse as these things were, we kept, as a rule, fat and sleek and as strong as mules. And that, too, in spite of the fact that we had no special arrangements for taking regular baths, and no very great effort was made to keep us regularly in clean clothes. No tables were used or allowed. In summer we would sit down on the ground and eat our meals, and in winter we would sit around inside the filthy stockades. Each man was his own dish washer — that is to say, each man was responsible for the care of his pan and cup and spoons. My dishes got washed about once a week!

Today, I am told, there are six or seven of these private camps in Georgia — that is to say, camps where most of the convicts are leased from the State of Georgia. But there are hundreds and hundreds of farms all over the State where Negroes, and in some cases poor white folks, are held in bondage on the ground that they are working out debts, or where the contracts which they have made hold them in a kind of perpetual bondage, because, under those contracts, they may not quit one employer and hire out to another except by and with the knowledge and consent of the former employer.

One of the usual ways to secure laborers for a large peonage camp is for the proprietor to send out an agent to the little courts in the towns and villages, and where a man charged with some petty offense has no friends or money, the agent will urge him to plead guilty, with the understanding that the agent will pay his fine, and in that way save him from the disgrace of being sent to jail or the chain-gang! For his high favor the man must sign beforehand a paper signifying his willingness to go to the farm and work out the amount of the fine imposed. When he reaches the farm, he has to be fed and clothed, to be sure, and these things are charged up to his account. By the time he has worked out his first debt, another is hanging over his head, and so on and so on, by a sort of endless chain, for an indefinite period, as in every case the indebtedness is arbitrarily arranged by the employer.

In many cases it is very evident that the court officials are in collusion with the proprietors or agents, and that they divide the "graft" among themselves. As an example of this dickering among the whites, every year many convicts were brought to the Senator's camp from a certain county in South Georgia, 'way down in the turpentine district. The majority of these men were charged with adultery, which is an offense against the laws of the great and sovereign State of Georgia! Upon inquiry I learned that down in that county, a number of Negro lewd women were employed by certain white men to entice Negro men into their houses; and then, on a certain night, at a given signal, when all was in readiness, raids would be made by the officers upon these houses, and the men would be arrested and charged with living in adultery.

Nine out of ten of these men, so arrested and so charged, would find their way ultimately to some convict camp, and, as I said, many of them found their way every year to the Senator's camp while I was there. The low-down women were never punished in any way. On the contrary, I was told that they always seemed to stand in high favor with the sheriffs, constables and other officers.

There can be no room to doubt that they assisted very materially in furnishing laborers for the prison pens of Georgia, and the belief was general among the men that they were regularly paid for their work. I could tell more, but I've said enough to make anybody heart sick. This great and terrible iniquity is, I know, widespread throughout Georgia and many other Southern States.

But I didn't tell you how I got out. I didn't get out — they put me out. When I had served as a peon for nearly three years — and you remember that they claimed that I owed them only $165 — when I had served for nearly three years, one of the bosses came to me and said that my time was up. He happened to be the one who was said to be living with my wife. He gave me a new suit of overalls, which cost about seventy-five cents, took me in a buggy and carried me across the Broad River into South Carolina, set me down and told me to "git." I didn't have a cent of money, and I wasn't feeling well, but somehow I managed to get a move on me. I begged my way to Columbia. In two or three days I ran across a man looking for laborers to carry to Birmingham, and I joined his gang. I have been here in Birmingham district since they released me, and I reckon I'll die either in a coal mine or an iron furnace. It don't make much difference which. Either is better than a Georgia peon camp. And a Georgia peon camp is hell itself!

Fleeing English Tyranny:
The Irish Cross the Atlantic

THE AGE OF JACKSON witnessed not only Indian removal and the expansion of slavery, but also the great migration of immigrants from Erin. The Irish did not want to come to America. But many felt they had no choice.

> Such troubles we know that have often
>   Caused stout Irish hearts to roam . . .
> And . . . sons from their homes were drove. . . .
> The hills and the valleys so dear to my heart;
> It grieves me to think that from them I must part.
> Compelled to emigrate far, far o'er the sea.[1]

The British "yoke" had been "enslaving" Ireland. Protestant landlords pushed Catholic peasant farmers from the land, and then the Potato Famine of the 1840s left them desperately hungry.

With bundles on their shoulders, the migrants were "laving dear old Ireland without warnin'" to "shtart for Philadelphia in the mornin'" and cross the "briny ocean." But before they left, they attended an "American wake" — a party hosted by the families. They said their good-byes and mourned what everyone knew would be a permanent separation.

> Sad was the day we said farewell,
>   Dear native land, to thee;

And wander'd forth to find a home,
Beyond the stormy sea.
Hard then our fate; fast flow'd the tears,
We tried to hide in vain,
At thought of those we left behind,
And might ne'er see again.[2]

After the "wake," the migrants traveled to Dublin and then to Liverpool, where they boarded crowded ships bound for America. The crossing was traumatic. "The emigrant is shown a berth," *The Times* reported, "a shelf of coarse pinewood, situated in a noisome dungeon, airless and lightless, in which several hundred persons of both sexes and all ages are stowed away on shelves two feet one inch above the other, three feet wide and six feet long, still reeking from the ineradicable stench left by the emigrants of the last voyage." During the nineteenth century, three million Irish crossed the Atlantic.[3]

Pushed from Ireland by economic hardships and famine, the immigrants were pulled to America by the Market Revolution's demand for labor. Yankees regarded the Irishman "as one made to work," reported the Reverend Michael Buckley, a visitor from Ireland. "Where they want labour they will engage Paddy as they would a drayhorse." An Irish worker recalled how he labored "so severely" digging cellars, "up before the Stars and working till darkness," "driven like horses" to be "a slave for the Americans." Working in the mines of Pennsylvania, Irish miners "sucked up" the black dust into their lungs as they dug the "bloody coal."[4]

Irish immigrants provided the labor for the construction of roads and canals for the Market Revolution. Watching them work on the National Road in Pennsylvania, a farmer described them as an "immortal Irish brigade, a thousand strong, with their carts, wheelbarrows, shovels and blasting tools, grading the commons, and climbing the mountainside . . . leaving behind them a roadway good enough for an emperor to travel over." Irish laborers helped to build waterways, including Connecticut's Enfield Canal, Rhode Island's Blackstone Canal, and most importantly, New York's Erie

A LARGER MEMORY

Canal, described by Reverend Buckley as "one of the grandest
pieces of engineering ever seen in the world" and "proof" of "Irish
talent." Standing knee-deep in water while cursing swarms of mos-
quitoes, the workers dug and shovelled earth as they sang:

> When I came to this wonderful rampire, it filled me
>   with the greatest surprise,
> To see such a great undertaking, on the like I never
>   opened my eye.
> To see a full thousand brave fellows at work among
>   mountains so tall,
> To dig through the vallies so level, through rocks for
>   to cut a canal.[5]

Irish workers built thousands of miles of rail lines such as the
Western and Atlantic Railroad from Atlanta to Chattanooga and the
Union Pacific segment of the transcontinental railroad.

More than half of the Irish immigrants were women. This massive migration of women was saluted in a song:

> Oh brave, brave Irish girls,
> We well might call you brave
> Should the least of all your perils
> The Stormy ocean waves.[6]

Irish immigrant women became ubiquitous as maids. In the
1850s, they represented 80 percent of all female household laborers in New York City. In 1900, 54 percent were classified as "servants and waitresses," compared to only 9 percent for Italian
female workers. Unlike Italian women who came to America with
their husbands or fathers, Irish immigrant women tended to be
unmarried and unattached to families. Hence, they were attracted
to work offering housing and meals as well as wages. Employment
in homes rather than in factories offered a healthier environment
and often paid more.

Tens of thousands of Irish immigrant women were employed
in factories. Irish women were preponderant in the New England
textile mills of Lawrence, Holyoke, Fall River, and other Massachu-

setts towns. In Lowell, the City of Spindles, they represented 58 percent of the total textile workforce. "The gray mills in Manchester [New Hampshire]," remembered Elizabeth Gurley Flynn, "stretched like prisons along the banks of the Merrimac River. Fifty percent of the workers were women. . . . Many lived in the antiquated 'corporation boarding houses,' relics of when the mills were built. Our neighbors, men and women, rushed to the mills before the sun rose on cold winter days and returned after dark. They were poorly dressed and poverty stricken."[7]

In the dusty and noisy mills, the women felt their heads become "empty of sense and their ears . . . deaf." Constantly standing and tying knots, they suffered backaches "until they lost their minds and ran amuck." Far from the rural countryside of Ireland, they had become tenderers of machines, their activities routinized and measured by the clock.

> When I set out for Lowell,
> Some factory for to find,
> I left my native country
> And all my friends behind.

> But now I am in Lowell,
> And summon'd by the bell,
> I think less of the factory
> Than of my native dell.

> The factory bell begins to ring
> And we must all obey,
> And to our old employment go,
> Or else be turned away.

> Come all ye weary factory girls,
> I'll have you understand,
> I'm going to leave the factory
> And return to my native land.

The "factory girls" also worked in dangerous conditions. On January 10, 1860, a terrible tragedy occurred at Lowell's Pemberton

Mill. A building suddenly collapsed, trapping nine hundred workers, mostly Irish women; then a fire broke out, adding to the terror and destruction. One hundred and sixteen women were seriously hurt while eighty-eight were killed. The list of victims included many daughters of Erin.[8]

Still, for many Irish women, America was a land of opportunity. "My dear Father," a daughter wrote from New York in 1850, "I must only say this is a good place and a good country. . . . [A]ny man or woman without a family are fools that would not venture and come to this plentyful Country where no man or woman ever hungered or ever will and where you will not be seen naked. . . ." Similarly, in the same year, Margaret McCarthy wrote home to her family, imploring, "Come you all Together Couragiously [sic] and bid adieu to that lovely land of our Birth" where there was so much misery, oppression, and degradation. She enclosed twenty dollars, urging her father to clear away from "that place all together and the Sooner the Better."[9]

For these women, America represented not only jobs and wages but also economic self-sufficiency — freedom from dependency on fathers or husbands. "I am getting along splendid and likes my work . . . it seems like a new life," one of them wrote to her younger sister in Ireland. "I will soon have a trade and be more independint. . . . You know it was always what I wanted so I have reached my highest ambition." Thomas McCann wrote home about his sister: "Maggie is well and likes this Country. She would not go back to old Ireland for any money." What Maggie especially valued was the "independence" she had found in America.[10]

Finding Her Voice for Militant Labor: Elizabeth Gurley Flynn

Born of Irish immigrant parents, Elizabeth Gurley Flynn joined the Industrial Workers of the World and became a fiery speaker at strike demonstrations and rallies across America from Bridgeport, Connecticut, to Butte, Montana, to Seattle, Washington. Alongside labor leaders like William D. "Big Bill" Haywood, Flynn spoke for the rights of migratory farm workers, miners, and factory laborers. After decades of activism, she published her life story in I Speak My Own Piece: The Autobiography of "The Rebel Girl." *Here she recounts growing up in a family dedicated to the labor movement and giving her first public speech for the labor movement in 1906, when she was only fifteen years old.*

THE IRISH WHO CAME to this country around the middle of the last century were far from happy. They sought but had not found freedom from religious and political persecution, nor a chance to earn a decent livelihood for their families. My father was very bitter about the hard conditions which prevailed here in his youth among the Irish. They were principally employed at manual labor — building railroads, canals, roads, and in mines and quarries. They lived in shanty towns, even in New York City. One such — consisting of 20,000 inhabitants — was located in what is now Central Park. They were excluded from the better residential areas. In my father's youth there were many signs on empty houses and factories seeking help: "No Irish Need Apply."

My father, who was then a laborer in the quarries, met my mother in the mid '80's. There were tight social lines drawn between the "lace curtain" Irish of my mother's family and the "shanty Irish" of my father's family. The difficulties he had in courting my mother are indicated by the fact that neither Gurleys nor Flynns came to their wedding. My father was determined to

A LARGER MEMORY

leave the quarry. All but one of his male relatives had died as a result of working there. My father carried the mark of the quarry to his grave. When he was a young boy, working in a quarry in Maine, carrying tools, the sight of one eye was destroyed by a flying chip of granite. He lived to be over eighty, "thanks to Mama," we always said, who encouraged him in his ambition. He had a keen mathematical mind and through self-study and tutoring, he passed the entry examinations at Dartmouth College in Hanover, New Hampshire. He attended the Thayer School of Engineering and made excellent progress. One of his classmates, later a professor at Ann Arbor, Michigan, told me of how he remembered Tom Flynn poring over his book in the failing light of evening, finally taking it to the window to catch the last rays of the sun. . . .

When he married, his family was highly indignant, but Mama remained at work, partially solving the economic problem for a few years. My father got work in 1895 in Manchester, New Hampshire, as a civil engineer for the Manchester Street Railroad Company, which was laying a track for a new mode of transportation, since torn up to make way for buses. . . . This was eighteen miles south of Concord, and we moved there. Here he took his first flyer into politics. He ran independently for City Engineer. He had joined the "Ancient Order of Hibernians" (A.O.H.) and marched in the St. Patrick's Day parade. He sported white gloves and a green sash over his shoulder, with golden harps and green shamrocks on it. We children were terribly impressed. We organized parades and pranced around in that sash till we wore it out. Undoubtedly he got the Irish vote but it was not enough to elect him. He was convinced that he lost because he was Irish and looked around for a job outside of New England. He took a poorly paid map-making job in Cleveland, Ohio. It was an uncertain, seasonal type of work. Collecting his pay in full depended upon how many orders the canvassers received for the finished atlases. Sometimes the operating companies failed or were fly-by-night concerns and in the end nothing was forthcoming. Somebody was always "owing Papa money."

118

Yet he worked hard, was out tramping around in all kinds of weather, with his small hand-drafting board, plotting in with red and blue pencils the streets, houses, etc. He worked at this for years, making maps of Cleveland, Boston, Baltimore, Newark, Trenton, Kentucky, Nova Scotia and many other places. At first we moved around as his jobs changed, from Concord to Manchester, to Cleveland, to Adams, Massachusetts, and finally to New York City. Our greatest fear was "Papa losing his job!" We enjoyed our peaceful life with Mama when she gave us all her attention. We knew that there would be no money when he was at home all day, and that he would become increasingly irritable and explosive. We were selfishly happy when Papa got a new job and went off to another town.

Our trip way "out west," to Cleveland, Ohio, was high adventure for three small New England children. I was then seven years old. It was a wearisome trek in a dirty day coach for my mother with a nursing baby. We landed at an old wooden station down by the lake shore. . . . We lived in a shaky little one-story house on Payne Avenue, named for a pioneer family. It had an outdoor toilet, which shocked us very much. It was reported to be the old Payne family homestead and had barred windows in the cellar, which was entered through a trap door in the kitchen floor. We were told the family took refuge there a century ago, and shot through the windows at attacking Indians. True or not, it made living there exciting. There were cable cars then in Cleveland and apparently some shift in gears was made at midnight. Anyhow the little frame house shook and rocked at that time every night, and we loved to pretend the Indians had returned or maybe it was the ghosts of the old Payne family. My father worked at home, using the front room for his big drafting boards, pantographs, blue prints, etc. It was our first direct contact with his work and with him, in fact. He earned $25 a week, but bread cost 3 cents a loaf and steak was 10 cents a pound. . . .

We finally arrived in New York City at the turn of the century — in 1900. My mother was tired of moving around and decided here we would stay. Our school terms had been interrupted and what little furniture we possessed was being smashed up in moving around. We came to Aunt Mary, a widow and a tailoress, who lived with her five children in the South Bronx. Soon they found a flat for us nearby. It was on the inside facing an airshaft, gas-lit, with cold water. The only heat was the kitchen stove. We three older children cried, we refused to unpack our toys, and were as heart-sick for the green hills of New England as any lonely immigrants for their pleasant native lands. We missed the fields, the flowers, the cows, and beautiful Greylock Mountain we had seen from our window. We hated the big crowded dirty city, where now our playgrounds were empty lots with neither grass nor trees. The flats where we lived, at 833 East 133rd St., are still in use, for "welfare families," I understand, although for a while they were condemned and boarded up. . . .

On cold winter days we'd huddle in the kitchen and shut off the rest of the house. We would do our lessons by a kerosene lamp, when the gas was shut off for non-payment. We'd undress in the kitchen, scurry to the cold bedrooms, all the children sleeping in one bed, where we put our coats over us to keep us warm. We might as well have lived in an isolated farm in the Dakotas for all the good the benefits of the great city did us then. Bill collectors harassed my gentle mother — the landlord, the gas man, the milk man, the grocer. Once she bought us an encyclopedia, on the installment plan. But she couldn't keep up the payments and our hearts were broken when we lost the beautiful books we treasured so highly.

Our front windows of this long tunnel-like apartment faced the smoky roundhouse of the New York, New Haven and Hartford Railroad. The great engines would chug in day and night and blow off steam there. Many railroad workers lived in the area. In particularly bad times they would throw off chunks of coal and then look the other way when local children came to pick up coal around the roundhouse. There were many accidents to railroad workers. Widows lived around us who had lost their husbands on that dangerous road, and their children starved while the road fought sometimes for years against paying damages.

There were many small factories, veritable sweatshops in the neighborhood, where children went to work as early as the law allowed and even younger. They made paper boxes, pencils, shirts, handkerchiefs (at three dollars a week and bring your own thread). There were larger factories employing adult labor — piano and refrigerator factories, a drug plant, and others. Mothers worked too and many children were left alone. Sometimes babies fell out of windows; one boy was killed when a huge sewer pipe rolled over him; a widow's only son fell from a swaying pole in a backyard, where he was putting up a clothes line, and was killed. Children lost legs on the railroad and under trucks on the streets. The wife of the corner saloon-keeper made huge kettles of soup for free lunch and sent bowls of it around to the poorest families. People helped each other as best they could. Truly, as some philosopher said, "Poverty is like a strange and terrible country. Only those who have been there can really speak of it with knowledge." . . .

In the early days of our life in the South Bronx, at the turn of the century, there were no amusements for children, or for adults, either. There were no movies — the nickelodeon started later — no radios, no television, not even the old-fashioned phonograph, which also came later, and by now is a museum piece. Reading was our sole indoor pastime, especially in the long winter nights. We walked over the Willis Avenue bridge to the East 125th Street library for books. We read everything we could understand, and some we did not, including all the traditional books of childhood of the day — Louise Alcott, Alice in Wonderland, Robinson Crusoe and Fenimore Cooper, Walter Scott, Mark Twain, George Eliot, and the New England poets. My mother was a kind but reserved woman. She did not allow us to go into other people's houses; she frowned on over-familiarity and gossip. But she was a good neighbor in time of need. She helped the sick, advised on domestic problems, and when she baked pies and cakes she shared them with the neighborhood children. It was a calamity to the area when she moved away to Brooklyn in the late twenties. My father ran for N. Y. State Assembly in 1918, on the Socialist ticket. He got over 6,000 votes and ran ahead of the Republican. But lots of people said: "Too bad it wasn't Mrs. Flynn that was running. She'd easily get elected! Everybody knows her!"

I attended the grammar school at P.S. No. 9 on 138th Street. It was a decrepit old building then, with toilets in the yard. . . . My teacher in an upper grade was James A. Hamilton, who was studying law and later became a New York State official. He fired me with ambition to be a constitutional lawyer and drilled us so thoroughly in the United States Constititution, and especially the Bill of Rights, that I have been defending it ever since. (I have been arrested at least ten times in my lifetime and in every instance the denial of the Bill of Rights had been involved.) I joined a debating society which Mr. Hamilton had organized, and took to it like a duck to water. I won a gold medal for proficiency in debating and one in English at graduation, in 1904. I also won a silver medal from the New York *Times* in 1903, for "Merit in an Essay on the City's History." I believe that originals of these essays are in the cornerstone of the New York *Times* building, for posterity to unearth. Typical subjects for debate then were: capital punishment; should women get the vote; and government ownership of the trusts. I remember arguing that women should vote — and strongly believing what I advocated. . . .

We were conditioned in our family to accept Socialist thinking long before we came in contact with Socialism as an organized movement. My father had voted for Eugene V. Debs, as the Socialist candidate for President, in 1900. We knew our father was opposed to the "two old parties," as he called them over fifty years ago. . . . One of my first debates in the public school debating society was on the subject "Should the Government Own the Coal Mines?" I enthusiastically took the affirmative. This grew out of the 1902 anthracite coal strike in Pennsylvania, led by John Mitchell. 150,000 miners demanded nine hours instead of ten and recognition of their union — the United Mine Workers of America. The strike, which lasted five months, hit New York hard. A coal shortage forced the curtailment of the "El" services, then run with coal engines. This was serious in those pre-subway days. The strike won general sympathy, especially after the head of the Operators' Association, George F. Baer, made his arrogant remark that "God in His infinite wisdom gave us possession of the coal mines." Ever after that he was called "Divine Right" Baer. An Arbitration Commission, appointed by President Theodore Roosevelt, awarded the miners a nine-hour day and a 10 per cent increase. They returned to their dangerous jobs, where daily they took their lives in their hands in the dark earth.

This debate was my first approach to the subject of public ownership of natural resources and industries. It appealed to me. I had begun to feel very strongly that in a rich and fertile country like ours, there was no excuse for poverty, unemployment, child labor and long strikes. My mother used to recite a poem, by Whittier I believe, which expressed our hatred of poverty. It ran something like this:

> "When Earth produces free and fair the golden
>   waving corn,
> And golden fruits perfume the air and fleecy flocks
>   are shorn,
> Yet thousands cry with aching head and never-
>   ending song,
> 'We starve! We die! Oh give us bread!'
> There must be something wrong!"

It was this "something wrong" I was bound to search out.

Needless to say, I was a terribly serious child for my years, the oldest of a poor family, who shared the miseries of the parents. When a family suffers poverty, when children hear their mother and even their father weep sometimes from despair as to how to feed their children, when all around are other suffering families — children cannot be light-hearted and happy. We saw "some way out" in the struggles of the labor movement and rejoiced in them.

The subject of labor struggles was not new in our household.

We had heard in our very early childhood of the so-called Molly Maguires, seventeen young Irish-American miners who had been executed in the 70's in the Anthracite area, for trying to organize a union and of how they were framed up by a Pinkerton detective — James McParlan. An old woman had told us as amazed children in Manchester, New Hampshire, about how the imprint of a hand on the jail wall, made by one of "those innocent lads, God rest their souls!" could not be erased. I heard this same weird tale many years later from people in Pottsville, Pennsylvania. We had heard of the Haymarket martyrs, hung in Chicago in the 80's during the eight-hour struggle, and of Eugene V. Debs, imprisoned for violating an injunction in the railroad strike of the 90's, and of the Danbury Hatters' case of 1902, when the union was fined $234,000 under the Sherman Anti-Trust law and the members had to sell their houses to pay it. We hated the rich, the trusts they owned, the volence they caused, the oppression they represented. . . .

When I was just past my fifteenth birthday, searching for a solution to poverty, my mother suggested I read Looking Backward, by a Massachusetts journalist — Edward Bellamy. It was about the year 2000, in a Socialist America. The author, who is portrayed as a sufferer from insomnia, had taken a sleeping potion in 1887 and had gone to rest in an underground soundproof chamber of his house, in Boston. The house was burned down, the one servant had died in the fire and it was assumed the young man had also perished. He lay there in a trance-like sleep for 113 years, to awaken in a new world when his resting place was unearthed by builders, The book portrayed an ideal society, due to the abolition of banks, landlords and capitalists. It was an imaginative description of what a Socialist America could be like, with collective ownership of all natural resources and industries and a full utilization of machinery, technical knowledge and the capacities of her people. It appealed to me as practical and feasible. It still does in its basic principles — though the year 2000 is now only 46 years away and Socialism should be that much nearer at least, in fact "just around the corner."

This book of Bellamy's pictured an American society built on the principle, "From each according to his ability, to each according to his needs." Some of it seemed quite fantastic then, such as pushing buttons in the wall and hearing plays and operas right in the room, but children can do it today with TV sets. This Socialist romance of the 19th century was read and discussed by millions of people throughout the world. It was translated into German, French, Russian, Italian, Arabic and Bulgarian. Bellamy Clubs were formed around the country. My mother had belonged to one, in Concord, New Hampshire. The book first popularized the idea of Socialism in this country. It was a biting criticism of capitalism, which hit home to many Americans and with which they agreed, in the days of rising monopolies. . . .

Another book I recall, which caused an immediate change in my life, was The Jungle, by Upton Sinclair. After reading it, I forthwith became a vegetarian! He wrote this book in 1906, to expose the terrible conditions of the stockyards workers and to advocate Socialism, as a remedy. But the public seized rather upon the horrible descriptions of filth, diseased cattle, floor sweepings and putrid meat packed in sausages and canned foods. The sale of meat fell catastrophically for the packers and demands for investigations and legal action rent the air. It was not so long after the scandals over poisonous canned meat sold to the U.S. Army, which caused many deaths during the Spanish-American War. Ella Reeve Bloor, then a young woman, was sent to Chicago by Sinclair, to gather data to reinforce his charges. Later, after the Pure Food, Drug and Inspection Act of 1906 was passed, as a direct result of Sinclair's book, she went to work in the plants again to check on whether the law was enforced and found the Beef Trust was ignoring it. This was the first time I heard her name — in 1906.

After graduation from grammar school, our debating society continued outside as the Hamilton Literary Society. We met weekly during 1905 at the home of a Dr. Cantor on East 143rd Street and were supervised by Joseph Weinstein, a college student, later a school teacher. Many newcomers from other schools joined, most of whom were Jewish. This was my first intimate contact with

Jewish people, and I liked them very much. I found them idealistic and progressive. Their mental curiosity and intellectual acuteness were stimulating. Our discussions encompassed every possible social problem. I began to realize that the Irish were not the only national group that had suffered persecution because of their religion, language and culture. . . .

Someone who took a special interest in my questions at the forums suggested to me that I read the publications of the Charles H. Kerr Company of Chicago and gave me for a starter the *Communist Manifesto.* I had not yet read anything by Marx or Engels. They did not have a wide circulation in English. It was part of a "Standard Socialist Series," which this company started in 1900. The *Manifesto,* by Karl Marx and Frederick Engels, was written in 1848.

I read it first in 1906. It was introduced as "evidence" of a criminal conspiracy against me and my co-defendants at the Foley Square trial, under the Smith Act in 1952. I also read in that long ago day, nearly a half century ago, *Socialism — Utopian and Scientific* and the *Origin of the Family* by Engels, and the pamphlets *Value, Price and Profit,* and *Wage Labor and Capital,* by Karl Marx. The Kerr company had issued Volumes I and II of *Capital,* in 1909. All of these books and pamphlets are today not only labeled "subversive" but are introduced by stool pigeons in trial after trial as Smith Act evidence, to show that we are "foreign agents" and advocate the violent overthrow of government. In 1906 they were considered part of an education by all progressive-minded Americans, as Wendell Willkie remarked to the United States Supreme Court.

When I began to accumulate scientific Socialist literature, my father seized upon it. He read everything by Marx and Engels he could lay his hands on. His knowledge of mathematics helped him to master them easily. He read them aloud to his family. He talked and argued about them with anyone who would listen — in the saloon, in the park, on the job. Scientific Socialism came as a balm to my father's spirit. It exposed the capitalist system in all its ugly naked greed, and its indifference to human welfare. It showed how it enriched the few and impoverished the masses of people. It explained what caused depressions, "bad times," economic crises.

Scientific Socialism made clear that it was not a poor man's fault if he is out of work; it's no proof of incompetence, laziness and lack of ability on his part, said Pop, "if some damned capitalist could not make a profit out of buying his labor power!" And you were not a "failure" because you did not climb to riches on the backs of your fellowmen. I believe, however, my long-suffering mother often felt that Pop overworked Karl Marx as an alibi for not looking for a job.

In 1906 the Bronx Socialist Forum, which our familly attended regularly, closed. We shifted our allegiance to the Harlem Socialist Club, at 250 West 125th Street. In good weather, open-air meetings were held on the corners of 7th Avenue and 125th Street — with women speaking for suffrage, and Socialist meetings arranged by this club. In winter the Socialist meetings were held in their headquarters, up two flights of stairs. We used to walk over from the South Bronx — carfares for a whole family were more than we could afford. Events took a sudden turn during my second year in Morris High School. I had lost a few months in school during that winter, due to an infected jaw from an abscessed tooth. During that period I had studied two more books, which helped to catapult me into Socialist activities. One was the *Vindication of the Rights of Women*, by Mary Wollstonecraft; the other was *Women and Socialism* by August Bebel. . . .

Someone at the Harlem Socialist Club, hearing of my debating experience and knowing of my reading and intense interest in Socialism, asked me to make a speech. My father was not much impressed with the idea. He thought they should have asked him to expound Marxism, on which he now considered himself an expert. I'm afraid my father would be labelled a "male-supremacist" these days. Once I stood up at a meeting and asked the speaker a question. He frowned upon such a performance. Couldn't I have asked him to explain, on our way home? But my mother encouraged me and I accepted the offer to speak. I tried to select a subject upon which my father would not interfere too much, something he did not consider too important. It was *"What Socialism Will Do For Women."*

Wednesday, January 31, 1906, is a date engraved on my memory, the occasion of my first public speech. It was a small place, holding not more than seventy-five people, but like the Mayflower, legends grew around it. That little boat would have rivalled the gigantic Queen Mary if she had carried all the ancestors now claimed as passengers. And my little hall would have been of Carnegie Hall proportions to accommodate all who have told me "I heard your first speech!" . . .

I was a slender serious girl, not yet sixteen, with my black hair loose to my waist, tied with a ribbon. I wore a long full skirt down to my ankles, as was proper in 1906, a white shirt waist and a red tie. I had labored to write my speech and had stubbornly resisted all attempts of my father and others to tell me what to say or to actually write it for me. Good or bad, I felt it had to be my own. I began to quake inwardly at first, facing an adult audience for the first time. But they were sympathetic and I was soon sailing along serenely. When I concluded, I asked for questions, as I had heard other speakers do. None were forthcoming. The audience apparently sensed that I was nervous. How they laughed when I said resentfully: "Just because I'm young and a girl, is no reason you shouldn't ask me questions!"

My speech was compounded of my limited personal experience, which I felt very acutely, however, and my rather wide reading. It was in the spirit of the Wollstonecraft book, which advocated the rights of women in 1792 — economic, political, educational and social. That was a period of ferment over "the rights of man" in America and Europe. . . .

My advent as a speaker caused no comment outside of the weekly Socialist paper, The Worker, which said: "In view of her youth, although knowing she was very bright, the comrades were prepared to judge her lecture indulgently; they found that no indulgence was called for, that she had a surprising grasp of the subject and handled it with skill." With this blessing I was launched on my career as a public speaker.

Strangers from a Different Shore: The Chinese

HE WAR AGAINST Mexico led to the transfer of California to the United States. In a plan sent to Congress in 1848 shortly after the Treaty of Guadalupe Hidalgo, policymaker Aaron H. Palmer predicted that San Francisco, connected by railroad to the Atlantic states, would become the "great emporium of our commerce on the Pacific." Chinese laborers, he proposed, should be imported to build the transcontinental railroad as well as to bring the fertile lands of California under cultivation. "No people in all the East are so well adapted for clearing wild lands and raising every species of agricultural product . . . as the Chinese." A year later, 325 Chinese arrived in California to join the Gold Rush. Their numbers inclined quickly — 20,000 by 1852 and 60,000 by 1870. They worked in the mines as well as the fields of California, and also helped build the transcontinental railroad. Ninety-five percent of the immigrants were men. By 1930, some 400,000 Chinese had made the Pacific crossing to America.[1]

Though they generally considered themselves sojourners, the Chinese showed signs of settling down from the very beginning. During the 1850s, Chinatown in San Francisco was already a bustling community. "The majority of the houses were of Chinese importation," observed a traveler, "and were stores, stocked with hams, tea, dried fish, dried ducks, and other Chinese eatables, besides copper pots and kettles, fans, shawls, chessmen, and all sorts of curiosities. Suspended over the doors were brilliantly-colored boards covered with Chinese writings, and with several yards of red ribbon streaming from them; while the streets thronged with Celestials [the name often used to describe the Chinese] chattering vociferously as they rushed about from store to store." A Chinese immigrant, arriving in San Francisco in 1868, found a thriving and colorful Chinatown, "made up of stores catering to the Chinese only." The people were "all in their native costume, with queues down their backs," and the entire street fronts of the stores were open, with groceries and vegetables overflowing on the sidewalks. Every morning, vegetable peddlers could be seen in the streets, wearing "loose pajamalike" clothes and "carrying two deep baskets of greens, fruits, and melons, balanced on their shoulders with the help of a pole."[2]

The Chinese were creating their own communities in America. They built altars to honor their gods and celebrated traditional holidays. During Chinese New Year in January or February, they first did their "Dah Faw Hom Muy," or housecleaning. The house could not be cleaned again until after the celebration, or else any good fortune arriving with the new year would be swept away. "Oh yes — we cleaned the house upside down," an immigrant recalled. "You know it was good luck to have plenty at the start of the New Year. We couldn't buy too much, but a bit of everything. And then there would be oranges and lishee [gifts of money wrapped in red paper for good luck]. We didn't have money for the lishee — we used dried nuts for money." Then the people ushered in the New Year with lion dances and firecrackers. During the celebration, whites also joined the festive throngs in Chinatown. As soon as the clock tolled off the last minute of the departing year, firecrackers exploded in a roaring, crackling din, filling entire streets with columns of smoke and sheets of fire to frighten away the evil spirits for the new year.[3]

For recreation, many men attended the Chinese theater. The first Chinese play in America was presented in 1852 when 123 actors of the Hong Fook Tong performed at the American Theater in San Francisco. In 1879, a Chinese theater was erected, a three-story brick building with a seating capacity for twenty-five hundred people. The price of admission was thirty-five cents. During performances, the men — sometimes a few hundred, sometimes a thousand — sat on benches in the gallery. Smoking cigars and cigarettes and eating mandarin oranges and melon seeds, they listened to the Chinese orchestra and watched the drama.

On Sundays, most of the men had no families to take on outings. They had "no homes in this country," observed Otis Gibson of San Francisco. They strolled the streets, he added, for they had "nothing to do, and nowhere else to go." At night and during the weekends, men played games like mah-jong. Tom Lee, a cook and houseboy, said: "No get lonely for home China, many China boys all same one family. Sometime have holiday. Put on Merican hat, shoe, tie, all same White man, walk to Stockton have good time."[4]

The future had seemed so promising to these men when they had left their villages for Gold Mountain:

> If you have a daughter, marry her quickly to a travel-
> ler to Gold Mountain,
> For when he gets off the boat, he will bring
> hundreds of pieces of silver.[5]

But these migrants found it difficult to earn hundreds of silver pieces in America. Then, after the enactment of the 1882 Chinese Exclusion Law, they were not allowed to bring their wives to the country many had begun to adopt. All they could do was to maintain ties with their "widows" through letters.

Two of these migrants, Lung On and Ing Hay, had come to America in the early 1880s. At first, they worked as wage earners and then opened their own general store. Gradually over the years, as they built their business and developed personal and social ties to their new community, they came to feel detached from their homeland and their families. In 1899, Lung's father commanded in a letter: "Come home as soon as you can. Don't say 'no' to me any more. . . . You are my only son. You have no brothers and your age is near forty. . . . You have been away from home for seventeen years, you know nothing about our domestic situation. . . . Come back, let our family be reunited and enjoy the rest of our lives." In a letter to "My Husband-lord," Lung's wife scolded

A LARGER MEMORY

her absent mate: "According to Mr. Wang, you are indulging in
sensuality, and have no desire to return home. On hearing this I
am shocked and pained. I have been expecting your return day
after day. . . . But, alas, I don't know what kind of substance your
heart is made of. . . . Your daughter is now at the age of betrothal
and it is your responsibility to arrange her marriage."

Her appeal must have moved her husband, for Lung wrote to
his cousin Liang Kwang-jin on March 2, 1905: "We are fine here,
thank you. Tell my family that I will go back as soon as I accumulate
enough money to pay the fare." But a few weeks later, Lung
learned from a letter written by his cousin, dated March 4, that
certain family events had already passed him by: "Two years ago
your mother died. Last year your daughter married. Your aged father is immobile. He will pass away any time now. Your wife feels
left out and hurt. . . . Come back as soon as you receive this message."[6]

Hundreds of thousands of migrants like Lung On and Ing Hay
stayed in America. Though married, they had become "bachelors."

"How Can I Call This My Home?": Lee Chew

There were no "Chinese laundrymen" in China; they became washers of clothes in America. Why? Lee Chew gave an explanation in this "lifelet," published in the Independent magazine in the early twentieth century. After living for decades in his adopted country, he still felt he could not call America his home.

———————➤ ◆ ———————

THE VILLAGE WHERE I was born is situated in the province of Canton. . . . When I was ten years of age I worked on my father's farm, digging, hoeing, manuring, gathering and carrying the crop. We had no horses, as nobody under the rank of an official is allowed to have a horse in China, and horses do not work on farms there, which is the reason why the roads there are so bad. The people cannot use roads as they are used here, and so they do not make them.

I worked on my father's farm till I was about sixteen years of age, when a man of our tribe came back from America and took ground as large as four city blocks and made a paradise of it. He put a large stone wall around and led some streams through and built a palace and summer house and about twenty other structures, with beautiful bridges over the streams and walks and roads. Trees and flowers, singing birds, water fowl and curious animals were within the walls.

The man had gone away from our village a poor boy. Now he returned with unlimited wealth, which he had obtained in the country of the American wizards. After many amazing adventures he had become a merchant in a city called Mott Street, so it was said.

When his palace and grounds were completed he gave a dinner

to all the people who assembled to be his guests. One hundred pigs roasted whole were served on the tables, with chickens, ducks, geese and such an abundance of dainties that our villagers even now lick their fingers when they think of it. He had the best actors from Hong Kong performing, and every musician for miles around was playing and singing. At night the blaze of the lanterns could be seen for many miles.

Having made his wealth among the barbarians this man had faithfully returned to pour it out among his tribesmen, and he is living in our village now very happy, and a pillar of strength to the poor.

The wealth of this man filled my mind with the idea that I, too, would like to go to the country of the wizards and gain some of their wealth, and after a long time my father consented, and gave me his blessing, and my mother took leave of me with tears, while my grandfather laid his hand upon my head and told me to remember and live up to the admonitions of the Sages, to avoid gambling, bad women and men of evil minds, and so to govern my conduct that when I died my ancestors might rejoice to welcome me as a guest on high.

My father gave me $100, and I went to Hong Kong with five other boys from our place and we got steerage passage on a steamer, paying $50 each. Everything was new to me. All my life I had been used to sleeping on a board bed with a wooden pillow, and I found the steamer's bunk very uncomfortable, because it was so soft. The food was different from that which I had been used to, and I did not like it at all. I was afraid of the stews, for the thought of what they might be made of by the wicked wizards of the ship made me ill. Of the great power of these people I saw many signs. The engines that moved the ship were wonderful monsters, strong enough to lift mountains. When I got to San Francisco, which was before the passage of the Exclusion act, I was half starved, because I was afraid to eat the provisions of the barbarians, but a few days' living in the Chinese quarter made me happy again. A man got me work as a house servant in an American family, and my start was the same as that of almost all the Chinese in this country.

The Chinese laundryman does not learn his trade in China; there are no laundries in China. The women there do the washing in tubs and have no washboards or flat irons. All the Chinese laundrymen here were taught in the first place by American women just as I was taught.

When I went to work for that American family I could not speak a word of English, and I did not know anything about housework. The family consisted of husband, wife and two children. They were very good to me and paid me $3.50 a week, of which I could save $3.

I did not know how to do anything, and I did not understand what the lady said to me, but she showed me how to cook, wash, iron, sweep, dust, make beds, wash dishes, clean windows, paint and brass, polish the knives and forks, etc., by doing the things herself and then overseeing my efforts to imitate her. She would take my hands and show them how to do things. She and her husband and children laughed at me a great deal, but it was all good natured. I was not confined to the house in the way servants are confined here, but when my work was done in the morning I was allowed to go out till lunch time. People in California are more generous than they are here.

In six months I had learned how to do the work of our house quite well, and I was getting $5 a week and board, and putting away about $4.25 a week. I had also learned some English, and by going to a Sunday school I learned more English and something about Jesus, who was a great Sage, and whose precepts are like those of Kong-foo-tsze.

It was twenty years ago when I came to this country, and I worked for two years as a servant, getting at the last $35 a month. I sent money home to comfort my parents, but though I dressed well and lived well and had pleasure, going quite often to the Chinese theater and to dinner parties in Chinatown, I saved $50 in the first six months, $90 in the second, $120 in the third and $150 in the fourth. So I had $410 at the end of two years, and I was now ready to start in business.

When I first opened a laundry it was in company with a partner, who had been in the business for some years. We went to a town about 500 miles inland, where a railroad was building. We got a board shanty and worked for the men employed by the railroads. Our rent cost us $10 a month and food nearly $5 a week each, for all food was dear and we wanted the best of everything — we lived principally on rice, chickens, ducks and pork, and did our own cooking. The Chinese take naturally to cooking. It cost us about $50 for our furniture and apparatus, and we made close upon $60 a week, which we divided between us. We had to put up with many insults and some frauds, as men would come in and claim parcels that did not belong to them, saying they had lost their tickets, and would fight if they did not get what they asked for. Sometimes we were taken before Magistrates and fined for losing shirts that we had never seen. On the other hand, we were making money, and even after sending home $3 a week I was able to save about $15. When the railroad construction gang moved on we went with them. The men were rough and prejudiced against us, but not more so than in the big Eastern cities. It is only lately in New York that the Chinese have been able to discontinue putting wire screens in front of their windows, and at the present time the street boys are still breaking the windows of Chinese laundries all over the city, while the police seem to think it a joke.

We were three years with the railroad, and then went to the mines, where we made plenty of money in gold dust, but had a hard time, for many of the miners were wild men who carried revolvers and after drinking would come into our place to shoot and steal shirts, for which we had to pay. One of these men hit his head hard against a flat iron and all the miners came and broke up our laundry, chasing us out of town. They were going to hang us. We lost all our property and $365 in money, which members of the mob must have found.

Luckily most of our money was in the hands of Chinese bankers in San Francisco. I drew $500 and went East to Chicago, where I had a laundry for three years, during which I increased my capital to $2,500. After that I was four years in Detroit. I went home to China in 1897, but returned in 1898, and began a laundry business in Buffalo. But Chinese laundry business now is not as good as it was ten years ago. American cheap labor in the steam laundries has hurt it. So I determined to become a general merchant, and with this idea I came to New York and opened a shop in the Chinese quarter, keeping silks, teas, porcelain, clothes, shoes, hats and Chinese provisions, which include shark's fins and nuts, lily bulbs and lily flowers, lychee nuts and other Chinese dainties, but do not include rats, because it would be too expensive to import them. The rat which is eaten by the Chinese is a field animal which lives on rice, grain and sugar cane. Its flesh is delicious. Many Americans who have tasted shark's fin and bird's nest soup and tiger lily flowers and bulbs are firm friends of Chinese cookery. If they could enjoy one of our fine rats they would go to China to live, so as to get some more.

American people eat ground hogs, which are very like these Chinese rats and they also eat many sorts of food that our people would not touch. Those that have dined with us know that we understand how to live well.

The ordinary laundry shop is generally divided into three rooms. In front is the room where the customers are received, behind that a bedroom and in the back the work shop, which is also the dining room and kitchen. The stove and cooking utensils are the same as those of the Americans.

Work in a laundry begins early on Monday morning — about seven o'clock. There are generally two men, one of whom washes while the other does the ironing. The man who irons does not start in till Tuesday, as the clothes are not ready for him to begin till that time. So he has Sundays and Mondays as holidays. The man who does the washing finishes up on Friday night, and so he has Saturday and Sunday. Each works only five days a week, but those are long days — from seven o'clock in the morning till midnight. . . .

The reason why so many Chinese go into the laundry business

in this country is because it requires little capital and is one of the few opportunities that are open. Men of other nationalities who are jealous of the Chinese, because he is a more faithful worker than one of their people, have raised such a great outcry about Chinese cheap labor that they have shut him out of working on farms or in factories or building railroads or making streets or digging sewers. He cannot practice any trade, and his opportunities to do business are limited to his own countrymen. So he opens a laundry when he quits domestic service.

The treatment of the Chinese in this country is all wrong and mean. It is persisted in merely because China is not a fighting nation. The Americans would not dare to treat Germans, English, Italians or even Japanese as they treat the Chinese, because if they did there would be a war.

There is no reason for the prejudice against the Chinese. . . . There are few Chinamen in jails and none in the poor houses. There are no Chinese tramps or drunkards. Many Chinese here have become sincere Christians, in spite of the persecution which they have to endure from their heathen countrymen. More than half the Chinese in this country would become citizens if allowed to do so, and would be patriotic Americans. But how can they make this country their home as matters are now? They are not allowed to bring wives here from China, and if they marry American women there is a great outcry.

All Congressmen acknowledge the injustice of the treatment of my people, yet they continue it. . . .

Under the circumstances, how can I call this my home, and how can any one blame me if I take my money and go back to my village in China?

"Like Country Pretty Much":
Kee Low

During the 1920s, scholars collected scores of interviews for a "Survey of Race Relations." They are housed in the archives of the Hoover Institution in Stanford, California. One of them was an interview with a Chinese immigrant, recorded on August 4, 1924. Kee Low had been in America for almost a half century when he was interviewed. Here he tells how he made America his home, and what he disliked but also liked about his adopted country.

———————————▶ ◀———————————

Yes, people treat me all right, but when I first come here, I associated entirely among my people. They think they have not been treated right. I arrived in San Francisco in 1876, 49 years ago. Come to San Francisco when country one hundred years old. People treat Chinese rotten then. Don't blame people much at that time. Chinese and European not educated as much then as today. More civilized today. People drive Chinese out of country, people not working, not enough experience. Chinese no experience. Getting more education and experience now.

Come to Seattle in 1879 on steamer Dakota from San Francisco to Seattle. Landed at Yesler's wharf. It ran at that time straight up to Main Street. That is the First Street now. It ran up to what is now Twelfth Avenue.

Wages pretty small about that time. A person working logging camps $45 to $60 a month. Before you could work in logging camp, you had to put a lean on the logs. Few Chinese work in the saw mill and coal mine. Railroad not much. Railroad at that time just built. Railroad between here and Black Diamond, New Castle, Tacoma and Puyallup. Only nine railroad in the state at this time. Railroad men, they get about $1.25 to $1.50 a day and board themselves.

People talking about Chinese working small wages. That's where they begin at, and they want to keep them out of the country. When they start, some Chinese picking hops out in Squaw Valley, and the trouble is people would have tried to drive them out, and at night they go out around Chinese tents, and they kill three at that time. I was there at that time. I see that. I know. The good men came out and stop them, and some of these men, they think what is right, they still living today.

But people want to keep Chinese out. I was living on the waterfront, and they told me to get out one day. Sunday morning, they come together and drive Chinese out. They drive me out, and I lived among five and six hundred Chinese. They want to get us out to San Francisco, to go on steamer, and we stayed on the wharf all night, and they bring us little black coffee and little bread in morning. We pretty hungry. The last day, some of the citizens, Judge Greené, Judge Hanford, United States Attorney, nice fellow want to help us. Let us do as we pleased, so we came out and stayed at the court house, then a frame building. Judge Greene told the Chinese that those who wanted to stay and make good citizens could stay, and those who wanted to go could go. One half wanted to go, and one half wanted to stay. Two hundred fifty want to get away. When the steamer get here, wasn't big enough to hold this many people at one time. Some has to go back to city and stay until next steamer.

There were so many around the streets that they had to have somebody to protect these people. Some of the hobos tried to make them go back to the wharf, but volunteers tried to keep these fellows away. They commenced shooting and kill one of them. So Chinese people get excited when gun begin to sound, so they throw shoes, blankets and everything and run. I was uptown myself. I didn't intend to go. I ran outside to see what happened because I was so excited. No see one person. Then I get excited. Call up one or two friends of mine and tell them get killed, and we better get out of the way. We run out in woods. Build fire. Pretty cold. I told friends, we got to protect ourselves. We got to get out of here. One say, "I don't know what I going to do." "Hell," I say, "I tell what I going to do."

Steamer leaving for Victoria tonight. I sneak down to wharf and see what time steamer left. The Starr only one steamer run and asked one of the men what time steamer left. He say 11 o'clock tonight. If I had to stay to 11 o'clock tonight, all right. There were some hops piled up on the wharf, you know, in bales. There was a hollow place in the center, and we hide in there. It was about 4 or 5 in the evening, and about 7:30 I heard a man on a horse tell the men to stop steamers to Victoria. I jumped out and asked watchman. No he know why city stop them.

No eat anything that day. Little later on another man rode by on a horse. Watchman told him we inside of hops and no eat all day. That man was Captain Hill. "John, John, come out." We come out. He said, "Have you eat anything today?" He said then we going to feed you. He took us up to the New Brunswick Restaurant. The man, he afraid to feed us because spoil his business. He then took us up to Second and Main to a few frame buildings. He bought us some sandwiches. About 11 o'clock we have meal and Chinese tea. Next day soldiers come from Vancouver, then we all right. We can walk around street.

Now I want to know why the people getting educated day by day. In order to get experience. When I first come to this country, only four steamers run between here and China. More than forty now. Look at the business we build between here and Asia. I think that some way the commercial relations getting clear and better.

But the law [1924 Immigration Act] make people sore. I afraid someday there will be trouble here. Don't know what to think of this new law treating Chinese this way. I have been here forty-nine years. I have been to China once. I live here long. No want to leave here. This climate suit me. People treat me good enough. Now like this, some of the merchants bring their family, and some of the native born bring their wives over, that all right. But this law in case my wife or children over there, I can never see them anymore. No pleasure for myself. This way I think very wrong.

Break up family. I hope they can do something better on this law and keep friendship closer and closer all the time.

I had some relations in California when I come over. They told me about country. When I get here, I work in cigar store. When I come to Seattle, I go into the laundry business. After trouble, I go back to laundry to pick up my things. They wouldn't let me have chance to stay there too long. The trunk, they rolled up and throw on wharf. They let us pick them up. Then I went to California. I work in cigar business. Then I come back work in Shanghai Cafe (Peking then when I started). I sold out and come here.

I did not marry until I went away from here about thirty years ago. I marry in Hong Kong. My wife come here two years later. My eldest boy, he die in China. The second one die and third die. Fourth in high school. He citizen. He have as much education as possible. I have not much education myself. When come here, I young, so I went to night school. I work in day time. I only study one year in China. Six or seven months school, that sort. I fifteen years old. I study pretty hard. Only can read little, not much writing.

I live outside Chinese district. Neighbors no cause trouble. I don't belong to any regular club. We have Chinese association. All Chinese belong no matter what state they come from. Disputes they cannot settle themselves, then try to settle by association. If no settle, go to court. Settle most disputes themselves. No like courts.

I member of tong. I don't pay no attention to it. No benefit at all. Join long time ago. Would not put an eye on it. Hard to get out once get in. Chinese minister ought to go to Senate to make law to stop these tongs, all trouble makers. I have been here so long, have no trouble with anyone — Chinese or American. Don't want to go to court or judge or any this government. In case I have to go like to testify against anyone to get just treatment, then I go. Don't like to go to immigration till know case real good.

Lots of times people say things to me, make remarks. That's what I talk about today when I go to China restaurant to get my lunch. Waiter, he say, "You ought to go down to first class restaurant." One time in Butte I went to one restaurant, the waiter wouldn't wait on me. I don't go to other restaurant. One time when I go to barber shop, barber say we only shave white people. Those are the main things I keep in my mind all time. Lots time people say things, no pay any attention. All bankers treat me fine. Businessmen all treat me fine. Well, I tell you one thing. I always pay my bills. They want to get my business.

Yes, I rather my boy get wife in China. Get more Chinese education over there. New law will stop that. Chinese no mind if marry white girl, but not good. You see how it is. Now you take Chinese, they born in this country, they educated. Might get along better with white girl, but not good. But Chinese born in China no get along. No understand Chinese customs. They no know old-fashioned Chinese way. People in China understand custom better. My little boy go to China school. Learned Chinese in China school.

I have trouble getting my wife here, but they know I all right cause I been here so long. Everybody know me well. Have little trouble with inspector. Fisher was his name. He tried to make trouble for me. He tell little small business, he think. I talk with Hustus, inspector at Pt. Townsend. He say he know I hard working man. You have right to get your wife in this country. . . .

Almost impossible to change Chinese way at once, now. Some want Chinese way. No use. But you got to have some old way. I think impossible to cut out everything at once. I think I pretty much first reformer with the bunch. They don't cut queue off. People laugh at me for cutting mine. I told those people who laugh, you cut yours someday. Someday, somebody will force you to cut yours off. My word proved true today.

I no think Chinese regard religion at all. Some years ago, Mohammedans from northern part of China, and some Catholics, many hundred years ago come to China. Any Chinese get Christianity, they call them fallen to the devil. Well, most don't belong to anything. Christianity more and more each day in China. First man in China cause revolution, he Christian. Hurt Christianity lot.

Some Chinese play lottery. Yes, this is gamble. They don't, people can't make living on them. Some go broke, just the same as American.

American so much divorce. No divorce in China. Very seldom. I leave there when fifteen and never see one. One hundred sixty thousand people and never see one. Chinese people not get anyone to write divorce. No place to write divorce. Nobody want anything to do with paper. Hard to get somebody to write divorce. Not right. Some man no treat family right, hard to get divorce in China. Don't like that. Too much here. Little quarrels don't amount to anything.

I am glad people go to China to teach Christianity. Good experience. They doing lot of good. Over here no make difference. Got to go American way whether want to or not. You got to go by the country.

My wife not talk very much English. She cannot read single letter in Chinese or English. I come from Canton Province. Speak Cantonese. . . .

You have lots of land in this country yet, cross Cascades. Ten or fifteen thousand men to work out ditch. They need nothing but water east of mountains. They could put in the ditch. Some Chinese send money back to help various political factions. Last legislature hurt lots of business. I think it all right maybe to keep out labor, but not students, wives, wealthy class. All right to keep out class works on railroads and logging camps, but not others. . . . Plenty work in this country. No use fighting. Plenty farm. They think too much about these labor men. Even this government listen too much to labor men. . . .

Like country pretty much. Independent. Happy. I don't want to send my boy over there.

"A Chance to Take Care of Myself":
A Chinese-American Daughter

The cultural tensions between the immigrant generation and the American-born generation of the Chinese have been the focus of contemporary writers like Maxine Hong Kingston and Amy Tan. Hidden away in a 1946 mimeographed publication, Orientals and Their Cultural Adjustment *(Fisk University) is "Story of a Chinese Girl Student." Here the student tells about the wishes of her father, her dreams for herself, and the choices she made when she was only sixteen years old.*

I WAS BORN IN San Francisco. My father was a merchant, now gone back to China. My mother was native born, but in those days, Chinatown was like a little bit of China. My mother grew up without learning a word of English and quite according to Chinese ideas.

My mother knew when she married my father that she was the "second wife," but the other wife was in China, had no children, and so probably would never bother her. Besides, it would not have made any difference if my mother had objected. What could she have done about it? That was the custom, and her parents decided all that.

Well, when my oldest sister was about 14, and there were about a half dozen other children, my father decided to retire from business and go back to China. He expected, of course, to take all the family with him, but my sister did not want to go. The stories that she had heard about interior village life in China were not exactly alluring, and she made up her mind to stay here, if she could. Of course, there were only two ways open to her: she would have to go, or stay here and get married, according to my parents' ideas. She decided the latter was the lesser of two evils.

In a way, she had two men to choose from, but as she had never

seen either of them, only their photographs, she took her parents'
advice. One was young, about twenty, and her parents put it this
way: "This man is young, he has his way to make, and he has a
large family of brothers and sisters. You would be a sort of slave
to all of them. This other man is fifty years old, but he can give
you everything. He has no family — better to be an old man's
darling than a young man's slave," or words to that effect. They
told her, too, that a young man would not be constant. He would
be running around with other women. It was far safer to take an
older man who would settle down.

Of course, she was married in the Chinese way — that is, the
man handed over to her parents a sum of money. Naturally, that
would be far larger with an older and richer man, but the parents
did not speak of that. Of course, though, their interest was for
her to marry the older man. Some of this money is supposed
to be spent for the bride's outfit, but, of course, not all. One reason
why my sister decided as she did was that she felt that she could
not stand it to keep on with such heavy work. As the oldest
daughter, she had always been overworked, never had any time
to herself.

My sister's story comes into my story, for she chose to have me,
her little six-year-old sister, go with her, and I was allowed to go.
She knew she was going to live among strangers, almost all of them
Americans, and she would be very lonely, so she was allowed to
keep me.

Her husband was a cook, one of those old cooks you hear so
much about, always grinning, the kind you hear Americans say
you can't get again. He had worked for lots of the pioneer American families, and he began when he was about nine. He came from
China when he was nine and wanted to go to school and get an
education. But he had just one hour of it. His father came into the
school, grabbed him by the scruff of the neck, and said, "There's
a lady out here who wants a little China boy to work, so come
on!" That was before they had a law about going to school. He
learned to cook in that family, but he was always sore. After awhile
he was a section boss in a lumber camp and made some money.

When he was fifty years old, he was a cook in a lumber camp at Weed, Oregon, and he married a wife fourteen years old. He had a horrible disposition, suspicious and jealous, and my sister's life was one long tragedy with him. My sister was very attractive and had a good disposition. Even in the short time that she had been at school, she had picked up American ways, and he resented all that.

My sister had never been at school at all, except sort of spasmodically for two years from eight to ten. Then, in those days, it was thought proper to take a Chinese girl of ten years out of school and teach her the duties of a wife. She never would have been sent to Mission School at all except that Deaconess Drant, who was the head of the Episcopal Mission School, took a fancy to her, called on my mother many times, and persuaded her to let my sister come. But even then she used to be kept home for all sorts of things. If any of us little brothers and sisters were sick, or anything, she always had to stay home.

Then at ten she had to stay home for good and never went back at all, just when she was beginning to like it the best, make some ties, etc. What seems remarkable to me is that she learned so much in those two years, and it affected her whole life. She used to tell me what she had learned and about Deaconess Drant and Miss Cameron, and what they had done for the girls, and she told me that if I ever had the chance, and could do it, to go to them, and they would help me out of any trouble.

So I grew up in a lumber camp. I think I have seen the best and the worst of American life. Everybody knew everything about everybody else. Everybody's wife was running around with someone else. The wife of the man who kept the saloon was interested in the bartender — oh, we heard all about it.

The men drank a good deal and were pretty coarse, but good-hearted. They used to call my sister, that little girl as she was, "Mother." They'd tell her things because they trusted her, and she sort of believed the best of them. They would cheat my brother-in-law when they could, but never her. They would come in and say, "Say, yesterday I was stewed — for a fact, lost all my money.

But say, I want to go to a dance, Mother. It's Saturday night. Let me borrow two-fifty, will yuh, and put it in my board bill?" So my sister would go quietly and take some money out of the cash drawer and charge it up, and they always paid it back.

But my brother-in-law was always hollering. He would begin at five in the morning and keep it up till nine at night. He was awful strict with me, too. Did I get out much? Well, it wasn't his fault if I ever did. I suppose the men used to jolly me along, call me "a little Chink," "Little Chatterbox," etc., the way they do my niece now. My sister had two children, a boy and a girl. My, they lead the "old man" a life, now!

When I was about fifteen, my father came back from China, stayed in America a year, and then decided to go back to China and take me with him. He said that I would be sent to school there, but I did not trust his promise because of the way that I felt he had brought about my sisters' marriages. One of my older sisters had been married in China against her will, after she had been just a very short time in school. I felt that if I went back with him, I would very shortly be married, and that I would not have anything to say about it. My sister knew that, and even with that little bit of teaching that she had had so long ago, before she was ten years old, she helped me. She told me if I ever came to San Francisco, to go to see Deaconess Drant and Miss Cameron. You asked me once if it is true that one can always believe a Chinaman's word when once it has been given. I don't know — I have only my own experiences, but I feel that they are a good deal like other people. They are human, and if they want a thing, they are very apt to try to get it. I know that they tell girls many things that they do not intend to fulfill. That is done all the time.

My father brought me to San Francisco and bought my ticket to China. But I had been away from my father for so long that I was not much afraid of him. He seemed to me just like a man, I was used to standing up for myself. I told him all the time that I wouldn't go, and finally, the night before the boat sailed, I told him that if he insisted, I would go up to the Mission and throw myself on their protection. But he did not believe me. He just said, "There is no use in talking, get ready to go on the boat tomorrow."

I was in the care of relatives who believed just as he did, that I ought to go and that I ought to get married, the sooner the better. But I was resolved not to marry, to have an education instead. My sister had asked me to see Miss Cameron about her own troubles, and I told my relatives I had to see Miss Cameron about her own [my sister's] troubles, and I told my relatives I had to go there for that purpose and went the next morning before the boat sailed.

I think it was rather wonderful that I could find the house at once, as I had not seen the place since I was six years old. When I had the nerve, the night before, to tell my father that I would go there, he had not believed that I could defy him. "The home will not keep you for life," he said. "I don't want it to keep me for life," I said. "I want a chance to learn, so that I can take care of myself!"

So Miss Cameron took me to Judge Muraski of the Juvenile Court, and I talked to him. I said that there were enough Chinese girls who would marry and bring children into the world who were of no more use than themselves. I did not want to marry, myself, but to do something that would be of some use to my people. I said that I wanted to study and do something. The judge said that I was native-born and could not be forced to go to China, and because there was a respectable person like Miss Cameron who would be responsible for me, I was permitted to stay. That was seven years ago, when I was sixteen.

I came back and called up my father by telephone because I knew he would be looking for me, and I thought well, I will save him that much trouble. No, I was not afraid up there; nothing could touch me, I knew. Isn't it wonderful? I told him not to look for me any more. I was not going, and the judge said I could stay. He came up in the afternoon with my brother to see me, but my father is more or less a gentleman, and he did not make any fuss. I told him I wanted to study, that I would never disgrace him, and that I hoped to be of value to my country.

Soon after my father went to China, we heard that he and my little brother, about nine years old, had been taken by the bandits. They did not make prisoners of the women in the party, but they held my father and my little brother for ten thousand dollars ransom. Of course, the family could not produce that at once, and while they were trying to raise it, my mother found the body of my little brother, killed and exposed on the hillside as a warning to hurry up with the ransom, or the same fate would befall my father. His face was terribly disfigured, but my mother knew him by his body and the clothes he had on, which she had made. That was terrible, but it did not touch me so much as I had never known that little brother. He was born over there.

My older brother took what money there was and returned to America to borrow money among the relatives. He finally raised enough to ransom my father and has spent his life working to pay it back. He is a common workman since he did not care for an education. My father would have given it to him, but he only got as far as the third grade. Then he said it was too much for him and went to work at fifteen washing dishes in a restaurant. He never got very far!

I went through the grammar grades, then the Lux High School, then worked for a year in the literary department of the Women's Board of Missions. About this time, a wonderful thing happened to me. I always feel a little bit as though I had been led by Providence.

I had gone down to Los Angeles to cheer up a friend. She was very unhappily married, and Miss Cameron thought that a visit from me might cheer her up, so I went down. While I was there, I met a Scotch friend of Miss Cameron's who asked me, among other things, what I wanted to do with my life. I told her that I wanted to become a medical missionary, and she was very much impressed, for it seemed she had always wanted to help someone to be a medical missionary. She wrote to Miss Cameron that she could not get me out of her mind, and that she would like to help me. She lived in San Mateo, where they had a junior college, and she offered to let me live with her, work and go to college. She would also pay me something.

At first I began with twenty dollars a month, but later it became twenty-five, and when there are six grown people in the family, she pays me thirty. But I may do something else, in case this lady loses interest in the idea. She said she would send me to college, but I don't think I ought to hold her to that, in case she loses interest in the idea. I work there during the school year, but during vacations I generally come up to the Mission to work — gives us both a rest from each other.

One thing I can say about my school and my friends in school, I have been very happy in my friends there. I hate to say anything that sounds conceited, but I want to say, just to show how fair the students have been to me, that I was the president of my class in the Lux High School, and in junior college, I am the first vice-president of the Association of Women Students. The girls lately gave me a surprise party. Wasn't that nice of them? I am the only Chinese student there, and they have been such good friends, all but one girl, and it turned out she liked me all right, but her parents wouldn't let her have anything to do with the Chinese. She was a kind of quiet girl, not much personality.

I think I feel more American really than Chinese, but still, what I want to do is to help my own people if I'm a medical missionary. I'll get them when they feel sick and are thinking about what they'll get when they die. Then I can appeal to them, make them think, and their relatives, too. They all will be in a more serious frame of mind. . . .

PART FOUR

A Multicultural Destiny

Introduction

IN 1891, THE Census Bureau announced that the frontier no longer existed. Americans had reached beyond what Jefferson had called the "Stony mountains" and were settling the entire continent from the Atlantic to the Pacific. Cities and towns dotted the face of America, from Boston to San Francisco. The United States had become the world's leading industrial nation: our economy produced more manufactured goods than both England and Germany combined. A manifest destiny had been realized.

What would the future hold for this industrial and urban America, now without a frontier? This question fascinated a young historian. At the 1893 American Historical Association meeting in Chicago, Frederick Jackson Turner presented a sweeping interpretation of "the significance of the frontier in American history." The end of the frontier, he observed, marked the close of a great historic movement. In the crucible of this westward expansion had been forged a lasting legacy. By providing "free land," the vastness of the continent had created the American character with its "inventive turn of mind," "restless nervous energy," individualism, and democracy. Continually beginning over again on the frontier — the "meeting point between savagery and civilization" — Americans had experienced "perennial birth" as they moved to the west with its new opportunities and continuous contact with the "simplicity of primitive society." Europeans originally, they had been "Americanized" by the wilderness.

The frontier is the line of most rapid and effective Americanization. The wilderness masters the colonist. It finds him a European in dress, industries, tools, modes of travel, and thought. It takes him from the railroad car and puts him in the birch canoe. It strips off the garments of civilization, and arrays him in the hunting shirt and the moccasin. It puts him in the log cabin of the Cherokee and the Iroquois. . . . Before long he has gone to planting Indian corn and plowing with a sharp stick; he shouts the war cry and takes the scalp in orthodox Indian fashion. In short, at the frontier the environment is at first too strong for the man. He must accept the conditions which it furnishes, or perish, and so he fits himself into the Indian clearings and follows the Indian trails. Little by little he transforms the wilderness, but the outcome is not the Old Europe. . . . The fact is that here is a new product that is American.

Embedded in Turner's frontier thesis was the notion of our national identity as white or European in origin. This pioneering people had been transformed into Americans in their encounters with the wilderness and the "Indians."

Although Turner was celebrating the winning of the West, he was also betraying a broadly shared feeling of uncertainty about the coming century. Without the expanse of the West and the availability of land, modern America was facing the grim prospect of explosive class conflict in an industrial society. Technological "progress," the "complexity of city life," and the "factory system" had become realities in the new industrial order. Would this new "age of machinery," asked Turner, usher in an era of social disintegration — an "age of socialistic inquiry"? The historian reassured a nervous society. "He would be a rash prophet," Turner proclaimed confidently, "who should assert that the expansive character of American life has now entirely ceased. . . . Movement has been its dominant fact, and, unless this training has no effect upon a people, the American intellect will continually demand a wider field for its exercise."[1]

Five years after Turner's announcement on the significance of the frontier, the "wider field" turned out to be an expansionist war that led to the annexation of the Philippines. The overthrow of Hawaii's queen by Americans opened the way to the U.S. incorporation of those islands. With possessions in the Pacific, America was placed on a collision course with Japan. The clash came on December 7, 1941, at Pearl Harbor. Japan's sudden attack swept our country into the whirlwind of World War II, a horrendous conflict already under way in Europe. The war against Nazi Germany with its ideology of Aryan supremacy forced us as citizens of a democracy to face the inconsistency between our ideals and our treatment of racial minorities.

This contradiction became the conceptual framework for Gunnar Myrdal's weighty study, entitled *An American Dilemma: The Negro Problem and Modern Democracy*, originally published in 1944. While waging this "ideological war" against Nazism, he declared, Americans should apply the principle of democracy more explicitly to racial inequality at home. "Fascism and nazism are based on a racial superiority dogma — not unlike the old hackneyed American caste theory — and they came to power by means of racial persecution and oppression." Therefore, Americans should stand before the whole world in support of racial tolerance and equality. "When in this crucial time the international leadership passes to America," Myrdal observed, "the great reason for hope is that this country has a national experience of uniting racial and cultural diversities and a national theory, if not a consistent practice, of freedom and equality for all. . . . The main trend in [this country's] history is the gradual realization of the American Creed."[2]

Affirming this creed of equality, President Franklin D. Roosevelt recognized the need to confront Nazism ideologically in order to rally Americans to the war effort. We were fighting, he declared, for the "four freedoms" — freedom of speech, freedom of worship, freedom from want, and freedom from fear. Our commitment to these ideals, he explained, condemned racism: "The principle on which this country was founded and by which it has always been governed is that Americanism is a matter of mind and heart. Americanism is not, and never was, a matter of race or ancestry."[3]

Americans of all ethnicities and races fought in this war to defend democracy. Blacks left their farms in the South and their homes in northern cities, Chicanos their barrios, the Chinese their Chinatowns, the Indians their reservations, and the Japanese Americans the internment camps. All of them made sacrifices for what blacks called the "war for double victory," the struggle against fascism abroad and racism at home. What Lincoln had described as "the mystic chords of memory" stretching from battlefields to patriot graves had become multiracial.

This national reaffirmation of our diversity and our dedication to the "proposition" of equality, forged in the fury of World War II, opened the way for the civil rights era of the sixties. The massive 1963 March on Washington and Martin Luther King's eloquent sharing of his dream of an America redeemed stirred the nation and led to the passage of the 1964 Civil Rights Act. A year later, President Lyndon Johnson went beyond this prohibition of discrimination when he issued Executive Order 11246. Aiming at "the full realization of equal employment opportunity," this law required firms conducting business with the federal government to take "affirmative action." Companies had to set "good faith goals and timetables" for employing "underutilized" qualified minority workers. In his 1965 speech at Howard University, Johnson explained why affirmative action was necessary:

> You do not take a person who, for years, has been hobbled by chains and liberate him, bring him up to the starting line of a race, and then say, "You are free to compete with all others," and still justly believe that you have been completely fair. Thus it is not enough to open the gates of opportunity. All our citizens must have the ability to walk through those gates.
>
> This is the next and more profound stage of the battle for civil rights. We seek not just freedom but opportunity — not just legal equity but human ability — not just equality as a right and a theory but equality as a fact and equality as a result.[4]

Thirty years later, however, equality as a fact remained a dream deferred for millions of Americans. A new structural discrimination was determining where minorities lived, went to school, and worked. Tremendous transformations had led to the economic hollowing out of major cities where an underclass of blacks and Latinos were entrapped and abandoned. The emergence of high-technology industries with their demand for educated workers had rendered large segments of the minority populations economically superfluous. Residential segregation had resulted in what Douglas Massey and Nancy Denton characterized as an "American apartheid."[5]

These structures of racial discrimination were shrouded by the myth of meritocracy. Championing individual responsibility and merit as American values, conservatives as well as many liberals attacked affirmative action as "reverse discrimination." They waged their political assault in California's Proposition 209, which forbade the state from using race and gender as a basis for university admissions, employment, and government contracting.

Within this context of a deepening racial divide and a widening backlash against affirmative action, President Bill Clinton gave his speech, "One America in the 21st Century," at the University of California, San Diego, on June 14, 1997.

America, declared Clinton, is a "multiracial" society. "The greatest challenge we face is the problem of race. Can we fulfill the promise of America by embracing all our citizens of all races? Can we become one America in the twenty-first century?" He noted that in fifty years there would be "no majority race." "Can we be one America respecting, even celebrating, our differences, but embracing even more what we have in common? Can we define what it means to be an American, not just in terms of the hyphen showing our ethnic origins but in terms of our primary allegiance to the values America stands for?

"In our efforts to extend economic and educational opportunity to all our citizens," Clinton insisted, "we must consider the role of affirmative action." Referring to Proposition 209, he explained: "Let me say, I know that the people of California voted to repeal affirmative action without any ill motive. The vast majority of them simply did it with a conviction that discrimination and isolation are no longer barriers to achievement. But consider the results. Minority enrollments in law school and other graduate programs are plummeting for the first time in decades. Assuming the same will likely happen in undergraduate education, we must not resegregate higher education."

Clinton observed that "the classic American dilemma" had become "many dilemmas of race and ethnicity." In addition to black-and-white antagonism, there were now conflicts between blacks and Koreans, and also a resurgent nativism against new immigrants from Asia, the Middle East, and Latin America. In his conclusion, Clinton reflected on whether our ethnically diverse nation would be "one America" in the twenty-first century: "More than thirty years ago, at the high tide of the civil rights movement, the Kerner Commission said we were becoming two Americas, one white, one black, separate and unequal. Today, we face a different choice: will we become not two, but many Americas, separate, unequal and isolated? Or will we draw strength from all our people and our ancient faith in the quality of human dignity, to become the world's first truly multiracial democracy? That is the unfinished work of our time, to lift the burden of race and redeem the promise of America."[6]

A hundred years after Frederick Jackson Turner, Clinton was again redefining America. Our manifest destiny was not to be a nation where European settlers and their descendants would transform themselves into Americans by clearing the wilderness and advancing "civilization" against "savagery." Rather, ours was a country with a multicultural destiny to carry forward what Lincoln called our "unfinished work" toward equality. Clinton's pronouncement on our nation's "multiracial" identity, however, was not new. Throughout the twentieth century, from the end of the frontier to the threshold of a new millennium, the voices of multicultural America have been affirming this truth all along.

Beyond the Pale: Jewish
Immigrants in a Promised Land

I N RUSSIA, JEWS WERE required to live in the Pale of Settlement,
a region stretching from the Baltic to the Black Sea. "Within this
area the Czar commanded me to stay, with my father and mother
and friends, and all other people like us," recalled Mary Antin,
who emigrated to America in the 1890s. "We must not be found
outside the Pale, because we were Jews." In their towns and villages, Jews were victims of anti-Semitic violence.[1]

Especially dreaded were the pogroms — massacres of Jews and
the destruction of their shops and synagogues. "I feel that every
cobblestone in Russia is filled with Jewish blood," an immigrant
bitterly remarked. "We lived then on the first floor of a small house
in Kiev," remembered Golda Meir, "and I can still recall distinctly
hearing about a pogrom that was to descend on us. I didn't know
then, of course, what a pogrom was, but I knew it had something
to do with being Jewish and with the rabble that used to surge
through town, brandishing knives and huge sticks . . . and who
were now going to do terrible things to me and to my family."[2]

By the beginning of World War I, 2 million Jews, one-third of
all of the Jews in Russia and eastern Europe, including the Russian-
controlled provinces of Poland, had emigrated, most of them to
the United States. Stories about freedom and a better life there were
"buzzing" all around them. The cry "To America!" roared like
"wild-fire." "America was in everybody's mouth. Businessmen
talked of it over their accounts; the market women made up their

quarrels that they might discuss it from stall to stall; people who had relatives in the famous land went around reading their letters."[3]

These new immigrants settled in the Lower East Side of New York City. In this vibrant immigrant community, pushcarts lined the streets, and a cacophony of Yiddish voices, "a continual roar," rose from the crowds. Everywhere there were peddlers. Carrying packs or pushing carts, they knocked on doors and cajoled housewives to buy their goods. Streams of people flowed down the streets. "Suspenders, collah buttons, 'lastic, matches, hankeches — please, lady, buy," peddlers shouted. "Bandannas and tin cups at two cents, peaches at a cent a quart, damaged eggs for a song, hats for a quarter, and spectacles warranted to suit the eye . . . for thirty-five cents." In this colony, Jews resided and worked "within that small compass, meeting only people of their own nationality." One immigrant recalled that living in the Lower East Side was as though "we were still in our village in Russia."[4]

But the Lower East Side was also different in a significant way. It was the center of the garment industry. Sewing factories filled the neighborhood, like a huge, spreading industrial beehive. On the Second Avenue elevated train, a passenger could ride half a mile through the sweater district. "Every open window of the big tenements, that [stood] like a continuous brick wall on both sides of the way, [gave] you a glimpse of one of these shops. . . . Men and women bending over their machines or ironing clothes at the window, half-naked. . . . Morning, noon, or night, it [made] no difference." From block after block of sweatshops came the "whir of a thousand sewing-machines, worked at high pressure from the earliest dawn till mind and muscle [gave] out together." Family members, from the youngest to the oldest, labored in "qualmy rooms, where meals [were] cooked and clothing washed and dried besides, the livelong day."[5]

In the sweatshops, the work was physically punishing. The section system gave the bosses power to set the pace of their workers, who sat in long rows with their "bodies bent over the machines." Each person completed an assigned task and then passed his or her part of the garment to the next worker on the line, while the foreman nagged everyone to hurry. "Most of them smoke cigarettes while they work," observed a contemporary; "beer and cheap whiskey are brought in several times a day by a peddler. Some sing Yiddish songs — while they race. The women chat and laugh sometimes — while they race." But many women were forced to work silently. "We were like slaves. You couldn't pick your head up. You couldn't talk. We used to go to the bathroom. The forelady used to go after us, we shouldn't stay too long."[6]

The immigrants worked in disciplined, harsh, and also unsafe conditions. "We are so crowded together that there is not an inch of space," one woman complained. "The machines are so close together that there is no way to escape in case of immergansie [sic]."[7]

An emergency did happen on March 26, 1911, when a fire suddenly exploded at the Triangle Shirtwaist Company. Eight hundred workers, mostly young women, were trapped in the burning building. "A stream of fire tore up through the elevator shaft and stairways to the upper floors. Fire instantly appeared at all windows, and tongues of flames crept higher and higher along the walls to where little groups of terrified girls, workers, stood in confusion." Screaming, struggling, they jumped from windows, some from the ninth floor, their bodies smashing on the sidewalks. Unable to escape, 146 young workers — mostly Jewish and Italian — died in the smoke and heat of the inferno. The deaths of the many young people stirred great grief. Fifty thousand mourners marched in a mass memorial parade in memory of their dead daughters.[8]

Facing such exploitations and dangers, the workers struggled to transform the circumstances of their labors and lives. After 1909, waves of strikes swept through the Lower East Side, as Jewish workers organized into unions, demanding higher wages and better working conditions. By 1920, the International Ladies' Garment Workers' Union had 100,000 dues-paying members, and 170,000 workers belonged to the Amalgamated Clothing Workers of America.

In their struggles, the workers had created a broadly based radical Jewish consciousness. "Until now there had been no more than a large scattering of Jewish immigrant workers who would sometimes cohere for a fierce outbreak and then crumble into isolated persons," Irving Howe noted. "The Jewish community in the United States was not really a Jewish community," remarked leftist Paul Novick, "it was just something in fermentation until the labor movement came along." The "uprisings" of this era sharpened a shared sense of becoming Jewish American.[9]

A Sweatshop Girl: Sadie Frowne

Female garment workers in the Lower East Side had complicated lives. A Jewish immigrant from Poland, Sadie Frowne related her experiences in an interview published as a "lifelet" in the Independent magazine in the early twentieth century. As she bent over the sewing machines, making repetitive motions hour after hour, she found her mind wandering. What should she do about her low wages? What should she wear when she goes to Coney Island? And what should she do about Henry and his proposal of marriage?

M Y MOTHER WAS a tall, handsome, dark complexioned woman with red cheeks, large brown eyes and a great quantity of jet black, wavy hair. She was well educated, being able to talk in Russian, German, Polish and French, and even to read English print, though of course she did not know what it meant. She kept a little grocer's shop in the little village where she lived at first. That was in Poland, somewhere on the frontier, and mother had charge of a gate between the countries, so that everybody who came through the gate had to show her a pass. She was much looked up to by the people, who used to come and ask her for advice. Her word was like law among them.

She had a wagon in which she used to drive about the country, selling her groceries, and sometimes she worked in the fields with my father.

The grocer's shop was only one story high, and had one window, with very small panes of glass. We had two rooms behind it, and were happy while my father lived, although we had to work very hard. By the time I was six years of age I was able to wash dishes and scrub floors, and by the time I was eight I attended to the shop while my mother was away driving her wagon or working in the fields with my father. She was strong and could work like a man.

When I was a little more than ten years of age my father died. He was a good man and a steady worker, and we never knew what it was to be hungry while he lived. After he died troubles began, for the rent of our shop was about $6 a month and then there were food and clothes to provide. We needed little, it is true, but even soup, black bread and onions we could not always get.

We struggled along till I was nearly thirteen years of age and quite handy at housework and shop-keeping, so far as I could learn them there. But we fell behind in the rent and mother kept thinking more and more that we should have to leave Poland and go across the sea to America where we heard it was much easier to make money. Mother wrote to Aunt Fanny, who lived in New York, and told her how hard it was to live in Poland, and Aunt Fanny advised her to come and bring me. I was out at service at this time and mother thought she would leave me — as I had a good place — and come to this country alone, sending for me afterward. But Aunt Fanny would not hear of this. She said we should both come at once, and she went around among our relatives in New York and took up a subscription for our passage.

We came by steerage on a steamship in a very dark place that smelt dreadfully. There were hundreds of other people packed in with us, men, women and children, and almost all of them were sick. It took us twelve days to cross the sea, and we thought we should die, but at last the voyage was over, and we came up and saw the beautiful bay and the big woman with the spikes on her head and the lamp that is lighted at night in her hand (Goddess of Liberty).

Aunt Fanny and her husband met us at the gate of this country and were very good to us, and soon I had a place to live out (domestic servant), while my mother got work in a factory making white goods.

I was only a little over thirteen years of age and a greenhorn, so I received $9 a month and board and lodging, which I thought was doing well. Mother, who, as I have said, was very clever, made $9 a week on white goods, which means all sorts of underclothing, and is high class work.

But mother had a very gay disposition. She liked to go around and see everything, and friends took her about New York at night and she caught a bad cold and coughed and coughed. She really had hasty consumption, but she didn't know it, and I didn't know it, and she tried to keep on working, but it was no use. She had not the strength. Two doctors attended her, but they could do nothing, and at last she died and I was left alone. I had saved money while out at service, but mother's sickness and funeral swept it all away and now I had to begin all over again.

Aunt Fanny had always been anxious for me to get an education, as I did not know how to read or write, and she thought that was wrong. Schools are different in Poland from what they are in this country, and I was always too busy to learn to read and write. So when mother died I thought I would try to learn a trade and then I could go to school at night and learn to speak the English language well.

So I went to work in Allen Street (Manhattan) in what they call a sweatshop, making skirts by machine. I was new at the work and the foreman scolded me a great deal.

"Now, then," he would say, "this place is not for you to be looking around in. Attend to your work. That is what you have to do."

I did not know at first that you must not look around and talk, and I made many mistakes with the sewing, so that I was often called a "stupid animal." But I made $4 a week by working six days in the week. For there are two Sabbaths here — our own Sabbath, that comes on a Saturday, and the Christian Sabbath that comes on Sunday. It is against our law to work on our own Sabbath, so we work on their Sabbath.

In Poland I and my father and mother used to go to the synagogue on the Sabbath, but here the women don't go to the synagogue much, though the men do. They are shut up working hard all the week long and when the Sabbath comes they like to sleep long in bed and afterward they must go out where they can breathe the air. The rabbis are strict here, but not so strict as in the old country.

I lived at this time with a girl named Ella, who worked in the same factory and made $5 a week. We had the room all to ourselves, paying $1.50 a week for it, and doing light housekeeping. It was in Allen Street, and the window looked out of the back, which was good, because there was a elevated railroad in front, and in summer time a great deal of dust and dirt came in at the front windows. We were on the fourth story and could see all that was going on in the back rooms of the houses behind us, and early in the morning the sun used to come in our window.

We did our cooking on an oil stove, and lived well, as this list of our expenses for one week will show:

Ella and Sadie for Food (one week)

Tea	$0.06
Cocoa	.10
Bread and rolls	.40
Canned vegetables	.20
Potatoes	.10
Milk	.21
Fruit	.20
Butter	.15
Meat	.60
Fish	.15
Laundry	.25
Total	$2.42
Add rent	1.50
Grand total	$3.92

Of course, we could have lived cheaper, but we are both fond of good things and felt that we could afford them.

We paid 18 cents for a half pound of tea so as to get it good, and it lasted us three weeks, because we had cocoa for breakfast. We paid 5 cents for six rolls and 5 cents a loaf for bread, which was the best quality. Oatmeal cost us 10 cents for three and one-half pounds, and we often had it in the morning, or Indian meal porridge in the place of it, costing about the same. Half a dozen eggs cost about 13 cents on an average, and we could get all the meat we wanted for a good hearty meal for 20 cents — two pounds of chops, or a steak, or a bit of veal, or a neck of lamb — something like that. Fish included butter fish, porgies, codfish and smelts, averaging about 8 cents a pound.

Some people who buy at the last of the market, when the men with the carts want to go home, can get things very cheap, but they are likely to be stale, and we did not often do that with fish, fresh vegetables, fruit, milk or meat. Things that kept well we did buy that way and got good bargains. I got thirty potatoes for 10 cents one time, though generally I could not get more than fifteen of them for that amount. Tomatoes, onions and cabbages, too, we bought that way and did well, and we found a factory where we could buy the finest broken crackers for 3 cents a pound, and another place where we got broken candy for 10 cents a pound. Our cooking was done on an oil stove, and the oil for the stove and the lamp cost us 10 cents a week.

It cost me $2 a week to live, and I had a dollar a week to spend on clothing and pleasure, and saved the other dollar. I went to night school, but it was hard work learning at first as I did not know much English.

Two years ago I came to Brownsville, where so many of my people are, and where I have friends. I got work in a factory making underskirts — all sorts of cheap underskirts, like cotton and calico for the summer and woolen for the winter, but never the silk, satin or velvet underskirts. I earned $4.50 a week and lived on $2 a week, the same as before.

I got a room in the house of some friends who lived near the factory. I pay $1 a week for the room and am allowed to do light housekeeping — that is, cook my meals in it. I get my own breakfast in the morning, just a cup of coffee and a roll, and at noon time I come home to dinner and take a plate of soup and a slice of bread with the lady of the house. My food for a week costs a dollar, just as it did in Allen Street, and I have the rest of my money to do as I like with. I am earning $5.50 a week now, and will probably get another increase soon.

It isn't piecework in our factory, but one is paid by the amount of work done just the same. So it is like piecework. All the hands get different amounts, some as low as $3.50 and some of the men as high as $16 a week. The factory is in the third story of a brick building. It is in a room twenty feet long and fourteen broad. There are fourteen machines in it. I and the daughter of the people with whom I live work two of these machines. The other operators are all men, some young and some old.

At first a few of the young men were rude. Whey they passed me they would touch my hair and talk about my eyes and my red cheeks, and make jokes. I cried and said that if they did not stop I would leave the place. The boss said that that should not be, that no one must annoy me. Some of the other men stood up for me, too, especially Henry, who said two or three times that he wanted to fight. Now the men all treat me very nicely. It was just that some of them did not know better, not being educated.

Henry is tall and dark, and he has a small mustache. His eyes are brown and large. He is pale and much educated, having been to school. He knows a great many things and has some money saved. I think nearly $400. He is not going to be in a sweatshop all the time, but will soon be in the real estate business, for a lawyer that knows him well has promised to open an office and pay him to manage it.

Henry has seen me home every night for a long time and makes love to me. He wants me to marry him, but I am not seventeen yet, and I think that is too young. He is only nineteen, so we can wait.

I have been to the fortune teller's three or four times, and she always tells me that though I have had such a lot of trouble I am to be very rich and happy. I believe her because she has told me so many things that have come true. So I will keep on working in the factory for a time. Of course it is hard, but I would have to work hard even if I was married.

I get up at half-past five o'clock every morning and make myself a cup of coffee on the oil stove. I eat a bit of bread and perhaps some fruit and then go to work. Often I get there soon after six o'clock so as to be in good time, though the factory does not open till seven. I have heard that there is a sort of clock that calls you at the very time you want to get up, but I can't believe that because I don't see how the clock would know.

At seven o'clock we all sit down to our machines and the boss brings to each one the pile of work that he or she is to finish during the day, what they call in English their "stint." This pile is put down beside the machine and as soon as a skirt is done it is laid on the other side of the machine. Sometimes the work is not all finished by six o'clock and then the one who is behind must work overtime. Sometimes one is finished ahead of time and gets away at four or five o'clock, but generally we are not done till six o'clock.

The machines go like mad all day, because the faster you work the more money you get. Sometimes in my haste I get my finger caught and the needle goes right through it. It goes so quick, though, that it does not hurt much. I bind the finger up with a piece of cotton and go on working. We all have accidents like that. Where the needle goes through the nail it makes a sore finger, or where it splinters a bone it does much harm. Sometimes a finger has to come off. Generally, though, one can be cured by a salve.

All the time we are working the boss walks about examining the finished garments and making us do them over again if they are not just right. So we have to be careful as well as swift. But I am getting so good at the work that within a year I will be making $7 a week, and then I can save at least $3.50 a week. I have over $200 saved now.

The machines are all run by foot-power, and at the end of the day one feels so weak that there is a great temptation to lie right down and sleep. But you must go out and get air, and have some pleasure. So instead of lying down I go out, generally with Henry. Sometimes we go to Coney Island, where there are good dancing places, and sometimes we go to Ulmer Park to picnics. I am very fond of dancing, and, in fact, all sorts of pleasure. I go to the theater quite often, and like those plays that make you cry a great deal. "The Two Orphans" is good. Last time I saw it I cried all night because of the hard times that the children had in the play. I am going to see it again when it comes here.

For the last two winters I have been going to night school. I have learned reading, writing and arithmetic. I can read quite well in English now and I look at the newspapers every day. I read English books, too, sometimes. The last one that I read was "A Mad Marriage," by Charlotte Braeme. She's a grand writer and makes things just like real to you. You feel as if you were the poor girl yourself going to get married to a rich duke.

I am going back to night school again this winter. Plenty of my friends go there. Some of the women in my class are more than forty years of age. Like me, they did not have a chance to learn anything in the old country. It is good to have an education; it makes you feel higher. Ignorant people are all low. People say now that I am clever and fine in conversation.

We recently finished a strike in our business. It spread all over and the United Brotherhood of Garment Workers was in it. That takes in the cloakmakers, coatmakers, and all the others. We struck for shorter hours, and after being out four weeks won the fight. We only have to work nine and a half hours a day and we get the same pay as before. So the union does good after all in spite of what some people say against it — that it just takes our money and does nothing.

I pay 25 cents a month to the union, but I do not begrudge that because it is for our benefit. The next strike is going to be for a raise of wages, which we all ought to have. But though I belong to the Union I am not a Socialist or an Anarchist. I don't know exactly what those things mean. There is a little expense for charity, too. If any worker is injured or sick we all give money to help.

Some of the women blame me very much because I spend so much money on clothes. They say that instead of a dollar a week I ought not to spend more than twenty-five cents a week on clothes, and that I should save the rest. But a girl must have clothes if she is to go into good society at Ulmer Park or Coney Island or the theater. Those who blame me are the old country people who have old-fashioned notions, but the people who have been here a long time know better. A girl who does not dress well is stuck in a corner, even if she is pretty, and Aunt Fanny says that I do just right to put on plenty of style.

I have many friends and we often have jolly parties. Many of the young men like to talk to me, but I don't go out with any except Henry.

Lately he has been urging me more and more to get married — but I think I'll wait.

Dear Editor: Letters from Jewish America — Problems and Advice

Over the decades, hundreds of Jews wrote letters to the editor of the Jewish Daily Forward, seeking advice and giving intimate details about their personal and family problems. The letters were the counterparts of "Dear Abby" letters. Though the problems were personal, they were also ethnic: individual lives intersected with the problems of assimilation, the Triangle Shirtwaist Factory fire, and also the Holocaust. What these individuals wrote and the editors answered reveals much about what it meant to be Jewish American.

A "Greenhorn" for a Husband (1907)

WORTHY EDITOR,

I was born in America and my parents gave me a good education. I studied Yiddish and Hebrew, finished high school, completed a course in bookkeeping and got a job. I have many friends, and several boys have already proposed to me.

Recently I went to visit my parents' home town in Russian Poland. My mother's family in Europe had invited my parents to a wedding, but instead of going themselves, they sent me. I stayed at my grandmother's with an aunt and uncle and had a good time. Our European family, like my parents, are quite well off and they treated me well. They indulged me in everything and I stayed with them six months.

It was lively in the town. There were many organizations and clubs and they all accepted me warmly, looked up to me — after all, I was a citizen of the free land, America. Among the social leaders of the community was an intelligent young man, a friend of my uncle's, who took me to various gatherings and affairs.

He was very attentive, and after a short while he declared his love for me in a long letter. I had noticed that he was not indifferent to me, and I liked him as well. I looked up to him and respected him, as did all the townsfolk. My family became aware of it, and when they spoke to me about him, I could see they thought it was a good match.

He was handsome, clever, educated, a good talker and charmed me, but I didn't give him a definite answer. As my love for him grew, however, I wrote to my parents about him, and then we became officially engaged.

A few months later we both went to my parents in the States and they received him like their own son. My bridegroom immediately began to learn English and tried to adjust to the new life. Yet when I introduced him to my friends they looked at him with disappointment. "This 'greenhorn' is your fiancé?" they asked. I told them what a big role he played in his town, how everyone respected him, but they looked at me as if I were crazy and scoffed at my words.

At first I thought, Let them laugh, when they get better acquainted with him they'll talk differently. In time, though, I was affected by their talk and began to think, like them, that he really was a "greenhorn" and acted like one.

In short, my love for him is cooling off gradually. I'm suffering terribly because my feelings for him are changing. In Europe, where everyone admired him and all the girls envied me, he looked different. But, here, I see before me another person.

I haven't the courage to tell him, and I can't even talk about it to my parents. He still loves me with all his heart, and I don't know what to do. I choke it all up inside myself, and I beg you to help me with advice in my desperate situation.

Respectfully,
A Worried Reader

ANSWER:

The writer would make a grave mistake if she were to separate from her bridegroom now. She must not lose her common sense and be influenced by the foolish opinions of her friends who divided the world into "greenhorns" and real Americans.

We can assure the writer that her bridegroom will learn English quickly. He will know American history and literature as well as her friends do, and be a better American than they. She should be proud of his love and laugh at those who call him "greenhorn."

* * *

Drawn to the Love of a Gentile Girl (1908)

Worthy Editor,

I have been in America almost three years. I came from Russia where I studied at a yeshiva. My parents were proud and happy at the thought that I would become a rabbi. But at the age of twenty I had to go to America. Before I left I gave my father my word that I would walk the righteous path and be good and pious. But America makes one forget everything.

Here I became an operator, and at night I went to school. In a few months I entered a preparatory school, where for two subjects I had a Gentile girl as teacher. I began to notice that the teacher paid more attention to me than to the others in the class and in time she told me I would be better off taking private lessons from her for the same price I paid to the school.

I agreed, and soon realized that her lessons with me were not ordinary. For example, I was to pay five dollars a month for two hours a week, but she gave me three lessons a week, each lasting two and sometimes three hours. Then I had to stop the lessons because I had no money to pay her. However, she wanted to teach me without pay, explaining that she taught not only for money but also because teaching gave her pleasure.

In short, I began to feel at home in her house and not only she but also her parents welcomed me warmly. I ate there often and they also lent me money when I was in need. I used to ask myself, "What am I doing? but I couldn't help myself. There was a depression at the time, I had no job and had to accept their aid.

I don't know what I would have done without her help. I began to love her, but with mixed feelings of respect and anguish. I was afraid to look her in the eyes. I looked at her like a Russian soldier looks at his superior officer and I never imagined she thought of marrying me.

A few weeks ago I took the Regents examinations for entering college. After the exams, my teacher told me not to look for work for a few weeks, but to eat and drink at their home. I didn't want to but she insisted and I couldn't refuse.

Many times upon leaving her house, I would decide not to return, but my heart drew me to her, and I spent three weeks in her house. Meanwhile I received the report on my examinations which showed that I had passed with the highest grades. I went directly to her to show her the report and she asked me what I planned to do. I answered that I didn't know as yet, because I had no money for college. "That's a minor problem," she said, and asked if I didn't know that she was not indifferent toward me. Then she spoke frankly of her love for me and her hope that I would love her.

"If you are not against it, my parents and I will support you while you study. The fact that I am a Gentile and you a Jew should not bother us. We are both, first of all, human beings and we will live as such." She told me she believed that all men and all nations were equal.

I was confused and I couldn't answer her immediately. In Europe I had been absorbed in the yeshiva, here with my studies, and I knew little of practical life. I do agree with her that we are first of all human beings, and she is a human being in the fullest sense of the word. She is pretty, intelligent, educated, and has a good character. But I am in despair when I think of my parents. What heartaches they will have when they learn of this!

I asked her to give me a few days to think it over. I go around confused and yet I am drawn to her. I must see her every day, but when I am there I think of my parents and I am torn by doubt.

I wait impatiently for your answer.

Respectfully,
Skeptic from Philadelphia

ANSWER:

We can only say that some mixed marriages are happy, others unhappy. But then many marriages between Jew and Jew, Christian and Christian, are not successful either. It is true, however, that in some mixed marriages the differences between man and wife create unhappiness. Therefore we cannot take it upon ourselves to advise the young man regarding this marriage. This he must decide for himself.

*　*　*

A Death at the Triangle Shirtwaist Factory Fire (1914)

Worthy Editor,

I am a girl twenty-two years of age, but I've already undergone a great deal in my life. When I was born I already had no father. He died four months before my birth. And when I was three weeks old my mother died too. Grandmother, my mother's mother, took me in and soon gave me away to a poor tailor's wife to suckle me.

I was brought up by the tailor and his wife, and got so used to them that I called them Mother and Father. When I grew up I learned from the tailor how to do hand sewing and machine sewing too.

When I was sixteen my grandmother died and left me her small dilapidated house. The rabbi of the town sold it for me for three hundred rubles and gave me the money.

In time one of the tailor's apprentices fell in love with me, and I didn't reject his love. He was a fine, honest, quiet young man and a good earner. He had a golden character and we became as one body and soul. When I turned seventeen my bridegroom came to me with a plan, that we should go to America, and I agreed.

It was hard for me to take leave of the tailor's good family, who had kept me as their own child, and oceans of tears were shed when we parted.

When we came to America my bridegroom immediately started to work and he supported me. He was faithful and devoted. I'll give you an example of his loyalty: once, during the summer in the terrible heat, I slept on the roof. But it started to rain in the middle of the night and I was soaked through to the bone. I got very sick and had to be taken to the hospital. I was so sick that the doctor said I could be saved only by a blood transfusion. My bridegroom said immediately that he was ready to give me his blood, and so, thanks to him, I recovered.

In time I went to work at the "famous" Triangle shop. Later my bridegroom also got a job there. Even at work he wanted to be with me. My bridegroom told me then, "We will both work hard for a while and then we'll get married. We will save every cent so we'll be able to set up a home and then you'll be a housewife and never go to work in the shop again."

Thus my good bridegroom mused about the golden future. Then there was that terrible fire that took one hundred and forty-seven young blossoming lives. When the fire broke out, the screaming, the yelling, the panic all bewildered me. I saw the angel of death before me and my voice was choked in my throat. Suddenly someone seized me with extraordinary strength and carried me out of the shop.

When I recovered I heard calming voices and saw my bridegroom near me. I was in the street, rescued, and saw my girl friends jumping out of the windows and falling to the ground. I clung to my bridegroom and rescuer, but he soon tore himself away from me. "I must save other girls," he said, and disappeared. I never saw him alive again. The next day I identified him, in the morgue, by his watch, which had my picture pasted under the cover. I fainted and they could hardly bring me to.

After that I lay in the hospital for five weeks, and came home shattered. This is the fourth year that I am alone and I still see before me the horrible scenes of the fire. I still see the good face of my dear bridegroom, also the black burned face in the morgue. I am weak and nervous, yet there is now a young man who wants to marry me. But I made a vow that I would never get married. Besides that, I'm afraid that I will never be able to love another man. But this young man doesn't want to leave me, and my friends try to persuade me to marry him and say everything will be all right. I don't believe it, because I think everything can be all right for me only in the grave.

I decided to write to you, because I want to hear your opinion.

Respectfully,
A Faithful Reader

ANSWER:

It is senseless for this girl to sacrifice her life in memory of her faithful bridegroom, since this would not bring him back to life. What the earth covers must be forgotten. She has suffered enough in her life already and is advised to take herself in hand and begin her life anew.

*   *   *

Jewishness Through Zionism (1932)

Dear Editor,

I am an immigrant from Russia, my wife is American-born, and we are both freethinkers. We have two grown children, a son and a daughter, who know they are Jews but never saw any signs of religion or holidays in our home. Even Yom Kippur is just another day to us. For the last twenty years we've lived among Christians and we socialize with them. Our children also go around with Gentiles.

Some time ago a Christian girl began to come to our house, seemingly to visit our daughter, but it was no secret to us that she was after our twenty-three-year-old son, with whom she was friendly. We said nothing about it, because we wouldn't have minded having her for a daughter-in-law.

Once the girl invited our son to a party at her house where all the other guests were Gentiles. They were all having a good time until one of the guests, whether in jest or earnest, began to make fun of Jews. I don't know what happened there, but I am sure they didn't mean to hurt my son, because none of them, not even his girl friend, knew that he is Jewish. But he was insulted and told the girl so. Then he told her that he is Jewish and this was a surprise to her.

My son left the party immediately and from that day on he is changed. He began to ask questions about religion, debated with me about things that formerly hadn't interested him. He wanted to know where I was born, how many Jews there are in the world, why the religious don't eat pork, where the hatred of Jews came from, and on and on. He was not satisfied with my short answers but began to read books looking for more information. My son also berated me for not giving him a Jewish upbringing.

His Gentile girl friend came to beg him to forgive her. She cried and explained that it was not her fault, but he didn't want to have anything to do with her because, it seems, he was deeply insulted. His head was filled with one thought, Jewishness. He found Jewish friends, he was drawn into a Zionist club and they worked on him so that he has come to me with a suggestion that I give up the business and we all go to Palestine. And since he sees that I am not about to go, he's getting ready to go alone.

At first we took it as a joke, but we see now that he's taking it very seriously. Well, my going is out of the question, I am not that crazy. But what can be done about him? I'm willing to give in to his whim. I'm sure that in Palestine he'll sober up and realize that not everyone who is Jewish must live in Palestine. My wife is carrying on terribly; what do I mean, allowing my son to travel to a wild country where Arabs shoot Jews? She says we should not give him the money for the trip. But our son says he will find a way to reach the Jewish Homeland.

My wife and I are very anxious to hear your opinion.

Respectfully,

A Reader

ANSWER:

Your son is a very sensitive and thinking person. Since he is an adult you must let him go his way and do what he wants to do.

* * *

On Speaking Yiddish (1933)

Worthy Editor,

I am sure that the problem I'm writing about affects many Jewish homes. It deals with immigrant parents and their American-born children.

My parents, who have been readers of your paper for years, came from Europe. They have been here in this country over thirty years and were married twenty-eight years ago. They have five sons, and I am one of them. The oldest of us is twenty-seven and the youngest twenty-one.

We are all making a decent living. One of us works for the State Department. A second is a manager in a large store, two are in business, and the youngest is studying law. Our parents do not need our help because my father has a good job.

We, the five brothers, always speak English to each other. Our parents know English too, but they speak only Yiddish, not just among themselves but to us too, and even to our American friends who come to visit us. We beg them not to speak Yiddish in the presence of our friends, since they can speak English, but they don't want to. It's a sort of stubbornness on their part, and a great deal of quarreling goes on between our parents and ourselves because of it.

Their answer is: "Children, we ask you not to try to teach us how to talk to people. We are older than you."

Imagine, even when we go with our father to buy something in a store on Fifth Avenue, New York, he insists on speaking Yiddish. We are not ashamed of our parents, God forbid, but they ought to know where it's proper and where it's not. If they talk Yiddish among themselves at home, or to us, it's bad enough, but among strangers and Christians? Is that nice? It looks as if they're doing it to spite us. Petty spats grow out of it. They want to keep only to their old ways and don't want to take up our new ways.

We beg you, friend Editor, to express your opinion on this question, and if possible send us your answer in English, because we can't read Yiddish.

Accept our thanks for your answer, which we expect soon,

Respectfully,

I. and the Four Brothers

ANSWER:

We see absolutely no crime in the parents' speaking Yiddish to their sons. The Yiddish language is dear to them and they want to speak in that language to their children and all who understand it. It may also be that they are ashamed to speak their imperfect English among strangers so they prefer to use their mother tongue.

From the letter, we get the impression that the parents are not fanatics, and with their speaking Yiddish they are not out to spite the children. But it would certainly not be wrong if the parents were to speak English too, to the children. People should and must learn the language of their country.

* * *

Hiding One's Jewish Identity (1933)

Worthy Editor,

Though my husband is a Zionist and I used to be a Bundist, we have already celebrated our silver wedding anniversary and lived the quarter century happily together.

We have five children, with whom all parents would consider themselves blessed. We gave them a good education, sent them to college, and they are all good, bright and cultured. We are in business, and until the depression we made a good living.

Two of our children are already married. One boy, eighteen years old, is studying at City College, one works in a department store with a college diploma in his pocket and earns such poor wages it's a shame to talk about it. But what can one do, when even this job was hard for him to get? And our twenty-one-year-old daughter did something that my husband, the

A LARGER MEMORY

Zionist, cannot stand. It's about her that I am writing this letter to you.

Our daughter graduated from college with high honors, but this did not help her find a job. She could not find work for a long time, but two months ago she got a very good job in an insurance company, and she brings home a check for thirty-five dollars every week. We should be satisfied, yet our world has turned upside down since she got the job.

My husband is very upset, because in order to get the job my daughter had to give her religion as Episcopalian. If they had known she was Jewish they wouldn't have hired her. She doesn't have typically Jewish features, and from her appearance she can be taken for a Christian. One of my sons says she also had to get a recommendation from a priest, because lately many Jewish girls say they are Christians in order to get a job. The priest's recommendation is the only way to assure the boss that he is not being fooled.

Our whole house is topsy-turvy. My husband insists that by all means she should give up the job. Our whole family is now divided into two sides. One side feels that our daughter has not committed a crime and hasn't wronged anyone. As far as her own conscience goes, it's not so terrible. Would going around jobless and having to come to her father or mother for a dollar be better?

I feel that I, myself, wouldn't do it, but I sympathize with my daughter. But my husband is terribly upset about the whole thing. We would like your opinion about our daughter's actions.

Your troubled readers,
F. and G.

ANSWER:

The father is entirely right in his stand against his daughter's actions, and his feelings about it are not necessarily caused by his being a Zionist. A Jewish father, whether he is a Socialist or a free-thinker, would also be against having his daughter posing as a Christian in order to get a job. But the fact is that the girl is already twenty-one years old. She certainly doesn't deserve a compliment for her dishonest behavior, but she has the right to act as she wishes.

184

Companies that do not hire Jews, though they have a large Jewish patronage, should be condemned.

* * *

A Christmas Tree in Our Son's Home (1941)

Dear Editor,

My husband and I came from Galicia to America thirty-three years ago right after we were married. At home I had received a secular education, and my husband had been ordained as a rabbi. However, he did not want to be a rabbi here, and since we had brought along a little money from home, we bought a small business and made a good living. My husband is religious but not a fanatic. I am more liberal, but I go to shul with him on *Rosh Hashanah* and *Yom Kippur.*

We have five children — two boys and three girls. The boys went to a *Talmud Torah,* and the girls, too, received a Jewish education. We always kept a Jewish home and a *kosher* kitchen.

Our eldest son is now a college teacher, tutors students privately, and earns a good deal of money. He is married, has two children, four and seven years old. They live in a fine neighborhood, and we visit them often.

It happened that on Christmas Eve we were invited to have dinner with friends who live near our son and daughter-in-law, so we decided to drop in to see them after the meal. I called up, my daughter-in-law answered the telephone and warmly invited us to come over.

When we opened the door and went into the living room we saw a large Christmas tree which my son was busy trimming with the help of his two children. When my husband saw this he turned white. The two grandchildren greeted us with a "Merry Christmas" and were delighted to see us. I wanted to take off my coat, but my husband gave me a signal that we were leaving immediately.

Well, I had to leave at once. Our son's and daughter-in-law's pleading and talking didn't help, because my husband didn't want to stay there another minute. He is so angry at our son over the

Christmas tree that he doesn't want to cross the threshold of their home again. My son justifies himself by saying he takes the tree in for the sake of his children, so they won't feel any different than their non-Jewish friends in the neighborhood. He assures us that it has nothing to do with religion. He doesn't consider it wrong, and he feels his father has no right to be angry over it.

My husband, besides having a temper, is stubborn, too. But I don't want him to be angry at our son. Therefore I would like to hear your opinion on this matter.

With great respect,
A Reader from the Bronx

ANSWER:

The national American holidays are celebrated here with love and joy, by Jews and Gentiles alike. But Christmas is the most religious Christian holiday and Jews have nothing to do with it. Jews, religious or not, should respect the Christmas holiday, but to celebrate it would be like dancing at a stranger's wedding. It is natural that a Jew who observes all the Jewish traditions should be opposed to seeing his son and grandchildren trimming a Christmas tree.

But he must not quarrel with his son. It is actually your husband's fault because he probably did not instill the Jewish traditions in his son. Instead of being angry with him, he should talk to his son and explain the meaning of Christmas to him.

*　*　*

Teaching Children about the Holocaust (1956)

Worthy Mr. Editor,

When I read the "Bintel Brief" in the Forverts it reminded me of how they used to run to the rebbe in Poland with all kinds of problems. And now, to come to the point about my problem:

Years have gone by since the sharp fangs of the mad beast destroyed a third of the Jewish people. Thanks to the Allied armies, the beasts in human form were defeated, but with those who were saved by a miracle the nightmares and aftereffects of the destruction remain.

186

When the living, the lucky ones, began to come out of their hiding places and regained a bit of their normalcy, they began to rebuild their shattered lives. So it was with me and my present wife. The murderers killed my first wife and our two children, and my present wife lost her husband and a child. When we met, we decided to marry, establish a home, and start to build a new life, since this was the thing to do.

Now we are here in America, we already have two children, may they be well, who are eight years old, and my wife and I often discuss whether we should tell them about the tragic past. I mean, about our personal losses, because I have told them about the general destruction. I feel we should not tell them yet about the loss of our own children, but wait until they are older. My wife, however, thinks the opposite, and sometimes she comes out with a half statement and the children are disturbed.

Now I ask you, who is right, I or my wife? Should the children be told everything now, or is there time yet? I believe you will give us the right answer.

Respectfully,

H.S.

Brooklyn

ANSWER:

Certainly we should tell our children about the holocaust, about the horrible massacres that the German murderers and those who helped them perpetrated on our people, and about the fact that the whole world was silent. Certainly we must see to it that the future generations know and remember what the German Amalek did to the Jews. But we agree with you that your little children, who are a great comfort to you after all your sufferings, do not need to be burdened yet with the anxiety and sorrow. It would be advisable for you and your wife to let it go until later, when they will be better able to understand the tragic history of the annihilation of the six million Jews.

Betrayed by Their Country:
The World War II Internment
of Japanese Americans

THREE DAYS AFTER Japan's attack on Pearl Harbor, FBI director J. Edgar Hoover informed Washington that practically all suspected individuals whom he had initially planned to arrest were in custody: 1,291 Japanese (367 in Hawaii, 924 on the mainland), 857 Germans, and 147 Italians. In a report to the Attorney General submitted in early February, Hoover concluded that the proposed mass evacuation of the Japanese could not be justified for security reasons.

Despite these intelligence findings, Lieutenant General John L. DeWitt, head of the Western Defense Command, decided that Japanese aliens as well as Americans of Japanese ancestry should be evacuated from restricted areas. Meanwhile, the West Coast newspapers stirred anti-Japanese hysteria. The *Los Angeles Times* editorialized: "A viper is nonetheless a viper wherever the egg is hatched — so a Japanese American, born of Japanese parents — grows up to be a Japanese, not an American." Patriotic organizations like the American Legion and farm growers associations joined the clamor for Japanese removal. On February 19, 1942, President Franklin D. Roosevelt signed Executive Order 9066, authorizing the removal of Japanese Americans from the West Coast.[1]

The army promptly began the evacuation and internment of 120,000 Japanese Americans, two-thirds of them citizens by birth.

After a brief stay in assembly centers, the evacuees were transported to ten internment camps — Topaz in Utah, Poston and Gila River in Arizona, Amache in Colorado, Jerome and Rohwer in Arkansas, Minidoka in Idaho, Manzanar and Tule Lake in California, and Heart Mountain in Wyoming.

Most of the camps were located in remote desert areas. "We did not know where we were," remembered an internee. "No houses were in sight, no trees or anything green — only scrubby sage-brush and an occasional low cactus, and mostly dry, baked earth." Housed in barracks, each family was assigned one room, twenty by twenty feet. The room had "a pot bellied stove, a single electric light hanging from the ceiling, an Army cot for each person and a blanket for the bed." The facility resembled both a military base and a prison. "Camp life was highly regimented and it was rushing to the wash basin to beat the other groups, rushing to the mess hall for breakfast, lunch, and dinner." The internees ate at long tables, and parents often sat at separate tables from their children. People were "crowded in a long line just like a snake," waiting "for a meal in the dust and wind." At school, the children began the day by saluting the flag of the United States and then singing, "My country, 'tis of thee, sweet land of liberty." Looking beyond the flagpole, they could see the barbed wire and the armed guards. "I was too young to understand," recalled George Takei, "but I remember soldiers carrying rifles, and I remember being afraid." Young married couples worried about having children born in the camps. "When I was pregnant with my second child, that's when I flipped," said a Nisei woman. "I guess that's when the reality really hit me. I thought to myself, gosh, what am I doing getting pregnant. I told my husband, 'This is crazy. You realize there's no future for us and what are we having kids for?'"[2]

These Japanese Americans had been denied by their own government their rights to due process of the law and equality as well as life, liberty, and the pursuit of happiness.

A Birthright Denied: Monica Sone

Born and raised in Seattle, Washington, Monica Sone was the daughter of Japanese immigrants. Suddenly, in early 1942, she and her family were evacuated by the federal government, first by bus to an assembly center in Puyallup, Washington, and then by train to an internment camp in Minidoka, Idaho. In her autobiography, Nisei Daughter, published in 1953, she described the distress and indignity they experienced in the forced removal from their home. They had to leave behind everything, including their dog Asthma.

I N FEBRUARY, EXECUTIVE ORDER No. 9066 came out, authorizing the War Department to remove the Japanese from such military areas as it saw fit, aliens and citizens alike. Even if a person had a fraction of Japanese blood in him, he must leave on demand.

A pall of gloom settled upon our home. We couldn't believe that the government meant that the Japanese-Americans must go, too. We had heard the clamoring of superpatriots who insisted loudly, "Throw the whole kaboodle out. A Jap's a Jap, no matter how you slice him. You can't make an American out of little Jap Junior just by handing him an American birth certificate." But we had dismissed these remarks as just hot blasts of air from an overheated patriot. We were quite sure that our rights as American citizens would not be violated, and we would not be marched out of our homes on the same basis as enemy aliens.

In anger, Henry [her brother] and I read and reread the Executive Order. Henry crumpled the newspaper in his hand and threw it against the wall. "Doesn't my citizenship mean a single blessed thing to anyone? Why doesn't somebody make up my mind for me. First they want me in the army. Now they're going to slap an alien 4-C on me because of my ancestry. What the hell!"

Once more I felt like a despised, pathetic two-headed freak, a

Japanese and an American, neither of which seemed to be doing me any good. . . .

On the twenty-first of April, a Tuesday, the general [John DeWitt] gave us the shattering news. "All the Seattle Japanese will be moved to Puyallup by May 1. Everyone must be registered Saturday and Sunday between 8 A.M. and 5 P.M. They will leave next week in three groups, on Tuesday, Thursday and Friday."

Up to that moment, we had hoped against hope that something or someone would intervene for us. Now there was no time for moaning. A thousand and one details must be attended to in this one week of grace. Those seven days sputtered out like matches struck in the wind, as we rushed wildly about. Mother distributed sheets, pillowcases and blankets, which we stuffed into seabags. Into the two suitcases, we packed heavy winter overcoats, plenty of sweaters, woolen slacks and skirts, flannel pajamas and scarves. Personal toilet articles, one tin plate, tin cup and silverware completed our luggage. The one seabag and two suitcases apiece were going to be the backbone of our future home, and we planned it carefully.

Henry went to the Control Station to register the family. He came home with twenty tags, all numbered "10710," tags to be attached to each piece of baggage, and one to hang from our coat lapels. From then on, we were known as Family #10710.

On our last Sunday, Father and Henry moved all our furniture and household goods down to the hotel and stored them in one room. We could have put away our belongings in the government storage place or in the basement of our church, which was going to be boarded up for the duration, but we felt that our property would be safer under the watchful eyes of Sam, Peter and Joe.

Monday evening we received friends in our empty house where our voices echoed loudly and footsteps clattered woodenly on the bare floor. We sat on crates, drank bottles of coke and talked gayly about our future pioneer life. Henry and Minnie held hands all evening in the corner of the living room. Minnie lived on the outskirts of the Japanese community and her district was to leave in the third and last group.

That night we rolled ourselves into army blankets like jelly rolls and slept on the bare floor. The next morning Henry rudely shouted us back into consciousness. "Six-thirty! Everybody wake up, today's the day!"

I screamed, "Must you sound so cheerful about it?"

"What do you expect me to do, bawl?"

On this sour note, we got up stiffly from the floor, and exercised violently to start circulation in our paralyzed backs and limbs. We jammed our blankets into the long narrow seabag, and we carefully tied the white pasteboard tag, 10710, on our coat lapels. When I went into the bathroom and looked into the mirror, tears suddenly welled in my eyes. I was crying, not because it was the last time I would be standing in a modern bathroom, but because I looked like a cross between a Japanese and a fuzzy bear. My hideous new permanent wave had been given to me by an operator who had never worked on Oriental hair before. My hair resembled scorched mattress filling, and after I had attacked it savagely with comb and brush, I looked like a frightened mushroom. On this morning of mornings when I was depending on a respectable hairdo so I could leave town with dignity, I was faced with this horror. There was nothing to do but cover it with a scarf.

Downstairs we stood around the kitchen stove where Mother served us a quick breakfast of coffee in our tin cups, sweet rolls and boiled eggs which rolled noisily on our tin plates. Henry was delighted with the simplicity of it all. "Boy, this is going to be living, no more company manners and dainty napkins. We can eat with our bare hands. Probably taste better, too."

Mother fixed a stern eye on Henry, "Not as long as I'm around."

The front doorbell rang. It was Dunks Oshima, who had offered to take us down to Eighth and Lane in a borrowed pickup truck. Hurriedly the menfolk loaded the truck with the last few boxes of household goods which Dunks was going to take down to the hotel. He held up a gallon can of soy sauce, puzzled, "Where does this go, to the hotel, too?"

Nobody seemed to know where it had come from or where it

A Birthright Denied: Monica Sone

was going, until Mother finally spoke up guiltily, "Er, it's going with me. I didn't think we'd have shoyu where we're going."

Henry looked as if he were going to explode. "But Mama, you're not supposed to have more than one seabag and two suitcases. And of all things, you want to take with you — shoyu!"

I felt mortified. "Mama, people will laugh at us. We're not going on a picnic!"

But Mother stood her ground. "Nonsense. No one will ever notice this little thing. It isn't as if I were bringing liquor!"

"Well!" I said. "If Mama's going to take her shoyu, I'm taking my radio along." I rescued my fifteen-year-old radio from the boxes which were going down to the hotel. "At least it'll keep me from talking to myself out there."

Sumi began to look thoughtful, and she rummaged among the boxes. Henry bellowed, "That's enough! Two suitcases and one seabag a person, that's final! Now let's get going before we decide to take the house along with us."

Mother personally saw to it that the can of shoyu remained with her baggage. She turned back once more to look at our brown and yellow frame house and said almost gayly, "Good-by, house."

Old Asthma came bounding out to the front yard, her tail swaying in the air. "And good-by, Asthma, take good care of our home. *Yoroshiku onegai shimasu yo.*"

A swallow swooped down from the eaves. "Oh, soh, soh, good-by to you, too, Mrs. Swallow. I hope you have a nice little family."

Mother explained that she had discovered the swallow's little nest under the eaves just outside Sumi's bedroom window, filled with four beautiful blue-speckled eggs like precious-colored stones. The swallow darted low and buzzed over Asthma like a miniature fighter plane. We watched amazed as it returned time and time again in a diving attack on Asthma. Mother said, "She's fighting to protect her family." Asthma leaped into the air, pawed at the bird halfheartedly, then rubbed herself against Mother's woolen slacks.

"Quarter to eight," Dunks gently reminded us. We took turns

ruffling Asthma's fur and saying good-by to her. The new tenants had promised us that they would keep her as their pet.

We climbed into the truck, chattering about the plucky little swallow. As we coasted down Beacon Hill bridge for the last time, we fell silent, and stared out at the delicately flushed morning sky of Puget Sound. We drove through bustling Chinatown, and in a few minutes arrived on the corner of Eighth and Lane. This area was ordinarily lonely and deserted but now it was gradually filling up with silent, labeled Japanese, standing self-consciously among their seabags and suitcases.

Everyone was dressed casually, each according to his idea of where he would be going. One Issei was wearing a thick mackinaw jacket and cleated, high-topped hiking boots. I stared admiringly at one handsome couple, standing slim and poised in their ski clothes. They looked newly wed. They stood holding hands beside their streamlined luggage that matched smartly with the new Mr. and Mrs. look. With an air of resigned sacrifice, some Issei women wore dark-colored slacks with deep-hemmed cuffs. One gnarled old grandmother wore an ankle-length black crepe dress with a plastic initial "S" pinned to its high neckline. It was old-fashioned, but dignified and womanly.

Automobiles rolled up to the curb, one after another, discharging more Japanese and more baggage. Finally at ten o'clock, a vanguard of Greyhound busses purred in and parked themselves neatly along the curb. The crowd stirred and murmured. The bus doors opened and from each, a soldier with rifle in hand stepped out and stood stiffly at attention by the door. The murmuring died. It was the first time I had seen a rifle at such close range and I felt uncomfortable. This rifle was presumably to quell riots, but contrarily, I felt riotous emotion mounting in my breast.

Jim Shigeno, one of the leaders of the Japanese-American Citizens' League, stepped briskly up front and started reading off family numbers to fill the first bus. Our number came up and we pushed our way out of the crowd. Jim said, "Step right in." We bumped into each other in nervous haste. I glanced nervously at the soldier and his rifle, and I was startled to see that he was but a young man, pink-cheeked, his clear gray eyes staring impassively ahead. I felt that the occasion probably held for him a sort of tense anxiety as it did for us. Henry found a seat by a window and hung out, watching for Minnie who had promised to see him off. Sumi and I suddenly turned maternal and hovered over Mother and Father to see that they were comfortably settled. They were silent.

Newspaper photographers with flash-bulb cameras pushed busily through the crowd. One of them rushed up to our bus, and asked a young couple and their little boy to step out and stand by the door for a shot. They were reluctant, but the photographers were persisent and at length they got out of the bus and posed, grinning widely to cover their embarrassment. We saw the picture in the newspaper shortly after and the caption underneath it read, "Japs good-natured about evacuation."

Our bus quickly filled to capacity. All eyes were fixed up front, waiting. The guard stepped inside, sat by the door, and nodded curtly to the gray-uniformed bus driver. The door closed with a low hiss. We were now the Wartime Civil Control Administration's babies.

When all the busses were filled with the first contingent of Japanese, they started creeping forward slowly. We looked out of the window, smiled and feebly waved our hands at the crowd of friends who would be following us within the next two days. From among the Japanese faces, I picked out the tall, spare figures of our young people's minister, the Reverend Everett Thompson, and the Reverend Emery Andrews of the Japanese Baptist Church. They were old friends, having been with us for many years. They wore bright smiles on their faces and waved vigorously as if to lift our morale. But Miss Mahon, the principal of our Bailey Gatzert Grammar School and a much-beloved figure in our community, stood in front of the quiet crowd of Japanese and wept openly.

Sumi suddenly spied Minnie, driving her family car. The car screeched to a halt and Minnie leaped out, looking frantically for Henry. Henry flung his window up and shouted, "Minnie! Minnie! Over here!" The bystanders, suddenly good-humored, directed her to our moving bus. Minnie ran up to the windows, puffing, "Sorry

I was late, Henry! Here, flowers for you." She thrust a bouquet of fresh yellow daffodils into his outstretched hand. Henry shouted, "Thanks — I'll be seeing you, I hope."

When our bus turned a corner and we no longer had to smile and wave, we settled back gravely in our seats. Everyone was quiet except for a chattering group of university students who soon started singing college songs. A few people turned and glared at them, which only served to increase the volume of their singing. Then suddenly a baby's sharp cry rose indignantly above the hubbub. The singing stopped immediately, followed by a guilty silence. Three seats behind us, a young mother held a wailing red-faced infant in her arms, bouncing it up and down. Its angry little face emerged from multiple layers of kimonos, sweaters and blankets, and it, too, wore the white pasteboard tag pinned to its blanket. A young man stammered out an apology as the mother gave him a wrathful look. She hunted frantically for a bottle of milk in a shopping bag, and we all relaxed when she had found it.

We sped out of the city southward along beautiful stretches of farmland, with dark, newly turned soil. In the beginning we devoured every bit of scenery which flashed past our window and admired the massive-muscled work horses plodding along the edge of the highway, the rich burnished copper color of a browsing herd of cattle, the vivid spring green of the pastures, but eventually the sameness of the country landscape palled on us. We tried to sleep to escape from the restless anxiety which kept bobbing up to the surface of our minds. I awoke with a start when the bus filled with excited buzzing. A small group of straw-hatted Japanese farmers stood by the highway, waving at us. I felt a sudden warmth toward them, then a twinge of pity. They would be joining us soon.

About noon we crept into a small town. Someone said, "Looks like Puyallup, all right." Parents of small children babbled excitedly, "Stand up quickly and look over there. See all the chick-chicks and fat little piggies?" One little city boy stared hard at the hogs and said tersely, "They're bachi — dirty!"

A Birthright Denied: Monica Sone

Our bus idled a moment at the traffic signal and we noticed at
the left of us an entire block filled with neat rows of low shacks,
resembling chicken houses. Someone commented on it with awe,
"Just look at those chicken houses. They sure go in for poultry in
a big way here." Slowly the bus made a left turn, drove through a
wire-fenced gate, and to our dismay, we were inside the oversized
chicken farm. The bus driver opened the door, the guard stepped
out and stationed himself at the door again. Jim, the young man
who had shepherded us into the busses, popped his head inside
and sang out, "Okay, folks, all off at Yokohama, Puyallup."

We stumbled out, stunned, dragging our bundles after us. It
must have rained hard the night before in Puyallup, for we sank
ankle deep into gray, gluttinous mud. The receptionist, a white
man, instructed us courteously, "Now, folks, please stay together
as family units and line up. You'll be assigned your apartment."

We were standing in Area A, the mammoth parking lot of the
state fairgrounds. There were three other separate areas, B, C and
D, all built on the fair grounds proper, near the baseball field and
the race tracks. This camp of army barracks was hopefully called
Camp Harmony.

We were assigned to apartment 2–1–A, right across from the
bachelor quarters. The apartments resembled elongated, low stables about two blocks long. Our home was one room, about 18
by 20 feet, the size of a living room. There was one small window
in the wall opposite the one door. It was bare except for a small,
tinny wood-burning stove crouching in the center. The flooring
consisted of two by fours laid directly on the earth, and dandelions
were already pushing their way up through the cracks. Mother was
delighted when she saw their shaggy yellow heads. "Don't anyone
pick them. I'm going to cultivate them."

Father snorted, "Cultivate them! If we don't watch out, those
things will be growing out of our hair."

Just then Henry stomped inside, bringing the rest of our baggage. "What's all the excitement about?"

Sumi replied laconically, "Dandelions."

197

Henry tore off a fistful. Mother scolded, "*Arra! Arra!* Stop that. They're the only beautiful things around here. We could have a garden right in here."

"Are you joking, Mama?"

I chided Henry, "Of course, she's not. After all, she has to have some inspiration to write poems, you know, with all the '*nali keli's.*' I can think of a poem myself right now:

> Oh, Dandelion, Dandelion,
> Despised and uprooted by all,
> Dance and bob your golden heads
> For you've finally found your home
> With your yellow fellows, *nali keli*, amen!"

Henry said, thrusting the dandelions in Mother's black hair, "I think you can do ten times better than that, Mama."

Sumi reclined on her seabag and fretted, "Where do we sleep? Not on the floor, I hope."

"Stop worrying," Henry replied disgustedly.

Mother and Father wandered out to see what the other folks were doing and they found people wandering in the mud, wondering what other folks were doing. Mother returned shortly, her face lit up in an ecstatic smile, "We're in luck. The latrine is right nearby. We won't have to walk blocks."

We laughed, marveling at Mother who could be so poetic and yet so practical. Father came back, bent double like a woodcutter in a fairy tale, with stacks of scrap lumber over his shoulder. His coat and trouser pockets bulged with nails. Father dumped his loot in a corner and explained, "There was a pile of wood left by the carpenters and hundreds of nails scattered loose. Everybody was picking them up, and I hustled right in with them. Now maybe we can live in style with tables and chairs."

The block leader knocked at our door and announced lunchtime. He instructed us to take our meal at the nearest mess hall. As I untied my seabag to get out my pie plate, tin cup, spoon and fork, I realized I was hungry. At the mess hall we found a long line of people. Children darted in and out of the line, skiing in the slithery

A Birthright Denied: Monica Sone

mud. The young stood impatiently on one foot, then the other, and scowled, "The food had better be good after all this wait." But the Issei stood quietly, arms folded, saying very little. A light drizzle began to fall, coating bare black heads with tiny sparkling raindrops. The chow line inched forward.

Lunch consisted of two canned sausages, one lob of boiled potato, and a slab of bread. Our family had to split up, for the hall was too crowded for us to sit together. I wandered up and down the aisles, back and forth along the crowded tables and benches, looking for a few inches to squeeze into. A small Issei woman finished her meal, stood up and hoisted her legs modestly over the bench, leaving a space for one. Even as I thrust myself into the breach, the space had shrunk to two inches, but I worked myself into it. My dinner companion, hooked just inside my right elbow, was a bald headed, gruff-looking Issei man who seemed to resent nestling at mealtime. Under my left elbow was a tiny, mud-spattered girl. With busy runny nose, she was belaboring her sausages, tearing them into shreds and mixing them into the potato gruel which she had made with water. I choked my food down.

We cheered loudly when trucks rolled by, distributing canvas army cots for the young and hardy, and steel cots for the older folks. Henry directed the arrangement of the cots. Father and Mother were to occupy the corner nearest the wood stove. In the other corner, Henry arranged two cots in L shape and announced that this was the combination living room-bedroom area, to be occupied by Sumi and myself. He fixed a male den for himself in the corner nearest the door. If I had had my way, I would have arranged everyone's cots in one neat row as in Father's hotel dormitory.

We felt fortunate to be assigned to a room at the end of the barracks because we had just one neighbor to worry about. The partition wall separating the rooms was only seven feet high with an opening of four feet at the top, so at night, Mrs. Funai next door could tell when Sumi was still sitting up in bed in the dark, putting her hair up. "*Mah*, Sumi-*chan*," Mrs. Funai would say through the plank wall, "are you curling your hair tonight again?

Do you put it up every night?" Sumi would put her hands on her hips and glare defiantly at the wall.

The block monitor, an impressive Nisei who looked like a star tackle with his crouching walk, came around the first night to tell us that we must all be inside our room by nine o'clock every night. At ten o'clock, he rapped at the door again, yelling, "Lights out!" and Mother rushed to turn the light off not a second later.

Throughout the barracks, there were a medley of creaking cots, whimpering infants and explosive night coughs. Our attention was riveted on the intense little wood stove which glowed so violently I feared it would melt right down to the floor. We soon learned that this condition lasted for only a short time, after which it suddenly turned into a deep freeze. Henry and Father took turns at the stove to produce the harrowing blast which all but singed our army blankets, but did not penetrate through them. As it grew quieter in the barracks, I could hear the light patter of rain. Soon I felt the "splat! splat!" of raindrops digging holes into my face. The dampness on my pillow spread like a mortal bleeding, and I finally had to get out and haul my cot toward the center of the room. In a short while Henry was up. "I've got multiple leaks, too. Have to complain to the landlord first thing in the morning."

All through the night I heard people getting up, dragging cots around. I stared at our little window, unable to sleep. I was glad Mother had put up a makeshift curtain on the window for I noticed a powerful beam of light sweeping across it every few seconds. The lights came from high towers placed around the camp where guards with Tommy guns kept a twenty-four-hour vigil. I remembered the wire fence encircling us, and a knot of anger tightened in my breast. What was I doing behind a fence like a criminal? If there were accusations to be made, why hadn't I been given a fair trial? Maybe I wasn't considered an American anymore. My citizenship wasn't real, after all. Then what was I? I was certainly not a citizen of Japan as my parents were. On second thought, even Father and Mother were more alien residents of the United States than Japanese nationals for they had little tie with their mother country. In their twenty-five years in America, they had worked and paid their taxes to their adopted government as any other citizen.

Of one thing I was sure. The wire fence was real. I no longer had the right to walk out of it. It was because I had Japanese ancestors. It was also because some people had little faith in the ideas and ideals of democracy. They said that after all these were but words and could not possibly insure loyalty. New laws and camps were surer devices. I finally buried my face in my pillow to wipe out burning thoughts and snatch what sleep I could.

A Birthright Renounced:
Joseph Kurihara

Joseph Kurihara, born in Hawaii of Japanese parents, was an American citizen by birth. After moving to California, he served in the U.S. Army during World War I, but at the outbreak of World War II, he was placed in an internment camp. The following statement, written in 1946, is in the Bancroft Library of the University of California. Kurihara describes why he made a "definite and absolute" decision at the end of the war.

I . . . WAS BORN in the little village of Hanamaulu, Kauai, on the first day of January 1895. At the age of two, my parents moved to Honolulu. . . . We, the boys of conglomerated races, were brought up under the careful guidance of American teachers, strictly following the principle of American democracy. Let it be white, black, brown, or yellow, we were all treated alike. This glorious paradise of the Pacific was the true melting pot of human races. . . .

[In order to study medicine, Kurihara moved to California. There he encountered many instances of discrimination, as for example, in Sacramento.] As my friend and I were ambulating in the residential district, a short distance away from the Japanese center, something came whizzing by, and then another and another. We noticed they were rocks being thrown at us by a number of youngsters. As we went toward them, they ran and hid. It was really aggravating. Feeling perplexed, I asked my friend, "Why do they attack us in such a manner?" He answered, "It's discrimination." No such thing ever happened where I came from. It was disgusting. At the time, I felt homesick for my good old native land, Hawaii. . . .

Disregarding the conditions, I pursued my studies for two years.
. . . Unexpectedly, my friend from Sacramento called and persuaded me to go east, Michigan as the destination. He vouched to
me that the American people east of Chicago were very friendly
and kind. They did not discriminate just because we were Japanese.
They would treat us as one of their equals. I could not believe it,
but the news was very tempting after experiencing much unpleas-
antness for two years. . . .

[Soon after arriving in Michigan, Kurihara decided to join the
army and reported to Camp Custer.] During this training period,
I was befriended by many, amongst whom were Dr. Homer Knight
of Charlotte and Mr. William Green, president of the Green Advertising Company of Detroit. I made several visits to their homes.
On every occasion, I was treated like a prince. I felt very happy.
Knowing that they were going out of the way to make me happy,
I solemnly vouched to fight and die for the U.S. and those good
people, whose genuine kindness touched the very bottom of my
heart. . . . In California my animosities against the Californians
were growing with ever increasing intensity, but here in Michigan,
my liking for the American people was getting the best of me. . . .

[Kurihara enlisted and was sent to France, where his unit was
ordered to march sixty-two kilometers to the front.] After our arrival, we made preparations for the drive on Metz, digging gun
pits and hauling ammunition. We waded through mud and slept
in a dugout, bothered by rats and dripping water that soaked
through the earth on our bunks. Water was scarce, making a bath
a luxury. The sticky mud became part of our breeches. I felt so
dirty I would have given my last penny for a bath. . . .

At the front, while making extensive preparation for the drive
on Metz, someone gave away the secret and told us that an armi-
stice was going to be declared on November 11. Oh, what a happy
tiding it was to us all! Thank God, peace again would be restored
to mankind. . . .

For seven months I was stationed in Coblenz with the army of
occupation. . . . I found out that the German people were just as
much human as any other race. They were no more beasts than

the rest of the people in this world. I learned to like these people because they were kind and sincere. A little German girl voluntarily washed my laundry and returned it neatly ironed. So I, in return, gave little Freida chocolate candies and other sweets, including some canned foods I secured from the supply sergeant. Soap was very scarce in Germany, so this too I requisitioned and gave to her.

At every mealtime, the little German girls and boys were lining the walk to the garbage can for whatever scraps the boys were throwing away. I could not bear to see these little ones suffer, so I always made it my duty to ask for as much as my plate would hold and gave it to them. . . .

I took advantage of the two-week furlough being granted during my stay in Germany and visited Cologne, Brussels, Ypres, Paris and numerous other historically important places. Wherever I went, I saw the ugly scars of war, reminding me of the cannibalistic deeds of man only more cruel and complete in civilized manner. It was horrible to think that the more the world progresses in science, the more devilish it gets. I shuddered from thoughts what the next war would be. . . .

[During the next two decades, Kurihara pursued various activities in the Los Angeles area. He completed degree programs at California Community College and Southwestern University, worked as an accountant in the Japanese community, operated small produce businesses, studied television and navigation, and worked as a navigator on a tuna clipper.]

On the day when war broke out (December 7), we were fishing around the Galapagos Islands. Naval orders from Panama instructed all American vessels on the coast to put in at once into Panama or into any friendly port. . . . On the way above Cedros Islands, which are approximately three hundred miles south of San Diego, we saw American planes scouting the sea and reporting the movements of all vessels. It was thrilling to see them flying around to determine the name of the boat. I felt proud of them. Above all I was happy to be back in sight of America without a mishap.

We entered San Diego Bay immediately after daybreak. In the bay, the boat was stopped and several officers in naval uniforms came aboard. They scrutinized the papers, and finding them satisfactory, they left, taking three of us along — two Portuguese and myself.

We were taken to the naval wharf and awaited orders, but none came. Around nine-thirty, we again were asked to board the official launch, and this time were taken back to our own ship. No sooner had I boarded the ship, a plain-clothes man yelled, "Hey! you Jap, I want some information. You better tell me everything, or I'll kick you in the ____." My blood boiled. I felt like clubbing his head off. It was just a hat-rack and nothing more.

"What did you call me? If you want any information from me, you better learn to address a man properly."

"Is that so?"

"Yes, and most positively."

[After being kept waiting for three hours without lunch, Kurihara was again questioned]:

"What do you think of the war?"

"Terrible."

"Who do you think will win this war?"

"Who knows. God only knows."

"Do you think Japan has the materials she needs to wage this war?"

"I never was there, so your guess is just as good as mine."

"Are you a navigator?"

"Yes, I navigated boats for the last eight years."

"Have you a navigator's license?"

"No, but I have a captain's license, which gives me the right to navigate."

"Have you been a good American citizen?"

"I was and I am."

"Will you fight for this country?"

"If I am needed, I am ready."

"Were you a soldier of any country?"

"Yes, I am a veteran of the Foreign War, U.S. Army."

"Okay, that's all. If you hear or notice anything suspicious, please report the matter to me."

"I will."

"You may go."

I was really famished. I had no other thought but to satisfy my hunger. . . .

I went to the employment department of the Consolidated Aircraft Corporation to apply for a position as navigator. I wanted to do my share as an American citizen. The best and most useful place which I could apply my knowledge was as a navigator to navigate the bombers across the country to New York, from thence to England. I had absolute confidence in this work. . . .

[At Consolidated Aircraft, Kurihara was told to call back every day although other applicants were being notified by mail. When he tried to get a job with the merchant marines, he was informed that they were not employing any Japanese. Next, he tried California Shipbuilding, where the employment manager said Kurihara would not be happy because of discrimination from the other employees. Finally, he went to Bethlehem Steel and was not even admitted into the yard by the guard at the gate.]

A friend from Terminal Island requested a loan of $500. Being a very trustworthy person, I went to the bank to withdraw the requested amount to help. The bank manager told me I had to get an okay from the F.B.I. office before he could let me have the money. If I were an alien, probably I could see the reason why, but since I am a citizen, I could not. My account was not frozen. We argued for awhile. He knew I was right, but he was afraid to give it to me. I decided to see the F.B.I.

[At the FBI office, an officer asked him many of the same questions he had answered after being taken from his boat. Impatient, Kurihara asked him what the questions had to do with the withdrawal.]

One of the other officers, a husky and powerful looking gentleman (a ruffian is better suited to him here), interrupted and said, "Say, you, I do not like your attitude. Understand?"

"Maybe you don't like my attitude, and if you want to know, I don't like the foolish questions I am asked."

"You don't? Well, you better like it."

It looked for a moment as if he was going to strike. I paid no attention to his threatening manner. I kept sitting calmly. Then the first officer asked me if I had any proof to show that I was an American citizen. In answer to this question, I pulled out a folder in my pocket and unfolded it. This folder was purposely made to hold the Honorable Discharge Certificate of the U.S. Army. This the officers unfailingly noticed. I handed my birth certificate to the officer which he scrutinized. The other officer at once changed his bullish attitude and spoke more politely thereafter. Before departing, the officer told me he didn't like it because my voice was rather loud. I told him it was my natural voice. He understood, and we parted with no harm done. [Eventually, he was permitted to withdraw the money.]

Having nothing to do with plenty of time, I wrote to my cousin discussing the war, and in it I denounced the Japanese militarists in no uncertain words. I do not believe in war. It is the most horrible thing on earth. I've seen the sufferings of the poor German girls and boys while in Coblenz, the destroyed cities and towns throughout the front, and the unendurable hardships the poor soldier boys had to go through. . . .

Since the last ray of hope had vanished, I decided to return to Los Angeles. During the ensuing week, Terminal Island was thrown into turmoil. All able-bodied men went to help the poor women on whose heads the world came crashing down. [All Japanese, both aliens and citizens, had been ordered to evacuate from the West Coast. In the case of Terminal Island, the men were taken away first.]

It was really cruel and harsh. To pack and evacuate in forty-eight hours was an impossibility. Seeing mothers completely bewildered with children crying from want and care, the peddlers taking advantage and offering prices next to robbery, made me feel like murdering those responsible without the slightest compunction in my heart.

The parents might have been aliens, but the children were all American citizens. Did the government of the United States intend to ignore their rights, regardless of their citizenship? Those beautiful furnitures, which the parents bought to please their sons and daughters, costing hundreds of dollars, were robbed of them at the single command — "Evacuate!" Here my first doubt of American Democracy had crept into the far corners of my heart with the sting that I could not forget.

Democracy had been my political affiliation before, and the first vote I casted. Having had absolute confidence in democracy, I could not believe my very eyes of what I had seen that day. America, the standard bearer of democracy had committed the most heinous crime in its history, indelibly imprinting in my mind, as well as in the minds of those children, the dread that even democracy is a demon in time of war. It is my sincere desire to see this government of the United States some day repair the wrong in full.

When the Army took command of the Western Defense area, it relieved me greatly because I really believed it was capable of handling the situation. There would be no more hysteria, and we Japanese, especially the Niseis [Japanese born in the United States] could settle down and go to work. But no sooner after it did, our rights as American citizens were shattered by General DeWitt. Frankly, I doubt his ability as a general.

[Kurihara had expected the Japanese American Citizens League to contest the evacuation orders. Instead, he was angered by what he considered a lack of courage on the part of the JACL leaders. At this time, he vowed to challenge them in the camps.]

On March 23, 1942, I left for Manzanar [an internment camp in southeastern California] with the second contingent of volunteers. I wanted to be there first since I was single and free to help those arriving later with children, so they could be comfortably installed.

The camp was in topsy-turvy condition. Life was really discouraging during the first two months. The wind blew with such ferocity that at times I thought the building was going to be carried away. Dust were everywhere. Sandstorms were so bad it obscured the sun. We, in fact, slept in the dust, breathed the dust, and ate the dust. Bath houses were in the stage of blue-print. For two weeks we had to go without a bath.

A Birthright Renounced: Joseph Kurihara

Manzanar enjoyed peace and tranquility for several months. It would have continued to enjoy peace and tranquility had not the J.A.C.L. brazenly made its appearance after it was quietly organized by those spineless leaders. . . . They called a meeting which I attended to fulfill the vow I had made to crush them wherever I met them. . . . Instantly, when the floor was opened for general discussion, I took the floor and started bombarding and blasting the organization to bits. The entire floor was electrified. After some verbal blasting I gave to Talkative Slocum (Tokutaro Nishimura), who not only interrupted my speech but threw mud at me, the hall resounded with such cheers, whistling and stamping, it was said the noise was heard throughout the center. I had turned the table with unquestionable success. . . .

[A few days after a national convention of the J.A.C.L. was held at Salt Lake City, one of its leaders was severely beaten. Harry Ueno was arrested on suspicion. Kurihara took up the fight to have him released. This resulted in what was called the "Manzanar Incident." Demonstrators denouncing J.A.C.L. leaders and the camp administration began rioting. Soldiers then fired machine guns into the crowd, wounding ten internees and killing two. Kurihara was arrested and thrown into jail. He was then taken to another internment camp in Moab, Utah.]

Mr. R. R. Best, the director, treated us very kindly. For a long time, we ate the same food in the same mess hall with the soldiers, enjoying the best. I have absolutely no complaint to make under this humane treatment we received. If all directors were like Mr. Best, I am sure the Japanese would have no cause to revolt. Such is the true and sincere opinion I entertained both in Moab and at Leupp, Arizona, under his administration. . . .

Mr. Robertson, who succeeded Mr. Best, was very kind to us. He was really a God-send. Though he was slightly more exacting, like Mr. Best he went out of his way to see that the boys got everything they had coming. I again commenced to see the beautiful side of the American people, which was completely submerged with hatred. The bitterness which dominated my feelings for months after the killing of those two innocent boys at Manzanar was so great I could have murdered any white man as if he were an animal. Was it time that healed it? No, it was the kindness of these two real Americans.

Through Mr. Robertson's efforts, we were transferred to Tule Lake on December 6, 1943. We were thrown into the stockade upon arrival, out of which I was released three days later and enjoyed the freedom of the camp once more. The faces of the little children were really consoling. If we only could be like them, this world would be void of trouble, I thought. . . .

In the face of my cooling animosity against this country, my American friends, especially Mr. Best, no doubt must have wondered why I had renounced my citizenship. This decision was not that of today or that of yesterday. It dates back to the day when General DeWitt ordered evacuation. It was confirmed when he flatly refused to listen even to the voices of the former World War veterans, and it was doubly confirmed as I entered Manzanar. We who already had proven our loyalty by serving in the last World War should have been spared. The veterans asked for special consideration, but their requests were denied. They too had to evacuate like the rest of the Japanese people, as if they were aliens.

I did not expect this of the Army. When the Western Defense Command assumed the responsibilities of the West Coast, I expected that, at least, the Niseis would be allowed to remain. But to General DeWitt, we were all alike. "A Jap is a Jap. Once a Jap, always a Jap." He must have felt great when he phrased it, but today no doubt he must be feeling ashamed of it. A great man does not manifest his feelings in such contemptuous words. I then swore to become a Jap one hundred percent, and never to do another day's work to help this country fight this war. My decision to renounce my citizenship there and then was definite and absolute. . . .

[In February of 1946, Kurihara sailed to Japan, a country he had not yet even visited.]

Fighting on the "Frontier" of the Pacific War: Native Americans

————————➤◆————————

I N AN ESSAY, "How We Felt About the War," published shortly
after the end of World War II, historian Allan Nevins observed:
"Probably in all our history, no foe has been so detested as were
the Japanese." He located the fierce fighting within the context of
American westward expansion: "Emotions forgotten since our
most savage Indian wars were awakened by the ferocities of Japanese commanders."[1] The Pacific islands had become America's
"frontier." "When I was a young boy," a soldier said, "we always
played cowboys and Indians, and when I landed on Guadalcanal
that's what I felt like — I was playing a game, it was not real.
Even though I knew it was real. . . ." Another soldier described
the Japanese attackers as "whooping like a bunch of wild Indians."[2]
Jungle combat against Japanese soldiers was often characterized as
"Indian fighting," and the perimeter outside of U.S. military control was called "Indian country."[3] Commenting on the fighting
skills of Japanese soldiers, Colonel Milton A. Hill stated that the
"Japs" were "good at infiltration, too; as good as Indians ever
were."[4] Recycling an old frontier adage, Admiral William Halsey
declared: "The only good Jap is a Jap who's been dead six
months."[5]

Many U.S. soldiers fighting in the Pacific were Native Americans.
One of them was Ira Hayes. In 1942, he left the Pima reservation
and volunteered for the Marines. But Hayes was not fully prepared

for the horrors of the Pacific war. At Bougainville, Hayes saw his fellow white soldiers mutilate corpses of Japanese soldiers. They sawed gold teeth from heads and dried out skulls. "In the mutilations," biographer William Bradford Huie wrote, "Hayes recognized that some of the fiendishness came from difference. He doubted his buddies would mutilate Germans in the same fashion. To Hayes the Japs were 'dirty bastards'; to his buddies they were 'dirty yellow bastards.' Not once, in letters or conversation, did Hayes call a Jap yellow."[6]

Hayes participated in the invasion of Iwo Jima. On February 23, 1945, after three days of bloody fighting, the Marines captured Mount Suribachi, a strategic viewpoint for the Japanese defense of the island. Hayes went up to the summit and was there for a staged second raising of the American flag. Joe Rosenthal took still photographs; one of them became the most famous wirephoto of World War II, instantly capturing the patriotism and emotions of the war.

As one of the flag-raisers, Hayes suddenly became a war hero. Hayes and two of the other Marines in the photograph were flown back to the United States to help lead the Seventh War Loan Drive. Hayes knew the photograph was a fraud. He had not been there for the first flag-raising. Disturbed by this publicity deception, Hayes felt uncomfortable. In Washington, D.C., Sergeant W. Keyes Beech was the official guardian for the bond tour. He explained to Hayes: "Chief, this is strange duty for you, and I know how you feel. You got to understand that a bond tour is show business. Show business is make-believe. You make up stories, and it's all right because it's for a good cause. And in this business you're representing the Marine Corps." Hayes asked: "What about this crock o' shit about the flag-raising?" "You let me and the reporters tell that story, Chief," Beech answered. "You forget it and smile and nod your head."[7]

The deception of the tour, combined with the tremendous publicity and pressure, took its toll on Hayes. His drinking became a problem. In Chicago in May, he was found drunk in a bar and had to be brought to sobriety by having ice water poured on him an hour before a scheduled flag-raising act. His commanding officer pulled Hayes from the tour and ordered that he be sent back overseas without delay.

After the war, Hayes wondered what he had fought for. Unemployed and depressed, Hayes drifted into the depths of alcoholic delirium and was frequently jailed for drunkenness and vagrancy. On January 23, 1955, Hayes was found on a street: drunk, he had fallen and "drowned" in his own vomit. "People shoved drinks in our hands and said we were heroes," he had remarked sadly. "On the reservation I got hundreds of letters and I got sick of hearing about the flag-raising, and sometimes I wished the guy had never made the picture."[8]

The Indian Hero of Iwo Jima:
Letters from Ira Hayes

In his letters to his family, Hayes told why he wished he were not famous. William Bradford Huie obtained these letters and included them in The Hero of Iwo Jima *and Other Stories, published in* 1959.

━━━━━➤ ◄━━━━━

August 29, 1942
USMC, San Diego

D EAR FOLKS:
    Gee, this is the first time I had a chance to write. So far I have had no luck as some boys have. It's swell here, cool in the day but kind of chilly at night. We're located here in the bay just beyond the city limits.

We arrived here Thursday evening. We were supposed to arrive that morning but the train was held up at Yuma.

There are quite a lot of Indian boys here. I met Marvin Jones and we are in the same platoon. We are in the same tent with another Indian boy from New Mexico.

Right now we have all our equipment, toilet articles, linens and everything. We are to stay here in boot camp seven weeks. That's where the new men have to toughen up. No liberty, no town for us. After seven weeks we'll be allowed to roam around in San Diego, which is four miles off.

The officers are really tough here, but we have to steady our-selves for tougher things to come.

I'm really grateful for the big dinner you gave me and the people you invited. Things those old men said are really helpful . . . about God taking care of you. . . .

214

They gave us a Marine haircut 1½ inches long and you should see me. . . .

From a guy who's very proud he's a
Marine and in his country's service

*   *   *

September 8, 1942

Dear Folks:

In case you don't know, the picture above is the famous Marine emblem and the words *Semper Fidelis* which means Always Faithful. And all of us are Always Faithful — we really are — to our country, our families, our people, and mainly our church. . . .

Our drill instructors are swell. When they get to know us better they are really nice, always joking with us. One of them is always fooling with me. Asking me where is my tomahawk and bows and arrows. Then he'll try to make fun of the Indians and we'll argue. He's trying to put Marvin and the other Indian boys from Oklahoma and myself on the boxing show Saturday night. He says he's trying to prove that Indians can fight better than most white men. Yes, it's really swell here. . . .

*   *   *

Camp Matthews, San Diego
September 20, 1942

Dear Parents and Brothers:

We arrived here yesterday, at Camp Matthews where the rifle range is. . . .

They put us here in the new barracks. . . . It's beautiful all around us . . . rolling hills and canyons where the targets are placed for the rifle ranges. . . .

The going will now get tougher every week. We'll be tired, blisters on our hands, shoulders, sore muscles all over from marching over the hills with rifles and packs. But we have to go through with it. We know what we are going into and we

215

ask no favors from our instructors. We take it in order not to let our loved ones at home down or our country or the service we are in.

This morning we marched to church. Anyone who did not want to attend did not have to go. But about half of us chose to go. We had a good sermon and a choir from Long Beach sang for us. When we marched back the men started singing Onward, Christian Soldiers and some of the boys started to cry and it was rather sad. I never knew white boys cried so easy. I knew us Indians cried. Now I think maybe white boys cry easier than we do.

Tomorrow we'll practice all the positions of shooting. . . . I'll try hard to shoot expert or marksman or maybe sharp-shooter in order to get a medal.

I'm glad you're proud of my picture in my uniform.

The fellows are swell chums and we lay awake into the night and they keep shooting questions at us Indians and we have to answer. They don't believe me when I tell them that I can't speak my own language but that I understand it. . . .

From a Marine who's anxious
to meet them damn Japs

* * *

April 9, 1943

Dear Folks:

You know by now that we have left the states and arrived safely overseas. All I can say is that we are across the equator, somewhere in the South Pacific. . . . I'm glad you sent me the clipping about the Memorial Service in honor of Richard. It must have been impressive where they said: Colonel Richard Lewis, United States Marine Corps, First Pima Indian killed in the War for the Four Freedoms. I wiped tears of pride out of my eyes. . . . Us Indians have so much to be thankful for, and so much to gain in this war.

* * *

November 16, 1943

Dear Folks:

We are now allowed to say where we have been since we left the States. We left on March 12th and arrived at New Caledonia March 24th. . . . We trained and jumped here for exactly six months. Our liberty town was 40 miles away, which was settled by a Frenchman. Noumea was the name, and it was also the capital. After six months in New Caledonia we shoved off for Guadalcanal which you know was a hot hell hole a year ago. We stayed there two weeks then shoved off to where we are now. This place is all right, but there's no liberty town. It's cool because we are right by the ocean. The fellows swim and fish in the streams.

* * *

February 16, 1944

Dear Folks:

Well, I'm back in Dago . . . arrived here Monday with the whole regiment. We get furloughs starting Monday for 30 long days. . . . We saw a lot of action which isn't a very good thing to remember. We lost some of our dear buddies, but they did not die in vain. We accomplished our missions. I'll get home the fastest way possible.

* * *

August 7, 1944

Dear Folks:

Well I was offered another chance to go to communication school and be promoted fast and get away from this rough life. But I said no. It kind of made me sore too. My place is with a gun. I didn't come in here to lead an easy life. They better get us overseas quick and the war would be over with. . . . Don't worry about me. I'm a man now, no young guy.

* * *

[On February 23, 1945, Hayes's life was suddenly changed when Rosenthal photographed the flag-raising atop Suribachi.]

* * *

May 10, 1945
[on Waldorf stationery]

Dear Parents and Brothers:

We just arrived here in NYC about 2 hours ago from Washington. It's now 6 o'clock in the evening and it's cloudy and raining like the dickens.

I can't hardly realize I'm here in the most famous hotel in the world. But I am.

Yesterday morning in Washington in front of the capitol we raised the flag which was the same one we hoisted up on Iwo Jima. We got it here in our room.

Four of us are on this trip. Gagnon, Bradley and Tech Sgt. Beech, who is watching over us and taking care of our traveling business. He's a swell guy and I like him.

Tomorrow is a big day. We go to the Roxy Theater in the morning and make an appearance. Then we go to Times Square to unveil the monument of the flag-raising on Iwo which is 25 feet high. And then the dinner to be held in our honor in the evening. Then we leave for Philadelphia and Boston and back here in New York. So you see we will be busy.

This tour is supposed to last until July 4th when we come back to Washington and make our last appearance. Phoenix is also on our list.

Your excited but happy son,

* * *

May 22, 1945
Hotel Statler, Detroit

Dear Parents and Brothers:

We [have] been here in Detroit for two days now and we leave tonight for Indianapolis and Chicago for one day. We spent three days in Chicago before, and Cleveland, Canton and Akron, Ohio.

In Chicago I had a dinner given in my honor by the National Congress of American Indians, and I met a lot of swell Indian folks. . . .

Yesterday I met a swell couple who were Indians. And last night their daughter came up to our apartment and presented me with a lovely Indian war club. It's really pretty, a foot and a half long with fancy carvings. . . .

* * *

[Hayes was drinking heavily on the tour and was suddenly ordered to be sent back to the Pacific.]

* * *

San Francisco
May 25, 1945

Dear Parents and Brothers:

This may shock you but do not be afraid. At the present I am in San Francisco, just got in this morning from Chicago, and leaving this evening for Pearl Harbor.

There's supposed to be some show out there, that's why Gen. Rockey wants me back there, just for it. Then back here again to rejoin Gagnon, Bradley and Beech. So do not worry.

* * *

June 1, 1945
Pearl Harbor

Dear Folks:

. . . I guess you know the story on me now. Trust me when I say I could not. . . . I figured that there were more guys over here who did more than I did. . . . Too many men are dead now whom I liked and knew personally. Most all the old guys are either wounded or killed. And I can never forget them.

I know there are lots of persons who think I am crazy for coming back when I could have stayed in the states forever. But as I said before I have reason for coming back the third time. Nobody would understand it but me. There was a strong urge in me to come back. And I felt it was my Lord, still by my side. And now I am back, more confident in myself and stronger in mind and I am unafraid. For I still have Christ to look up to.

The bond tour was really lots of fun for a while. We found out it would not be so easy after a week on the road. We done the same old stuff. It got so boring and tiresome. And the people were so bothering. I couldn't stand much more, especially newspaper reporters and photographers.

Over here I feel a lot better. I feel like my own self, just another Marine, and that's the way I want it.

* * *

June 18, 1945

Dear Folks:

. . . When I go back I know people will forget this flag deal. And then I'll feel a lot happier.

* * *

[1953]

Dear Folks:

Well, I guess you know what happened. The whole country knows now. I got drunk, woke up in jail. No shirt, no shoes. The judge gave me $25 or 17 days in the workhouse. Before they gave us prison clothes they called me up and said Warden Sain wanted to talk with me. He asked if I was really the man who raised the flag on Iwo Jima. I told him yes and he told me I would be out very soon. We had our pictures taken for the Tribune. He bought me new shoes, new slacks, new shirt. Then the Sun-Times came and bailed me out and took me to see the editor and I guess I owe him everything. He talked to me for a long time and said he was going to have a doctor look me over and cure my drinking, so I gave in. They took me to the Hopecrest San. where they cure drunks. In 5 to 7 days they will help the patient to hate any kind of liquor. I was there 5 days and took 10 treatments and 16 shots in the arm. My last four treatments were rough, but I was forced to take it if I really wanted to help myself, and of course I did.

Like I said I was pretty sick. I threw up whiskey, gin, beer, and wine they forced on me, and automatically hated the taste of all of them. I'd be so sick for a couple of hours after.

So I was cured in their eyes. They had done their part. Now the real test is up to me. This hateful taste for liquor will go away in a month. So all I need is the will power. Some go back to drinking; but most do not. This was a private-owned hospital and is in the rich man's district and cost $313 but they charged us $270 as a favor to me. I am still taking vitamins and different prescriptions for 6 or more weeks. As of now my blood system is free of alcohol.

So you see what a position I'm in. People have put their trust in me — so many people and so much trust — and now I've got to do good.

Your son and brother, Ira

Transplanted in Chicago:
The Polish

THE VERY FIRST Poles arrived in Jamestown in 1608, along with some Germans to work in the colony's timber industry. But their population remained small until 1870, when a mass migration began that would lead to the movement of 2 million by 1914. In significant numbers, these migrants went back to their homeland: the return rate was 40 percent. The purpose of their journey was to earn money for a better living in Poland. Migratory men sang about the experience of separation from their families:

> When I journeyed from Amer'ca
> And the foundry where I labored. . . .
> Soon I came to New York City,
> To the agent for my passage. . . .
> Then I left Berlin for Krakow;
> There my wife was waiting for me.
> And my children did not know me,
> For they fled from me, a stranger.
> "My dear children, I'm your papa;
> Three long years I have not seen you." [1]

But many of these men returned to America with their families and stayed. The 1924 National Origins Act restricted immigration from Poland. Fifty years later, there were 5 million Polish Americans, 400,000 of them living in Chicago — a community that as early as the turn of the century had come to be known as the "American Warsaw."

Bilingual Education in Polonia

Born in Poland, this woman grew up in a Polish neighborhood of Chicago. No name is attached to her life story, which is in the Immigration History Research Center, University of Minnesota. As a young girl, this Polish immigrant attended a Catholic school, where she was instructed in both Polish and English. Bilingual education is nothing new: it helped open the door to America for her and many others.

———————→ ◆———————

T HE MONTH WAS DECEMBER, the year 1913, and I was eight and a half years old when I got my first glimpse of the Statue of Liberty and America. We, my mother, my aunt Weronika and my two brothers, Karol, 10, and Jozef, 5 years of age, disembarked a large ship loaded with trunks, wicker hampers and bundles of all description and were ushered to a barn-like building on Ellis Island. . . .

We were third-class passengers, and the five of us occupied one tiny cabin with four bunk beds. At that time the ships had no stabilizers and most passengers became seasick soon after the ship went into motion. Many of them, like my mother and my aunt, never left the cabin until the ship reached its destination. Except to take some bread and tea, they ate practically nothing. The vomiting of seasick people was uncontrollable. The crew came with water hoses to wash down and disinfect the cabins and passageways several times a day. My brothers and I had no such problems. We ran all over the ship, looked into every nook and cranny, made friends with other children and worked up tremendous appetites. The meals were served in two shifts. When the bell rang announcing the first serving, the Dubiel youngsters were there. They were also there for the second sitting. No one minded since most of the adults did not show up for the meals.

[After our arrival] I remember the long train ride from New York and also meeting my father at the railroad station in Chicago. This was a reunion after five years of separation. . . . About this long separation between my mother and father I must write in some detail. I am sure they wanted to be together, but Mother felt it would not be wise to give up the home and farm they both worked so hard to preserve. Then too, she was apprehensive as to what life in the distant and unknown America would be. Dad came to America to earn some money to pay off the mortgage on the farm, and Mother, with money coming regularly from Dad, did an exceedingly good job in managing the farm. . . .

I recall in wintertime, during the long evenings, she occupied herself by doing beautiful needlework, which later adorned our house — bedspreads, billowing pillows, tablecloths and curtains. She loved flowers and had a showy flower garden in the summer and many potted plants in the house in the winter. The decision to leave her little domain was a difficult one, but leave she did. Dad, much as he loved Poland, strongly believed that America was truly a land of opportunity for all and especially his own children. . . .

I remember riding the Milwaukee Avenue streetcar and getting off on Noble Street in Chicago. Two short blocks and we reached our destination — 1420 W. Division Street, where Dad rented a four-room, two-bedroom flat. This was to be our home for the next seven years. . . . Dad was earning $12.00 a week as a presser in a tailor shop.

Our living quarters consisted of a living room, kitchen and two bedrooms. The toilet was three flights down in the hall. The stairway was always dark, as the building next to us was also four stories high and the narrow passageway allowed little daylight. We generally had to grope our way going up or down the stairs. At night a tiny gas light flickered, illuminating the entrance. The hallway separated the front 6-room flats from the rear 4-room flats. The length of the building extended to the alley, so there was no room for even a blade of grass or a tree to grow. Besides the four rooms I mentioned, our flat had a tiny 4x4 room meant to be a clothes closet. But with a full-sized window facing west, it could only be used as a catch-all. In the years that followed, this little room became my own escape room. Here I read, dreamed my childish dreams and often cried. The transplant from the life in the country to a city tenement was not easy for me. . . .

Our little flat also contained a space intended for a so-called "skylight," but since it was boarded by the attic floor, the little nook became a book depository and our future library. Karol was a great collector, and although we could not afford to buy books, he would scrupulously clip the installments of novels which ran daily in the Polish papers, and by putting the clippings together, he accumulated quite a collection of novels and works of outstanding authors.

Father never discouraged our love of books. In fact, shortly after our arrival, he made a point of obtaining a card to the Polish National Alliance Library. The library catalog had section "A" books for children, section "B" educational, and "C" books for adults. I have since forgotten the name of the kindly librarian who came to know us well. I recall his kindly face and his manner of handling the children. When selecting books, we would often request a book from "C" section. Invariably they were "out." The old gent then substituted our choice and thus guided us into reading books proper for our age. How wonderful was the world of books! And how beautifully the Polish authors wrote. We often read the works of other authors in translation, such as Conan Doyle's "Sherlock Holmes" and Charles May's great stories of adventures in far-off lands and many others.

We arrived in America in the middle of December and did not start school until after Christmas holidays. Holy Trinity church and school were only a block away from our home. I shall never forget my first day in school. Sister Rozalia, the superior, took me to my classroom and presented me to my new teacher. As was the custom in Poland, I attempted to kiss the sister's hand, which she withdrew to my utter embarrassment. In Poland I was to enter third grade. Here I was placed in the first grade, as was Karol. However, it was not long before he and I began skipping grades, and by the age of 14, we were ready to graduate with the rest of the 14-year-olds.

The pastor, Fr. Kazimierz Sztuczko, was not only a saintly man but wise and a great Polish patriot. He not only looked after church affairs, but also guided and took personal interest in the educational program of the grade and high school, thus bringing them to the highest level of any parochial school in the city. The grade school had a very large enrollment so the boys and girls were always in separate classrooms. Sister of Nazareth taught the girls. The boys were taught by them only up to the sixth grade. Beginning with seventh grade, the teaching was taken over by the Holy Cross Order of Brothers. The brothers also staffed the high school faculty.

When Karol and I began attending school, we would come home bursting to tell what new English words we had learned. And we had our difficulties! Insofar as our schoolwork went, we both were making good progress, but we encountered so many new words and phrases which we did not understand. In the beginning we used to play games. I would say, "Karol, bet you don't know the word for 'piec' in English." He would say, "No, do you?" "Certainly, it's called stewart" — or so I thought because our kitchen stove displayed a trademark "Stewart."

We frequently argued about the pronunciation of words, and thus slowly, little by little, we were learning to speak English. Considering that at home we spoke Polish, heard only Polish in church, read only Polish papers and books, it was a wonder that Karol and I learned the language well enough to graduate — and with honors. Josef did not have these problems. He learned to speak English before he started school. Actually Karol and I were star pupils of our graduating class. . . .

In those days, the schedule of studies in a Polish parochial school was as follows: each and every school day morning mass, more prayers in the classroom, followed by a few minutes of calisthenics. On alternate days this was followed by catechism and Bible history, both in Polish. Then came arithmetic in English. After recess, we had Polish reading, writing, grammar and history. The afternoons were devoted to English studies — reading, spelling, grammar,

American history, and in the higher grades, literature and civics. Once a week the girls had lessons in needlework. The boys attended gym classes. I still have the pillow I made in eighth grade. . . .

Beginning in seventh grade, the girls were taught shorthand, typing and correspondence, i.e., how to write and answer a business letter. This so-called "business course," as far as I know, was taught only at Holy Trinity school. In those days, most of the girls, after finishing eighth grade and reaching the age of 14, would seek employment. Father Kazimierz Sztuczko, pastor of the parish, initiated the program to encourage them to continue the course in evening schools and try for better jobs. Many did — I did. . . .

As I mentioned before, learning the English language was not easy for Karol and me. We were "greenhorns" from the old country. The nuns, instead of speaking English to us, preferred to speak Polish, perhaps to practice their own Polish. The children in school were first-generation Americans, and although not as fluent in Polish as Karol and I, could speak the language. Then too, the section of Chicago where we lived was the heart of Polonia. Except for some Jewish store-keepers, who also spoke Polish, the neighborhood had only Polish immigrants. They were the ones, who with their meager earnings, built magnificent churches and schools, founded fraternal organizations and erected the fine buildings which housed them — the Polish National Alliance, Polish Roman Catholic Union, Polish Women's Alliance, Falcons and many other societies and groups. At that time there were three Polish dailies in Chicago (Dziennik Chicagoski, Kaiennik Zwiazkowy, and Dziennik Ludowy) plus a number of weekly and monthly publications. . . .

While the neighborhood's largest stores were owned by Jews, the Poles operated many small businesses — restaurants, jewelry stores, bookstores, shoe stores, music stores, as well as groceries, bakeries and butcher shops. Across the street from us, the butcher's name was Mr. Gnatek. Translated his name meant "bones," an apt name for a butcher. As now, then too, saloons were practically on every corner. In summer, the usual accompaniment to supper for most men, including my dad, was beer. Children were not allowed in saloons, but they had a side entrance through which a child could slip a pail and five cents and was handed a cold foamy beverage. . . .

Third of May, Polish Constitution Day, still observed by Poles all over America, meant to us the biggest parade of the year. It always began with church services at Holy Trinity Church. Starting at Noble Street, the parade proceeded down Division Street to Humbolt Park to gather around the statue of Thaddeus Kosciuszko. The program and speeches went on all afternoon. The park was filled with hundreds of people who came to see the parade — bands, floats, representatives of organizations and church societies with banners and flags, hundreds of children and adults in colorful Polish costumes from various regions of Poland, Scouts, and Falcons in uniform. One year this celebration presented my first big thrill. I happened to have the longest hair of any girl in eighth grade and was chosen to be on the float representing Poland. My hair was unbraided, and I wore a queenly robe and crown.

My father's wages in the tailor shop were small, and there were five of us to feed, clothe and house. It wasn't long, therefore, that Mother, who was very good with the needle, found herself working in the same tailor shop with Dad. Her job greatly helped to supplement Dad's earnings, especially since expenses kept mounting as we children grew older. After graduating eighth grade, Karol was enrolled at Holy Trinity High School. When in grade school, the tuition for the three of us was only $1.00 a month. The tuition in high school was naturally considerably higher and so were the books. Then too, my parents were extremely hospitable. Seldom a Saturday or Sunday passed by when there were no guests. Relatives, friends and neighbors all enjoyed coming to our home. Dad was a great conversationalist, well read and informed. Also when in company, he had a great sense of humor and wit. With the family he was much sterner and a strict disciplinarian.

Mother and Father worked five and a half days a week, and much of the housework had to be done by Karol and me. We took turns scrubbing the floors. We helped Mother with her weekly wash, which was done in the kitchen and mostly in the evenings. For that we used two wash tubs, a washboard and a hand-operated wringer. The clothes had to be boiled in a large basin on the stove, rinsed, starched and hung in the attic. Saturdays I cleaned and dusted our flat and took turns with our next door neighbor scrubbing the third flight stairs. . . .

Karol's friends were also my friends. During summer vacations our recreation consisted of going to nearby parks — Eckhardt and Pulaski. The parks were small, but each had a playground, swimming pool and gym. Karol and I read a lot, played cards and roller skated. My girl friends and I went swimming, played jacks, skipped rope and took long walks. We always looked forward to the 4th of July, the fireworks and the shooting from real, real revolvers. Occasionally, my parents took us to a picnic given by some lodge or church society. We then traveled by street car to some grove located on the outskirts of Chicago. Some of the children in the neighborhood attended nickel shows. Those were the days of great silent movies. We seldom had the necessary five cents, but I was luckier than my brothers. Aunt Hania loved the movies and frequently took me with her. Saturday matinees were the big thrillers. Serials, such as "The Peril's of Pauline," kept us in suspense until the next week's episode. . . .

After my graduation from eighth grade, at the age of 14, I was ready to become a working girl. . . . At graduation I was given the first award, and the nuns personally came to our house to induce my father to send me to high school. Dad believed in higher education, but on his income the best he could do was to provide a high school education for my brothers. As for me, a girl, my future role was to be that of a wife and mother, and homemaking did not require a high school diploma. . . . Dad also had a job waiting for me in his tailor shop. I was to be a baste puller — nothing to it — but I hated the job and the surroundings.

After a few months, I quit the job, but not before securing another one. . . . My first job did not present any special challenges, not even a chance for promotion. Daily, I scanned the "Want Ads" looking for something better. Finally, one day I came across something which I thought was just the thing for me. Peter Fahrney, makers of patent medicine, needed a typist with knowledge of Polish. I was only 14 and a half. They advertised for someone 16 or over, but I was big for my age and could easily pass for 20. I applied for the job and was accepted. This work I loved — a spacious, clean office and wonderful co-workers. Much as I liked my work, one had to be practical.

When, two years later, there was an opening for a job in the Polish National Alliance offices with better pay and close to home which meant saving on car fare and lunches, I took the job and stayed there until my marriage. My own pay was turned intact to my parents for as long as I lived under their roof. There was no such thing as "paying board" as most parents had to depend on the earnings of their children to get by. Each week I was given $1.00 for spending money. This covered the price of entertainment, treats, cosmetics and other "foolishness." Since beginning to work at 14, my first one-week vacation was given to me when I was 18. In the meantime, Karol did us proud in high school by winning the much coveted scholarship to Notre Dame University, where he began his premedical studies. . . .

Charles (Karol) became a doctor. Joseph recently retired as one of the vice-presidents of a large Chicago bank. . . . I am now a widow. Of my three children, my daughter, a Ph.D., studied at the Sorbonne and in Poland, speaks English, Polish, French and has a working knowledge of Russian. She was a college professor for a number of years and is now the chief administrator of a Milwaukee high school. My older son is a communication specialist for A.T.&T., and the other son is a librarian.

A Stepchild of America:
Thomas Napierkowski

In 1971, Napierkowski received his Ph.D., and then taught at the University of Wisconsin and the University of Colorado. His life story was published in 1976 in Growing Up Slavic in America, *edited by Michael Novak. He became more aware of his own ethnic identity when he began teaching a course on African-American literature.*

───────────▶ ■──────────

I WAS BORN Polish-American thirty-two years ago in South Chicago. . . . For me, probably the greatest advantage of being born and raised in South Chicago was that it made my early years of growing up Polish-American relatively easy. In very subtle ways, but ways which I have since realized were profound, South Chicago nurtured my identity; and although that identity has exposed me to moments of intense pain and bitter anger in American society, it has also provided the most rewarding aspects of my life.

The family was, of course, the source of my identity. The atmosphere of our home was ethnic. The foods we ate, the sounds we heard, the rituals we observed were heavily, but not exclusively, Polish. Perhaps the only ethnic crises I ever faced at home were my occasional rebellions at not getting enough "American" food like chili and pizza. These rebellions were sometimes tolerated, infrequently indulged, but most often squelched. It is ironic that today my children crave with amazing frequency the daily fare which I didn't always appreciate. The Polish meals which highlighted the year were the Christmas Eve dinner (Wigilia) consisting of traditional meatless dishes and the Easter morning breakfast which, after the gloom of Lent, gloriously reintroduced us to the tastes of ham, sausages, and baked goods.

The sounds emanating from our home were a potpourri of languages, music, and shouts. My parents spoke Polish, but the language most commonly used was English. Circumstances dictating the use of Polish ranged from the visits of relatives, an almost daily occurrence, to occasional attempts at concealing something from us children. Obviously, then, my parents did not teach us Polish; what we learned, which was not inconsiderable, was what we picked up from its frequent usage at home and in the neighborhood. Musically, our radio and phonograph were put to amazingly eclectic use. Depending on the time and day, the various strains of Bill Haley and the Comets, Marion Lush and the Polka All Stars, or a Chopin polanaise might be heard drifting from our window. Shouts, laughter and cries were also quite common. In usual Slavic style, we were a rather emotional and demonstrative family. Laughter and tears, anger and affection were freely given vent. Unlike most Anglo-Saxons we wept quickly, went quickly from weeping to laughter and back again; we were often headstrong and hasty, sinning, repenting and then sinning and repenting again.

This picture of my home life would be incomplete without mentioning my father whose influence over me in all areas, including ethnicity, has been pervasive. My father was in my youth and remains today a man of tremendous power and crushing charm. A steel worker for forty years, he was part of an all Polish crew of loaders who shipped more steel in an eight-hour turn than any other crew in the history of his plant. Among the many affronts on my identity which I have since suffered, few arouse my rage as much as those which caricature my father and men like him. To his credit, and his disadvantage, his measure of success and worth has always been gauged on his care of his family. There have been times in his life when he should have looked to himself first; but he has steadily, to a fault, refused to do it.

Ethnically, my father was a perfect model. Aware of the numerous cases of discrimination against Polish-Americans both in the steel mills and in other areas of his experience, he, nevertheless, remained quietly but confidently proud of his Polish-American identity and certain of the American dream. There were, however, two things which inevitably provoked his powerful person to wrath and disdain: openly expressed contempt for his Polish identity and the cowardice of Poles who Anglicized their last names. ("If it was good enough for my father, it's good enough for me," was the only justification he felt necessary to settle the matter.) My father's faith in America but equally firm pride of his Polish heritage have more than once been the major consolation in the many battles I have experienced since leaving his house.

A significant benefit of beginning my education at St. Mary Magdalene Grade School was that the attitudes of my teachers and the atmosphere of the school reinforced those of our home. I was, therefore, spared the trauma, not uncommon among ethnic children, of having the values and norms taught at home attacked in school. Here my identity was nurtured both by direct and subtle means.

Although our curriculum and the majority of our texts primarily reflected the Anglo-Saxon culture of America, time was also found to teach us a little about Polish history and to remind us of the numerous Poles and Polish-Americans who helped to make America great. The 1608 arrival of Polish craftsmen in Jamestown (twelve years before the landing of the Pilgrims at Plymouth Rock), the contributions of Kosciuszko and Pulaski to the American victory in the Revolutionary War, and the fatalities of Polish-Americans during World War I were among the bits of information we learned which American education ignores or quickly passes over. . . .

The final constituent part in the composition of my identity was our church. In the days of my youth, every canonical service in which the Catholic Church authorized the use of vernacular languages was available in our parish in both Polish and English. Most often, in fact, Polish was the preferred language. The sermons in four of the seven Sunday Masses offered at our church were in Polish. In addition, our liturgy catered to the feasts, rites, and hymns special to Polish Catholicism which attempts to touch the heart and appeal to the senses as well as satisfy the intellect. From the vantage point of today, it seems outrageous that so many American Catholics still regard this strain of their religion as backwards or ineffectual when the Church of Poland remains the most vibrant, vital and popular brand of Catholicism in the officially atheistic East or secular West — something which Aleksandr Solzhenitsyn has commented on with admiration.

Like so many immigrant churches, our parish was also the center of social life outside the home. And here again the ethnic factor was always at play. Holy Name dances admitted modern tunes; but obereks, krakowiaks, and polkas were more commonly heard. And parish bazaars and carnivals featured the same Polish dishes against which I sometimes rebelled at home.

In short, although I, like all non-WASP children, was aware of a discrepancy between my life and the usual image of American life presented in the media, textbooks, and political speeches, the impact of this realization was greatly reduced for me. All the most important institutions in my life — family, school, and church — reinforced my identity and minimized the conflicts.

All of this changed, however, when I left South Chicago. It was then that the massive assault on my identity began.

Fortunately my initiation was rather gentle. It took place in high school at Quigley, the day school, prep seminary of the Archdiocese of Chicago. It was here that I first encountered people, students and faculty, who saw in my Polish identity reason to hold me in contempt. Needless to say, this was a difficult thing to handle. I was, after all, as good as anyone. I had been taught this, and I confidently believed it. Why did others fail to recognize such an obvious truth? These attacks, however, were not too frequent; and my adolescent mind soon came up with angry retorts which assuaged my damaged pride. Slightly more nebulous, and hence less easy to understand, was my sudden immersion in an Anglo-Irish brand of Catholicism which brooked no compromises.

After graduation from Quigley, I left the seminary system and worked a year to finance my education. It was then up to the University of Wisconsin at Oshkosh. My selection of this particular college was quite deliberate. I knew a girl at Oshkosh — and could afford the tuition. For whatever reasons, perhaps the ethnic makeup of the state and the lower middle-class background of the majority of its students, Oshkosh generated only low key pressure on my identity. There were occasional jokes about my name and put downs about my background, but they didn't affect me too much — and my responses to such encounters were becoming automatic. I thought I had become immune. Nevertheless, it was always something of a relief to return to the steel mills of South Chicago during the summers.

In December of 1964 I married the girl who lured me to Wisconsin; and in January of 1966, one semester after my wife's graduation and one week before the birth of our first child, I received my bachelor's degree. During that spring my wife and I applied to a number of graduate schools. We were both offered and accepted NDEA fellowships to the University of Colorado. After a final five-month stint back in the steel mill, we three — Harriet, our young son and I — set off for Boulder.

Our years at the University of Colorado were beautiful. In addition to our graduate degrees, we picked up two more sons and dozens of close friendships. And in typical ethnic fashion, I cried the day we left the state to move to my first teaching position. It was also, however, during these years that the full fury of this nation's contempt for me broke loose.

The turmoil of the late sixties required a scapegoat, and it was the people of the South Chicagos of the nation who were singled out. Racism, the Vietnamese War, the population explosion, the decay of American cities, and the pollution were the faults of white ethnics. Invariably they were presented in the media or general conversations as unintelligent hardhats who spent most of their time drinking beer, waving the flag, and planning moves to the suburbs to escape black neighbors. Even when they were not being blamed for any social evils, these people were still pictured as ignorant dolts, devoid and probably incapable of any culture.

Initially my reaction was disbelief, but very quickly a deep strain of alienation set in which has never since completely left me. Every component of my identity was under attack. My Polish background pegged me as a member of one of the "historically downtrodden, atavistic, and stagnant races" which Senator Henry Cabot Lodge and others like him opposed admitting into this country. My Catholic religion made my loyalty to America suspect to some and my liberal credentials invalid to others. And my blue collar origins indicated that I was a member of that class of whites who preserve their meager economic and social integrity at the expense of Blacks.

It must be granted that many of my associates were willing to except me from membership among the guilty and benighted. I was, after all, a refugee from the unfortunate circumstances of my birth; or such, at least, was the concession they were willing to make. This, however, only deepened my despair and fueled my rage. Nothing in my background prompted special guilt for America's dilemmas, or shame for my origins or identity. What was inferior about Polish culture? Why should the shortcomings of Catholicism be singled out for peculiar scrutiny? How could the powerless people of South Chicago be blamed for perpetrating such extensive social evils? The reports which I was receiving about my background simply didn't jive with my experiences; and I refused to renounce it.

In the midst of my anger and confusion, help came in a totally unexpected way. While still in graduate school, I was asked to help develop and to teach a course in Black-American literature — a gamble, I assume, based upon my sympathy for the Civil Rights Movement. My acceptance provided an invaluable opportunity to study and learn from the works of Black-American writers ranging from Booker T. Washington to LeRoi Jones. From this came my first meaningful insights into my own status and condition in America.

A recurring and important theme in Black literature is the significance of the past. Writer after writer insists upon the need for a sense of history if one is to properly appreciate the present. Although it now seems so obvious, it had never before dawned on me that an appreciation of history is as vital for Polish-Americans and other ethnics as it is for Blacks.

What were the Partitions of Poland? Where did your family come from? What have you ever done for America? Even with the advantages of my ghetto upbringing, strong sense of family pride, and university training, I was ill-prepared to answer such questions. Polish history was anathema. Many educators, even in South Chicago, feared it would retard assimilation; and others were convinced it contained nothing of value for Western Civilization. The thought of inquiring into the circumstances of my family's immigration never occurred to me, and no one ever volunteered the information. So strong were the prejudices generated by foreign birth that one of my aunts denied her birth in Poland until the day she died. And virtually everything I was ever taught during my higher education about American history was designed to prove that the pilgrim forefathers and their children were responsible for the moral, political, and technological greatness of the nation. No mention was made of any serious contributions by Blacks, immigrants, or foreigners. Furthermore, the hostility of Anglo-Americans — epitomized by the Ku Klux Klan's multifaceted campaigns against "Koons, Kikes, and Katholics" — was conveniently forgotten; instead we were taught the inscription on the Statue of Liberty. Yet the answers to such questions contained the keys to my identity and status. If I was to understand them or expected others to understand, answers had to be found.

Black literature also helped me realize the function of stereotypes and racial-ethnic humor in American society. Blacks are heathen savages who, in Africa, dwelled in poverty and sin. Blacks are naive innocents incapable of caring for themselves. Blacks are vengeful demons menacing our homes and families. These stereotypes have been used during various periods of our history to justify slavery, disenfranchisement, and segregation. Poles are political subversives and enemies of democracy. Poles are racists. Poles are flag-waving patriots. As with stereotyping of Blacks, these images have been used to justify defamation of and discrimination against Poles. It doesn't matter that in both cases the images contradict themselves; the only prerequisite is that they demonstrate the legitimacy, indeed the moral rectitude, of our policies. In light of this, the viciousness of our preoccupation with racial and ethnic humor becomes clear. These jokes supply an endless stream of negative stereotypes about their subjects — stereotypes which by their moronic images deny the very humanity of their victims and allow the majority to feel superior to the minority. Stephen Fetchit [sic] and "the dumb Polack" are the same character whose identity depends on the choice of a victim.

In addition to such intellectualizations, the classroom provided a different type of comfort. Most of my students were Black; and in the evening section many were older — thirty years of age or more. The majority of White students were of lower middle-class origins. These men and women brought to our discussions of the literature in question a wealth of experiences rarely available in a university classroom. Both in class and in the rap sessions which frequently followed, the students, Black and White, revealed backgrounds and insights reminiscent of South Chicago. We didn't always agree; but we did deal with each other and the literature honestly and with mutual respect. The atmosphere was one which made me feel at home. . . .

El Norte: Up from Mexico

IN 1848, THE TREATY of Guadalupe Hidalgo ended the war against Mexico and transferred over one million square miles to the United States. Together with Texas, the area amounted to one-half of Mexico. Suddenly, the border had been moved, and the Mexicans in the "occupied" territory found themselves "thrown among those who were strangers to their language, customs, laws, and habits." Today, most Mexican Americans belong to the migrations that began in the early twentieth century.[1]

To the immigrants from Mexico, the United States was "El Norte." A land across the river, this country became the stuff of boundless dreams for Mexican migrants. In growing numbers during the early twentieth century, they began to cross their northern border. Like the Japanese immigrants who were arriving about the same time, they saw America as a land of opportunity. In the villages and towns where they had been born and expected to live out their lives, they welcomed their brothers and friends returning from the United States. Look, they exclaimed, at their "shoes and good suits of clothes."[2]

In Santa Barbara, California, a Mexican recounted the immigration fever that had swept through entire villages. People wrote to friends and relatives back home: "Come! come! come over it is good here." The news set off a chain reaction that brought "others and others." In this way, just one person had led to the migration of twenty-eight families from his village. A land of promise in the north was beckoning. "Since I was very small I had the idea of going out to know the world, to go about a lot in every direction,"

Jesús Garza recalled. "As I had heard a lot about the United States it was my dream to come here."[3]

Most of the migrants were from the agricultural labor class, and they were predominantly young. Between 1900 and 1930, the Mexican population in the Southwest grew from an estimated 375,000 to 1,160,000; the majority of them had been born in Mexico. The greatest surge occurred during the 1920s, when nearly half a million Mexicans arrived. They settled in Texas, Arizona, New Mexico, and California, and spread as far away as Michigan and Illinois.

> Don't condemn me
> For leaving my country.
> Poverty and necessity
> Are at fault.
> Good-bye, pretty Guanajuato
> The state in which I was born.
> I'm going to the United States
> Far away from you.[4]

The migrants were pulled here by the lure of employment and higher wages. "We left Durango because work was very scarce," Pedro Villamil recalled, "and we were told that one could get good money in the United States and there was work for whoever wanted it." An immigrant worker in California said: "Where I came from I used to work ten hours for $1.25. . . . Then I came here and they paid $1.25 for eight hours — it was good."[5]

Most of the migrants worked in agriculture. In California, farmers turned increasingly to Mexican labor as immigration laws such as the 1908 Gentlemen's Agreement and the 1924 Immigration Act excluded Asian labor. A cotton grower in California's Imperial Valley declared that the farmers needed Mexicans as stoop laborers: "We mean to get Mexicans for the work and get all we need."[6]

Work in the fields was backbreaking. Rosaura Valdez described how much work it took to pick a hundred pounds of cotton: "I'd have a twelve-foot sack, about this wide. I'd tie the sack around my waist and the sack would go between my legs and I'd go on the cotton row, picking cotton and just putting it in there. . . . So when we finally got it filled real good then we would pick up the sack, toss it up on our shoulders, and then I would walk, put it up there on the scale and have it weighed, put in back on my shoulder, climb up a ladder on a wagon and empty that sack in."[7]

Farmwork was seasonal and migratory, with men and women following the crops. Where they would live at any given time was determined by where the jobs were. "We went to Calipatria [California] and the whole family of us engaged in cotton picking," said Anastacio Torres. "When the cotton crop of 1919 was finished we went to Los Angeles and then I got a job as a laborer with a paper manufacturing company. They paid me $3.40 a day for eight hours work. I was at that work for some time and then returned to the Imperial Valley for lemon picking."[8]

Conditions in the migrant labor camps were squalid and degrading. "Shelters were made of almost every conceivable thing — burlap, canvas, palm branches," reported a minister describing a camp in the Imperial Valley. There were no wooden floors, and chicken yards adjoined the shelters. Next to the houses was a huge pile of manure with children tumbling in it as though it were a haystack. "There were flies everywhere. . . . We found one woman carrying water in large milk pails from the irrigation ditch. The water was brown with mud, but we were assured that after it had been allowed to settle that it would be clear and pure. . . . There were no baths." The growers felt no responsibility for the housing conditions or the welfare of their workers. They thought of Mexicans as "here today and elsewhere tomorrow." Commenting on his Mexican laborers, a farmer bluntly stated: "They have finished harvesting my crops, I will kick them out on the country road. My obligation is ended."[9]

When the work disappeared during the Great Depression, nearly half a million Mexicans were "repatriated." But the demand for their labor returned with World War II and has continued to this day.

Searching for a Door to America:
Jesús Garza

In 1931, sociologist Manuel Gamio published a collection of oral histories in The Mexican Immigrant: His Life Story. In these personal accounts, the immigrants described their experiences migrating to El Norte and living here. One of them, Jesús Garza, tells why he liked to return to Mexico but only to visit.

⎯⎯⎯⎯⎯⎯▶ ◀⎯⎯⎯⎯⎯⎯

SINCE I WAS very small I had the idea of going out to know the world, to go about a lot in every direction. As I heard a lot about the United States, it was my dream to come here. . . . I was in school where my father was a teacher but when the revolution came and months went by without their paying him and there was a lot of trouble, my father resigned. He then started a store but I went on in a school where an uncle of mine was a professor. This uncle, however, didn't take much interest in my learning so I quit school and studied at home and helped my father in the store. . . .

When I was about twenty I decided to leave home and come here. I waited one day until my father went out and then I took money out of the strong box, gold coins especially. I took out enough to take me to San Antonio and took the train for Nuevo Laredo. I crossed the border there. I had no trouble, although it was the first time I had come. I paid my $8, passed my examination, then changed my Mexican coins for American money and went to San Antonio, Texas.

When I arrived there, I looked for work but couldn't find any so that I went to [a labor contractor]. They said it was to go and work on the tracks. I didn't know what that was but I contracted to work because my money was giving out. I only had three dollars left. I gave one to the contractor, and he then took me with a lot of Mexicans to a railroad camp.

I worked all day, but as I wasn't used to such a heavy kind of work I thought of leaving. I could hardly finish out working that first day. I thought I was going to die because the work was so hard. At night I asked the boys slyly where Dallas, Texas, was or some other large city and they told me down the tracks and said that if I wanted to go I should catch a freight train and go as a tramp. But I didn't let them suspect anything but told them I was only fooling. I also asked them how one could get there on foot and they said by following the tracks but that one should be careful and cross the bridges in a hurry so that a train wouldn't overtake one. In that part of Texas there are many bridges. On the next day, without their noticing it, I left on foot, and went down the tracks. I left at about seven in the morning and reached the outskirts of Dallas at about six in the evening. It was already getting dark and I only had a dollar with me as I hadn't even gotten my day's pay.

On reaching the outskirts of Dallas, I saw a man who seemed to me to be a Negro and at the same time a Mexican and I thought of speaking to him. As I didn't know English I said to myself, if he is a Negro he isn't going to pay any attention to me. Finally I spoke to him in Spanish and it turned out that he was Mexican, although to tell the truth he looked like a Negro. I told him how I had come and he said that I could spend the night there in his house. He gave me something to eat and a mattress on which to sleep.

On the next day the same man took me to the house of an old man who rented rooms. The old man received me very kindly into his home and gave me a room. When I told him that I didn't have either money or a job he said that I shouldn't worry. I could pay him when I had some. I was there about a month without working and the man and his wife, both of them quite old, took as good care of me as though I was paying them. They gave me food, my room, and even cleaned my clothes. They had some children now grown up.

Finally I managed to get work laying pipes and I was working

243

for two weeks earning $2.50 a day. Then they laid me off because they said that I wasn't strong enough for hard work. . . . Then a Mexican advised me to look for work in the hotels and restaurants because that fitted me, but I couldn't find that, because it is necessary to speak English for those jobs. Then I got a job with an electric company. . . . They wanted me to go down into a well with a pick and make it deeper. I think that it was 20 meters deep and I also had to wheel stones. This work was so hard that I could hardly finish the day, for at about four o'clock in the afternoon the foreman wanted me to lift a rock so big that I couldn't even move it much less lift it. He then said that if I couldn't do that it was better that I quit so that I asked for my time, and they gave me $2.50.

I kept on looking for work and in about three days I found one in a restaurant as "vegetable man" (peeling vegetables). I stayed there about two months and on account of a Mexican who went to tell the manager that I couldn't do that work they fired me. Then I went to another restaurant and hotel and there they gave me a job as dish-washer. I was then learning a little English. When they needed a new "vegetable man," I told the foreman that I could do the work and he gave it to me with an increase in pay. I think that they paid me $45 a month and my food. That boss was an American but very good and he told me that he was going to teach me how to do everything so that when anyone was missing I could take their place. He taught me to be a cook and to do all the work of the kitchen, bake, etc. He even increased my pay until I was getting $75 a month and my food.

By that time I stopped living at the house of the old man of whom I have told you. That was because I don't like to live at the edges of the town. In the outskirts there are no police nor authorities and one can be assaulted and even killed and no one will notice it. But I have remained very thankful to that old man and I told him that I would always be his friend and would go to visit him. I paid the old man there $4 a month but then I found a good friend with whom I took in the downtown district a room for which we paid between the two of us $15 a month, $7.50 each. I worked ten hours a day and he did also. My pal was Mexican and we cared for each other more than brothers. When one didn't have money the other did and we helped each other in everything. . . . Once I told my friend that we should go to Mexico but he said not, because he was in love with a girl who was his sweetheart.

I then told the boss to give me my time. The boss asked me why I wanted to go and if I wanted permission to go he would let me go for two weeks or a month. I then told him that I was going to Mexico to see my people. He answered that if I was going I should know that I always had my job there anytime that I should come back.

I then went to Aguascalientes taking a lot of clothes with me and a little money. I went to my home and my parents were very happy. But I found everything different, very dull, and very changed. I no longer wished to stay there but to return to Dallas. Then without my people knowing it I left again leaving all of my clothes for I only brought what I had on and a little money. I came to Ciudad Juarez and from there I went to El Paso without any trouble. There I sent a telegram to my boss in Dallas. He answered saying that my job was ready for me there.

I was all ready to go to Dallas when some friends told me that Los Angeles was very pretty, that one could earn a lot of money there and a lot of things, so that I took the train to Los Angeles. But as I came on the train I got sick and I decided to stay in Phoenix for I was afraid of getting sicker. As soon as I was well I began to look for work. Earlier I didn't mind being without work for weeks but now I did.

I soon found work at a sanatorium of the city, there in the outskirts. They paid me $65 a month and my board and room but I worked more than 10 hours for as soon as a patient came I had to give him water and food and had a lot of trouble. Once a patient got hard-boiled because I was late with the food. It wasn't my fault for the cook was late. I told him so and he said, "Shut up, Mexican." I then called him "a son of a viche" and he said that he was going to ask to have me fired. I told him all right and then went to the doctor and asked him to give me my time. Then I told him what had happened and he told me not to answer the patients, not to pay any attention to them for they were like children or crazy people and said that the reason why we Mexicans don't get ahead is because we can't get used to staying in one place. I told him to give me my time and that was all, for I wasn't used to have anyone shout at me. He gave me my time but he told me that when I wanted to come back he would give me work.

Then I got a job as a "vegetable-man" but when the boss saw that I knew how to cook and everything he raised my pay to $75 and put me as a cook together with the other cooks who are Americans or Greeks. I am the only Mexican there is in this hotel. The only thing is that here we don't have a day off as there is little business they have a few cooks and they can't substitute very easily. Only once in a while when I ask for rest do they give it to me and put a boy in my place. . . .

I want to go back to Aguascalientes but only to visit and then come back. I have two wool suits in which to go out on the streets and two pairs of shoes, my felt hat for the winter and I buy a straw one in the summer. I also have trousers and shirts to work in the kitchen with. All told I live very happily here. I don't lack anything and I am free. I write very often to my family, especially to a sister who is the one who cares for me most. I send her money once in a while and I also have my savings in the bank for it is better to be foresighted. I would also like to quit being a cook and enter the theater for I think I could work as an artist singing and dancing. That is my ambition, to be an artist.

I have learned a little English on account of all that I have heard and because I have happened to always work with Americans and hearing and speaking English all day but I have never gone to school. . . . A short time ago I received a letter from a friend of mine in Dallas telling me that he had married and that I should go there to live with him and he would get me a girl so that I wouldn't be alone. I am not thinking of getting married now, but if I ever marry it will be with a Mexican even though she be born in the United States. I don't think that an American can care for one like one of one's own blood, nevertheless to have a good time

I like the Americans because they are cleaner. I have been with American prostitutes and nothing has ever happened to me but the other day I went to a Mexican and I got sick with gonorrhea and other social diseases and had to go to the doctor. I won't go back to the Mexicans, it is better for me to go to the Americans.

I am Catholic and although I almost never go to Mass or pray, I do keep Holy Thursday and Friday every year for I am accustomed to do that. At home I was very Catholic but that was on account of my parents.

I haven't learned to cook Mexican style. I only cook American style and I have gotten used to eating American food. Only when I am hungry for it do I go to eat Mexican style in some restaurant in this city. In one of those restaurants I have my sweet-heart. Her mother is the proprietor. My sweet-heart is the waitress but she is very pretty. She is from here in Arizona but she is Mexican.

A Song of El Norte: Camelia Palafox

The migrants from Mexico are usually represented in the mass media as statistics, nameless, faceless, and also voiceless. In his paper based on an oral history completed in an Ethnic Studies course at the University of California, Berkeley, in 1997, Jose Palafox breaks this silence by retelling the life story of his mother. Camelia Palafox crossed the border illegally and worked hard to make El Norte her home. As a young woman, she wanted to become a singer; she never realized this dream. But she succeeded in many other ways. Her life of struggle became her "song."*

E VER SINCE I WAS little I used to tell myself that I would be a singer. I have always loved music. Everywhere there was a party, I used to sing. I wasn't shy at all. Because people always clapped, I assumed I was a good singer. I was twenty-two when I got a job at a local record store in Tijuana, Mexico. While working there, I got to meet many university students. I used to get excited when some of the students who studied theater and art would tell me that I had a good voice. One of them, Mario, asked me: "Wouldn't you like to sing with a university group?" One day he invited me to his university to see his group rehearse. The director of the group saw me and asked me if I wanted to fill a position they needed. He asked me to scream "I hate you!" as loud and as real as possible. So I did. "Perfect," he said. "Come back tomorrow and you can begin rehearsing with us." I was happy that they asked me to join their group. It wasn't a big theater group that was well known or anything. We sang and performed in small clubs in Tijuana and people would pay us whatever they could or wanted. Becoming a professional singer is something I always wanted to be. But working at the record store and performing did not bring in enough money for the family. That is when I decided that work-

* Some of the names have been changed.

ing in the U.S. with my sister Chela was probably the best thing I could do to help out the family financially. I knew that it would mean no more singing and acting, but that wasn't really a choice of my making.

When we lived in Mexicali, Mexico, my mother married Juan. He was very supportive of the family, economically. We were actually well off then. I think it was the physical abuse that led my mother to eventually leave him. He would hit her a lot. We would never see him hitting her, but we would see the bruises afterwards. That's how we came to Tijuana from Mexicali. My mother had heard from friends that living near the border wasn't such a bad idea. There were more jobs and one could cross into San Diego, work in the daytime and return back home with more money. I was born in 1954. By the time I was seven years old, we had moved to Tijuana.

Many things changed when we moved. I remember when we used to play hopscotch at night in the streets of Mexicali. We would also play marbles. I was pretty good at that. I would always beat the boys at that game. Our parents would watch over us as they watered the streets to try and keep the dirt from blowing all over the place. I remember when we first arrived at Tijuana, and we kids didn't have that much space to play like we used to. In Tijuana, one could only play in one's own yard. Eventually we invented our own games with what little room we had. . . .

Once in Tijuana, I started to learn a little bit more English. I had learned a little bit before, but I got much better at speaking it by taking free classes at night. That's where I met Cataro. He was a young painter with the ambition of becoming a professional painter. His main problem was that he was extremely shy. He was a very timid guy. I used to tell him, "Why don't you take your paintings to the malls, banks, universities, and to other places where you can exhibit them. If you want to sell your work, then you have get out there and show it to people." We both supported each other and gave each other hope in our involvement in the arts. He would always tell me that I was a good actor and singer. I would always tell him how beautiful his paintings were. Cataro came from a very poor family but with strong family values. I remember when the theater group couldn't practice at the university one night because somebody else was using [the rehearsal space]. The group asked Cataro if we could rehearse at his place. Cataro had a big space in his backyard and he didn't have a problem with us going there.

Eventually, the theater group toured our state [Baja California Norte, Mexico]. I got a scholarship for being the best actress of all Baja California. The scholarship was a full-paid tuition to study in Mexico City. I remember when I got the scholarship, the theater group director, Professor Orozco, looked at me with a happy and sad face. He was happy for my achievements, but he was upset because he knew that at the time I had my first child, José, and that it would be really hard for me to go. And sure enough, I had to reject the scholarship. It would have been too hard for me to take José with me to a different city.

José's dad, Enrique, at first did not want me to have the baby. I understand we were both young and that we weren't ready for something like this to happen, but what could I do? Enrique wanted me to have an abortion. I was scared because, for one, abortion in Mexico has always been illegal and he wanted me to get an abortion from one of his friends. I didn't tell anyone about my pregnancy. My mom didn't find out until I was six months pregnant. When I did tell her, she was very supportive. I remember her telling me: "How can I not accept what comes from you?" I was eighteen when I had José. Enrique didn't want any responsibilities of being a father. He didn't even bother to try and register José with his last name. Last I heard was that he had remarried and had two girls. Nevertheless, I worked and took care of my son by myself. I don't regret my decision, but I would have liked to have traveled to Mexico City and see many things there.

After I had José, I got a job at a flower store. Later on, I got a job at a local record store. That was my favorite job. I remember when my friend told me that the store was hiring. I got dressed in my best clothes and went for an interview. They asked if I knew English and told them that I did know a little bit. Because nobody else knew any English, I got the job. Also, I knew the hip songs, and all the new bands. Later on, I figured that in order to make more money, I needed to work in the U.S.

I remember what a hassle it was when my sister Chela and I worked in San Diego and had to travel back and forth every day from city to city. At times, it was kind of dangerous. I remember when my mother first got a job in San Diego. She also cleaned houses in the richer part of the city. Taking her to work was always something else. When she first came to the U.S., she always wanted to remember the directions to places according to two things: where the nearest McDonald's was and where the freeway entrances were. She would say, "Yeah, I know where the house is at. It's by the McDonald's." Never wanting to realize just how many different freeways and McDonald's there were all over the city, she insisted that we find the nearest McDonald's, and we would arrive at our destination. Once, on our way to Coronado, an expensive part of San Diego, we had to cross a large bridge, the Coronado Bridge. At the end of the bridge, people had to pay a toll. Well, my sister and I decided to joke with my mother and tell her that we accidentally took the wrong exit and that we were on our way through a U.S. Customs checkpoint. "Stop! Turn around, turn around," she started to scream. We didn't realize how scared she would get. We told her we were just joking and apologized. But the damage was already done. She was crying because she did not have papers and didn't want to get deported back to Mexico.

Chela, the oldest of us, was seventeen when she started working at an egg factory in the U.S. She used to get up at 5:00 A.M. to go to work. It wasn't until she started cleaning houses that I decided to go with her and help. Crossing into San Diego with her passport, she became a little more familiar and confident with the city. At first though, she would cry a lot. She used to get really lonely there. By bringing me with her, I would help her clean the houses faster, and therefore we were able to do many more houses. Cleaning houses for one or two days in San Diego would earn us the same amount of money that we would get if we worked in Tijuana for one whole week.

With that amount of money, I was able to give my mom about eighty dollars a week. That was a lot of money in those days — around 1979, 1980. But in reality, that was not enough money for all of our expenses. Twelve of us lived in our little house in Tijuana. We had to worry about paying for our drinking water, paying for our trash to get picked up, paying for gas, food, utilities; there were many expenses. Also, most importantly, our school uniforms were expensive and every school year we had to worry about buying new ones. Working in San Diego and bringing home dolares [dollars] was one solution.

I think that if it wasn't for Chela first coming to San Diego, helping the rest of the family get jobs here, we wouldn't be where we are. I mean, she was the one that first took the initiative to come all alone, knowing very little English, and hardly knowing anyone in the area. I think she was brave to do something like that. Our family always tried to figure out different ways to survive. Of all my sisters, I was the only one who — for whatever reason — did not get a passport to be able to cross legally into the U.S. I was sad about that. But we always figured out a method to get me to work in San Diego. Most of the time I used my sister Pily's passport. Since we were both short and looked the same, I crossed with that passport for about two years. I never had a problem until one day when they discovered that I wasn't the person I was saying I was.

When Chela and I would cross the border, we usually had dirty laundry with us. We used to make it seem like we were just going to San Ysidro, the U.S. border city north of Tijuana, to wash our clothes and quickly come back. I guess this particular agent, a younger woman, didn't fall for our story and began to ask a lot of questions. We both got really nervous. She began to question me about the person in the passport I had. "This isn't you in the passport, is it?" she asked me. I told her that it was me. She responded by telling me that if I was lying to her, and she found out, she would rip up the passport. She would give me one more chance to tell the truth, or I would have to face the consequences. As stubborn as I was then, I reiterated that I was not lying and that it was my passport. She grabbed my passport, took it to her supervisor and came back and told me that I shouldn't have lied. She grabbed Chela's passport and ripped it up into little pieces for attempting to bring someone across on a false identity. That's when I begged her not to rip up my passport. I lied again and told her that I had grabbed my sister's passport without her permission and that it wasn't her fault. I begged her not to rip up the passport. She saw that Chela was crying. She told me that it was my lucky day because she would not rip it up. She said that she would keep the passport and would hold it until the rightful owner, Pily, would come with her identification and pick it up. Chela and I returned home crying.

Pily eventually got her passport back, but Chela would now have to figure out a new way to cross, without a passport of course. I always had the illusion of having my own passport and not having to be nervous about being caught without papers. Eventually we figured out ways to get across. Most of the time we crossed as "U.S. citizens." We had learned a little English while in Tijuana from watching TV and listening to the radio. We also learned English from a neighbor in Tijuana who had family in the U.S. Little by little, we learned enough English to get by.

Cleaning houses in San Diego was hard work. It was good money, but sometimes the people we worked for tried to take advantage of us. Once, I cleaned a house all by myself. I cleaned the kitchen, washed clothes, swept the floor, cleaned the windows; I even fixed the yard to make it look better. After I was done, the owner of the house, an older white lady, said she was going to give me fifteen dollars, but because she paid taxes, she would only give me twelve dollars and fifty cents. Can you imagine?! I clearly remember walking home crying. But what could I do? She said she always paid taxes, but she didn't bother to ask for a Social Security number from me. I thought that that was just the way it was here. And even if I wanted to say anything, what would I say? Anyway, I spoke very little English. I took the money and never said anything to her.

About that time, Chela and I started working as waitresses in a Mexican owned restaurant in San Diego, El Poste. With two jobs, we could send more money home to our kids. I was always ashamed of having to work as a waitress there. Maybe because it was such a drastic change from hanging out with university students and musicians to hanging out with old, drunk men who constantly harassed the women at work. I felt ashamed that just because we were waitresses, most of the men felt they could make us do anything they wanted us to do. I didn't want my friends in Tijuana to find out that I worked in San Diego as a waitress. I also didn't like to wear our work uniform. It consisted of a very short mini-skirt. It was uncomfortable.

Most of the customers there were Mexican. That is where I met my second husband, Octavio. Like many of the other customers at the restaurant, Octavio had no papers. Every once in a while *la migra* [the INS] would arrest a bus load of undocumented people. Sometimes they would go undercover and check out the scene. Next thing you knew, people were running all over the place. I was lucky because most of the time when they came, I was either off work or was on the way there. I think it was pure luck that I didn't get apprehended by the INS like some of my co-workers. I remember when we would ask each other at work: "What happened to so and so? What happened to his sister? Why didn't she come back to work?" We just assumed that the INS got them or something. We hoped that they would come back the next day.

I felt ashamed that I didn't have papers. I felt inferior. Even just to go to the store, I was scared to ask for stuff. Instead, I would ask somebody else to ask for me. I thought that if people found out that I didn't speak English, that they would know I didn't have papers. I was scared that I would get put in a van with other people. I felt like we would get treated like animals, as if we were the dogs, and they [INS] were the dogcatchers. I don't know, maybe I thought the INS was everywhere because I looked out for them a lot. Still, I think that even if one is undocumented, they should have rights and not have to be scared all the time. It shouldn't matter if one is legal or illegal, in the end they are human beings and should be treated as such.

Because the owners at my job were Mexicans, they would try

and help their fellow countrymen as much as possible. One thing that really helped us was that the owner would cash our checks. Since most of us didn't have bank accounts, it was hard to cash our checks. Our boss was good to us most of the time. But, sometimes the manager, Gilbert, would keep extra funds away from us workers. For example, when we got "bonuses" from work, he would pocket some of the money for himself and would never tell us about what was supposed to be given to us. Just because many of us didn't speak English or had no documentation to prove our U.S. citizenship, didn't mean he could do what he did. About ninety percent of the people that cleaned the building were Mexican and the other percentage, mostly white, worked at the main office. Most of us Mexicans needed all the money we could get. Most of us had to support families in the U.S. and Mexico.

Because we would get off of work so late from working at the restaurant, sometimes we would drive back home to Tijuana at around 3:30 A.M. I knew that it was dangerous for two women to be driving around that time. One night, on our way home after work, our car broke down on the freeway. We were terrified. What were we supposed to do? We couldn't call anyone. Everything was closed since it was so late. One young guy stopped and offered to help us. I think he was a gang member. Chela, being the oldest, decided that I should return back to Tijuana and she would stay close by at a friend's house. We asked him if he could give me a ride to the border and drop Chela at her friend's house. He helped us with our stuff and drove us to where we needed to go. He was a good kid. We ran many risks like that at first, but that's what happened to a lot of people who had just moved here.

It wasn't until 1979 that I decided that it was time to try and bring my son, José (who was five years old), to the U.S. I missed him a lot. Around that time, Chela, Octavio, two of his friends, and I were living in a small apartment. We lived very crammed and could barely fit. We had planned on waiting to get a bigger house before we would bring any more of our family members. I couldn't wait. The only time I saw José was on the weekends when I would go to Tijuana and visit him. It was luck that a friend's husband was able to cross him as a U.S. citizen with no problems at all. For my other three brothers, crossing ended up being a little harder. My two younger brothers, Miguel and Gerardo, nearly got lost crossing the desert. It makes me cry just to think about it. Sergio, he was another story. Whenever he would try and cross at the port of entry, he was always scared to even try, and crossing through the mountains or any other place, he would always get caught. And every time he was asked by the authorities to give his name, he would say: "José Luis Rodriguez," "Camilo Cesto," "José José," etc., all names of famous Mexican singers.

By the time José came to the U.S., I was working more at home. I mostly stayed at home feeding the kids and watching over them. I would get seven dollars for each kid that I took care of. José had started going to elementary school. Sometimes he would come home and ask me why all professors were named "teachers." Another time he told me in Spanish that they had a prostituta [prostitute] at school. I couldn't believe it! I thought that maybe it was some sort of sex education thing or something. I still thought they were too young to be learning about these things though. I later learned that what he meant was that a substituta [substitute] had come to his class for that day.

I tried not to go out as much because of fear of being apprehended by the INS. I always remembered that Octavio had been deported at least eight times. They would chase him a lot. I didn't want the same to happen to me. Especially since I was beginning to get settled with my son, and I was pregnant with my second child, Mariana. I knew things were rough for all of us immigrants, but I think male immigrants had it especially difficult. I think it is because for us women immigrants, we could stay at people's houses. This is what I did when I cleaned houses. Sometimes I would spend the night at the owner's house. For immigrant men, it would be a little harder for Americans to do this and feel safe. Sometimes when Chela and I responded to ads in the paper about house cleaning, some of the owners, mostly men, wanted other things and not really house cleaning. Unless they were the regular people we cleaned for, we never knew what kind of people they would be. We came across many sick people.

At times, when Chela and I would see other undocumented people on the street, we tried to help them as much as we could. Once, we picked up some *Salvadoreños* from the street and took them to our house. There, we let them phone their families in Los Angeles to let them know they were OK. Since Chela knew how to cut hair, she gave them a haircut. We gave them more American looking clothes with lighter colors and hats with American logos like Nike. They also took our advice and got some sunglasses for the ride up to Los Angeles. They looked so different after we changed their appearance. Ever since we helped them, their mother has been so grateful to us. She calls us all the time to thank us. It felt good to help them.

Now that I'm a U.S. citizen, I feel a little safer because I know things are only going to get worse in the future for undocumented immigrants and minorities. Also, as a U.S. citizen, one can vote and have their voice be heard. I think it's really important for Latinos to get their citizenship and be able to vote. I'm really proud that I've never had to get handouts from the government. I'm glad I never had to get on welfare or anything like that. But now that I'm more conscious of my aging, I realize the importance of getting my U.S. citizenship just in case I might need something in the future. I also got José to get his U.S. citizenship. Since my other three daughters were born here, the only ones I worry about now are Octavio and my mother. Hopefully they can fix their papers soon.

I often think about how some Americans think that too many Mexicans have come to the U.S. They say that we should go back. But go back to where? I tell them that no matter how many border police they put at the border, the people will come because of the necessity. The necessity is far too much and people need to survive. And the truth is that the Anglos were the ones to come from Europe, and then they took this land. So who are the real Americans? I'm not afraid to tell them this.

Since I currently work at a retirement home for elderly folks, I have witnessed how some of the older immigrants are being treated. With the new laws, the government is cutting their monthly payments. Many can't buy their medicine anymore. Many talk openly about suicide. It's a shame that our government doesn't see their humanity. They just see them as numbers. Where will they go when they get kicked out of the home? The management at work has not made things easier for them either. Since many of the immigrants' only source was Medicare and S.S.I., many who have lost this are now being replaced with older people who have an insurance that will pay for their stay at the retirement home.

If these old people worked for thirty-five years of their lives, there must be some way to accommodate them. It's a matter of priorities. They also worked and paid taxes all their lives. Why must this change come? What our government is doing now is really bad. I mean, I love this country because of all the good things it has done for me and my family. I never really had the oppportunity to continue school in Mexico. I went only to sixth grade. I wanted to finish my education and maybe get a better career. I would have liked to have been a lawyer. I've always liked helping people. But, because we had to start work at such a young age to support the family, we never really got the chance for a better career. Another thing was that, because of the large size of our family, we had to work more and study less.

What I really like about my new job is that I'm helping others. I love doing that. I come home from work, and I feel good because I know I did something to help somebody. It's almost like being a social worker. I'm not only helping people in need by feeding them, but I'm also helping them spiritually. We are helping them get connected with reality. By reading them the paper, by telling them personal stories, anecdotes, all of this brings more life into their lives. They are so attentive to everything that one is telling them. Even to the clothes that one is wearing. Sometimes they tell me: "Oh, Camelia, your earrings match with your shoes." "Camelia, you look really good today!" I'm really happy at my job. I'd like to stay there for a while.

When I found out that my son had been accepted to UC Berkeley, I was really happy. This was something that I had always wanted: an opportunity to go to a university. At first, I was a little scared about my son going to another city. I was scared that he would change. I thought that he would think differently of his family. Also, he was going to another city! I didn't even know what the weather was like there. Besides going to Los Angeles once, I had never traveled outside of San Diego. Until I visited him in Berkeley for the first time, I realized that yes, he was in another house, living with other people, but I knew our house in San Diego would always be his first house.

At first, I really didn't see how serious José took his studies. To me, he looked so busy and happy just the way he was. He played music and was heavily involved with political groups. I remember when he was first arrested at a protest in 1991. They were protesting an INS detention center in Los Angeles. I was terrified to think of him being in jail. But, worst of all, I worried about him getting blacklisted and never being able to fix his papers. After going to court, I realized that, compared to some of the other kids who had gotten arrested for other things, I didn't feel so bad because what he had done was not for personal reasons, but for the benefit of his people, for us.

My other three daughters, Mariana, Angela, and Marlene, are still in school. But I don't think they put as much emphasis on school as they should. I know that Marlene, the youngest of all three, will someday have a good career. As a mother, I can tell the go-getters from the lazy ones. All three are very intelligent. Mariana, the oldest, also helps me a lot financially. Sometimes after school, she helps me clean houses, and we get them done earlier. I would like them to go to college but I can only pressure them so much.

I want them to study hard now so they won't have to work in the same manner that I do. An important aspect in giving my children a better chance in life was enrolling them at good elementary schools. When I enrolled José at Spreckless Elementary, we had to wake up at 6:00 A.M. every day to catch the school bus. The school was very far away from where we lived but, I knew that if I enrolled him in the schools around our neighborhood, José would not suc-ceed. I remember looking at the schools around our neighborhood and noticing that they had no computers, no new books, and also it just seemed that some of the teachers didn't care about the future of the kids. Nevertheless, giving my children an opportunity at a good education is something I have always fought for.

I know how important it is to get a degree to get anywhere in this country. Even for my job, I had to take special classes, go to school for seventy-two hours and pass a test. I did not think I would pass the test. I understood the questions, but I couldn't write the answers in English. So what I did was tell the person that was giving the test my situation. She told me not to worry. She said that she would help me. She was Filipino. She suggested that I write the answers in Spanish and that she would later translate them. I don't think she ever translated them. Nevertheless, I passed the test. I was happy because I could now work at a retirement home. This is a better job. There are a lot more benefits than I had ever had working anywhere else.

Sometimes I wonder what the future has in store for us. I think of my family, and I see that we have lived a good life. I have my mother living with us in the U.S. My kids are in school. I have a good job. Besides his drinking problem, Octavio is a good man. He is a quiet man — except when he drinks. I don't know how long we will live together. What can I say? I think it might have something to do with his background. He is from Tuxpan, Nayarit. The culture, the customs from people of southern Mexico are a lot more conservative than from the border region. The men there are more machistas. I don't blame him for that, but, what really gets me is that men there start to drink alcohol at such a young age.

I know Octavio has been drinking all his life, but our hard life in the U.S. has only made him drink more. I stopped counting how many times he was arrested and put in jail for his drinking problems. I know that he is very bitter and angry at this country. He feels repressed here. He always talks about going back to his little town in Tuxpan, Nayarit. Physically, he is also hurt. He once lifted some heavy equipment at work and ever since then, his back

hurts. The doctors tell him it's permanent. The lawyer that supposedly helped us only got Octavio ten thousand dollars and then he
took like four thousand dollars for expenses. After we paid for old
bills that had accumulated, we were left with three thousand dollars. Can you imagine having your back messed up for the rest of
your life, getting fired, and then you are given three thousand dollars to start all over? This is why he drinks a lot. He drinks to ease
the pain and anger he has. But, I should say that he has given our
family a house to live in. He has given me three healthy and beautiful girls. I see that many people — including many Anglos — are
trying to get housing. There are many homeless people struggling
out there, trying to survive. I am very thankful for what we have.

At times I wonder what would have happened if I were to have
accepted the scholarship to study in Mexico City when I was
younger. Sometimes I get sad to think of all the hard work that I
have done for others. What about me? I too would have liked to
travel, continue singing, read, and just do things for me. I don't
regret anything, I just feel like I'm getting old and I want to experience other things in life besides work and work. I have faith that
things will be better. One has to always have hopes, or else they
won't get anything done. That's how I see life.

Twice a Minority: María Jiménez
Joins the Army

In an interview published in Mexican Voices / American Dreams: An Oral
History of Mexican Immigration to the United States, *by Marilyn P.
Davis, María Jiménez tells what it is like to be a minority and also a woman in
the U.S. military. Impressively, she is a mother, too.*

I'M NUMBER SIX CHILD. There's nine living. My mother had
twelve children. There were six girls and six boys, if everybody
had lived, which would have been a lot of fun.

Oh heck, it was fun growing up. I always had fun. We would,
oh God, my sister was a good schemer. We used to do all sorts
of stuff. My mother would go grocery shopping once a week. And
when my sister was old enough Mom left her in charge of all of
us. The grocery store was an all-day event. It probably took my
folks about an hour or an hour and fifteen minutes to get over there
and then another hour and fifteen minutes back. To say nothing of
the time they spent at the store. And I'm sure they wanted to sneak
a moment to themselves also. I remember they'd be gone the better
part of the day. So my sister — we would do all sorts of things
to the house — but she had us all so under control.

One time we cleared out all the furniture in the living room,
moved it up against one wall. And the house was set up so that it
was kind of like a rectangle. The living room had three doors: the
front door coming to it, a door that led into one of the bedrooms,
and a door that led into the kitchen. Then there was a bedroom,
another bedroom, and the kitchen. They all had connecting doors.
No hallway, just all connecting doors. So we moved all the furniture to one side of the living room, pulled the mattresses off the
beds, put them in the living room, had all the pillows, all the blan-

kets, the whole living room was just padded. And we'd get up and run around the house, get to the beginning of the mattresses, do flips, get up and run around the house again, do flips, and we did this for hours. We did different flips, and by the time everybody got to do two or three turns, you had a good half hour there.

Then my sister had it timed, I mean, almost exactly. She said, "Okay, that's it." Everybody cooperated and put everything back away and folded everything back up, put the furniture back, cleaned it all off, and when my mom would show up we'd all just be, you know, sitting around waiting. We'd all run out and help bring the groceries in.

I don't know how it was for my sisters, the older ones, but I remember this distinctly. I received a comprehensive English lesson the summer before I started school. We were all in the driveway, it wasn't paved and my sister had a stick, and she kept writing words out for me and telling me what they were. She was teaching me everything I knew in Spanish in English, in one summer, trying to get me to the point where I knew most of my vocabulary in English. I don't know why they did such a comprehensive lesson on me. They probably said, "She's not going through what we went through." So, anything my sisters did for me, I did for my brother, and then my brother would do for my older brother, and it just kind of went all the way down the line.

Okay, the school that I went to nobody ever talked about college. I didn't know what a college was. See, I didn't go to high school in the same town I went to elementary school, because they didn't have a high school in my home town. I had to go ten miles to go to high school. That's when I started hearing about college and college and college. So you go from an environment like that to a university in a class of 400 or 500 people in the auditorium and you look around and you're the only nonwhite in the whole room. You're the only nonwhite. My God!

We were migrant workers. When we went up north we were minorities, but for some reason we never even saw blacks. We always ended up in these little rural areas where it was all white.

Everybody went. That was fun, except you work your butt off.

You think about it now and say, "Jesus Christ, how did we get eleven people in the station wagon with clothes for everybody?" Blankets, work clothes, church clothes, one set for church and three sets to go to work, and then you could take a couple of pair of shorts, and then you had to take plates and spoons and silverware and glasses and pots and pans and everything that you needed.

When we stayed in Michigan it was what you call un campo, which is all migrant workers. They assign you a little house. It's kind of like a little wood-frame, one-room thing. You have the kitchen/living room area, then a half wall like a T with one sleeping area and another one behind it. And it's Army bunk beds. We had four bunks, and my dad and brother slept in the car. I think they did that just to get away from everybody.

You had to take everything that you needed, all of that in a station wagon. I don't know how we did it, I really don't. I try and picture what it looked like to somebody else, seeing this car, fully loaded with Mexicans, rack on the top, riding low. That's where all the jokes come from.

My dad was the kind of man who was rarely around. As a matter of fact, I have very few memories of him before the eighth grade. Then it was only because we used to get into arguments. But when I was a kid I could name on one hand the memories I have of him. He was always working. I don't blame him, he had a lot of pressure. He had a lot of kids.

But since I started noticing it, my mom and dad's relationship has always seemed rather rocky. Consequently, he stayed out a lot. He's your typical Mexican male, I'm going out with the boys and you stay home with the kids. She dresses him so he can go out. I guess if you grew up with the mentality to put up with something like that, you can. He got past that, but it took a few years.

My mother used to come in our room; the girls slept in one room and the boys in another. She would come in right before lights out and talk to us. "Don't let what's happening to me happen to you all." Her talks got really intense once my sisters started dating. "Don't let him go out and you don't know where he is, and you don't know how to drive, and one of your kids is sick and you don't know how to get them to the hospital." Let's see, I must have been about ten or eleven when I started hearing this. Like nightly.

Well like I said, I didn't know what college was. And it was really weird because you don't want to say, "What's that?" People are going to say, "Where did she come from, the moon?" You don't want to ask questions but you want to find out. So you pull your ear when people are talking about it. But then my sister graduated from Pan Am [Pan American College]. So okay, that's what college is. Then when my sister Virginia went to UT, we went to drop her off and I said, "Wow!" You know, her dorm and Texas stadium. We walked around a little bit and everybody was like, "This is all right!" I thought, "I could get used to this sort of thing."

When I finished high school I got a full-time job. That was when I decided I didn't want to be a secretary. This was the pits, data entry. There were ladies there, like our supervisor, a woman in her fifties, making like maybe $200 more than we were. She had been there forever. Extremely boring.

After doing that for almost a year, my sister called me. "What are you doing with your life? You want to move to Austin?"

I said, "Sure."

So I went up there in September, got a job, night shift, five o'clock to one, computer, CIT data entry work.

So my sister says, "Well, as long as you're here, do you want to go to school?"

"I don't know." I didn't know what the hell I was doing, so I decided to talk to an admissions counselor.

The guy was from El Paso. I walked in and he said, "Where you from?"

"The Valley."

"All right!" and we started talking in Spanish. We had a good time just talking. He said, "Well, you want to come to school?"

"I don't know. I don't know if I'd fit in here."

He says, "Ah, don't worry about it. After a while you'll feel like this is home. Listen, give it a chance." He was really good. "Have you taken the SAT? Why don't you take it, there's one coming up in November; you can have your results by December. If you make it you can start in January. Take the test. What have you got to lose?"

"OK, I'll take the test."

He told me to call him as soon as I got the results and we'd see. When I called him he says, "That's great! You really scored that high? That's a great score, you're in."

This is someone that came from a town of 1,250 people. It was like, my God! Here I am, a little speck of dust in the middle of this whole thing. So I started, I was learning something for a change, and I just kept on going. I went straight through, every summer, every fall, every spring. I worked like crazy to make it through. Working fifty-seven hours a week plus taking twelve hours of college, I remember thinking, "When the hell am I going to sleep?"

I majored in accounting. I had wanted to go into dental, but after my first biology class I said, "This isn't going to work." I didn't have the science background to compete. The projected job market said accountants were going to be in need for the next ten to fifteen years. It was a logical major.

Anyway, everybody was graduating but I didn't want to do what everybody was doing. Friends that had graduated with my sister would come back into town and you could tell they were miserable. They hated it, nine to five, fight the traffic in the morning, fight the traffic in the afternoon. It didn't appeal.

The military was something I wanted to do when I was in high school, since my junior year when I got an offer from the air force academy. But my parents didn't let me accept. The reason I've stayed in is because I liked it. The money is not that great. People that graduated with me are doing a lot better in the private sector. There's pros and cons to everything. It's longer hours. It's not a nine to five job. That's what I like about it.

You can be a minority twice over in the military and you can be a minority twice over in the private sector; you're still a minority. I mean what are females going through in the private sector? They do the same job as a male and they get paid less. Here, in the military, I'm a female, I do this job, I have a counterpart, same rate, same time and service as I am, he's a male. We get paid the same. He has the same benefits as I do.

I have always been rather realistic, I guess. If you can tell me what you expect out of me I will do it. As long as the goals you're setting for me are within reach, even if I have to work my butt off to do it, I will do it. But if you tell me I have to do something that I know there is no way I can do it, then that's where my motivation just completely goes down the drain. Rarely do you ever get that kind of request in the military. You might think you can't do it, but you can. Like if somebody had told me I would be rappeling off of a twenty-foot tower, I'd say, "Ha!" But once I got in there and saw how it was I said, "Hey, this actually looks like fun." You start feeling more confident and the next thing you know you're coming down that thing and, "Can I go again?" Which I did. It builds a lot of confidence. If you had told me six years ago that I was going to run four miles: "In your dreams, I can hardly run one."

My problem was expressing myself, not on paper, not one-to-one, but in front of twenty, thirty, or more people. And now, hey, that's no biggie. I'll get up in front of an auditorium. I teach army stuff. The latest class that I've taught was the M18 A1 claymore mine. It's an antipersonnel mine. There are certain things that every soldier needs to know how to do. Once a year you get tested on the stuff. And the one thing that everybody messes up on is the claymore mine. There are so many little steps, and if you do one step before you do the other step you could blow yourself up. That's why it's graded so strictly. I did the grading. I taught the class.

A lot of the other classes were much faster. They called me in on it. I told them, "You want me to do it? You want me to do it right? It's going to take time. I can be out here two days, I don't care if that's what it's going to take." You'd be amazed at how many people didn't know the claymore and had been in the service for six or seven years. They were supposed to learn this way back in basic. I felt great because the people that I taught did really well.

267

People actually noticed. The head guy said, "Hey, you know what y'all doing, givin' your own guys the grades or something." It was like, oh no, you got a female teaching something that has to do with infantry.

Being in the army made a difference when I had my children. I was working at the club when I had my first child, so I wore civilian clothes. When I got to the point where I couldn't deal with sixteen-hour days anymore, my boss changed my schedule. I'd come in at ten o'clock and leave at five. Then I'd get my time off to go to the doctor, and if I really felt bad I'd call in. That was accepted. But it wasn't until the last month that I got so huge. It was waddle, waddle, waddle. But up until then I was working days, nights, everything. In the kitchen I always had my snacks, and they made sure I got my vegetables.

I liked my doctor too. Same doctor for both kids. I liked her, we talked all hours. But I've always been fighting not to be typical and what do I come up with? A boy and a girl. That's it. That's all I want.

I'm going to be in Georgia for nine months! Nine months! The whole reason for me getting out of the enlisted side of the house is that I don't feel I'm being fully utilized. I want something more challenging and believe me, Officer's Candidate School is going to be a challenge.

I keep telling myself it's worth it. It was a hard decision. Oh my God, we went back and forth about it for six months, before I finally decided. My husband is supportive though. He's not your typical Mexican.

My husband is taking care of the kids. They are moving to Austin to stay with our family. He will take care of them for this next nine months, and when we find out where we will be stationed it will be his turn. He wants to go back to school. My little boy needs to be in preschool because of what he's going to be up against as far as what the other kids know once he does get to school. See, he's never been in an environment where there's been more than two other kids. He doesn't know how to socialize. He knows about sharing with his sister, but now this will give him a chance.

I just don't want them to be spoiled. I saw a lot of kids that just wasted their parents' money. Spoiled rotten. Parents paying another semester's tuition and they're spending their time at the lake, drinking. I want to make sure I can help them, but I don't want them to end up taking everything for granted. I don't have a plan yet to achieve that goal, but that's what I want.

Beyond Ellis Island: The Italians

———▶ ◀———

"MOST ITALIANS REMAIN in the United States from two to five years," reported Victor Von Borosini in "Home-Going Italians," published in a 1912 issue of *Survey*. Between 1900 and 1920, 3 million immigrants from Italy arrived. Many of them were sojourners. Their plan was to make money and then go back to their villages. The rate of return migration for Italians was 50 percent. But, after the 1924 National Origins Act restricted further immigration from Italy, many of them became settlers, making homes in their adopted land. Still, as Catholics and Southern Europeans, these immigrants found that mainstream society did not always accept them into the "melting pot."[1]

Italian immigrants experienced ugly stereotyping. "You don't call . . . an Italian a white man?" a construction boss was asked. "No, sir," he answered, "an Italian is a Dago." They were said to be criminally inclined and violent. "The knife with which he [the Italian] cuts his bread," a prison authority commented, "he also uses to lop off another 'dago's' finger or ear. . . . He is quite as familiar with the sight of human blood as with the sight of the food he eats." Italian workers also found themselves restricted in employment opportunities. The Bricklayers' Union of New York, for example, successfully pressured the city to exclude unnaturalized Italian immigrants from working on the construction of the subways.[2]

Italian Americans were rudely taught the lesson of their marginality during World War II, when the United States was at war with Japan, Germany, and Italy. Shortly after the attack on Pearl Harbor, the military and policymakers questioned the loyalty of Italian Americans. In February of 1942, government authorities identified about ten thousand Italian immigrants who had not become naturalized citizens as "enemy" aliens and excluded them from specified restricted zones in the West Coast for reasons of "military necessity." Four months later, this policy of restriction was rescinded, and on October 12, the government announced that Italian aliens would no longer be classified as "enemies." In San Francisco, one Italian remarked scornfully about how he had suddenly become an American again. While California's attorney general Earl Warren urged a congressional committee to evacuate and intern Japanese Americans, he advocated the removal of the restriction aimed at Italian immigrants. Italians, he observed, were just like everybody else: they were Americans.[3]

But to be "American" presented dilemmas and challenges for many of these immigrants and Italians born here. Did becoming and being American mean breaking from ties to Italy? What did it mean to grow up as children of immigrant parents?

Growing Up Between Two Worlds: Joanna Dorio

Earlier we examined the intergenerational tensions between a Chinese father and his American-born daughter. Here Joanna Dorio gives an account of her experiences in an interview published in 1991 in Grandmothers, Mothers and Daughters, *a book edited by Corrine Azen Krause. College educated, Dorio became a teacher and the head of a modern language department, but she was still unmarried. Growing up in a traditional family, her parents had restricted her social life. Her father, she says, did not understand that in America dating was usually the way to find a marriage partner. In this story, Dorio tells how, at age thirty-five, she finally worked out this problem with her father.*

I WAS BORN IN Pittsburgh on August 4, 1931. We lived on the North Side in Pittsburgh, and we had an eighteen-room house. In that house there were three families — our family, my father's brother and his family, my father's sister and her family — and each of us had six rooms. Twelve children were raised very much like brothers and sisters rather than cousins, and we all shared everything in that house.

Each family had its own kitchen, and each family ate in its own home. But the great thing about that was if you didn't like what was served at your house, you could always run upstairs or go to the front of the house and have dinner with the other family and find maybe you liked what they were having better. The mothers shared laundry facilities, and, of course, the mothers helped each other raising the children. There were always baby-sitters available, because we could always count on one of our aunts to baby-sit if our parents had to go somewhere.

In our immediate family I had three brothers, two of them older than I, and I had one brother that was younger. There was a big difference in the way boys and girls were treated. There was definitely that idea that a girl is different than a boy, and I remember many times being upset about something and my mother would say, "Well, remember now, they're boys and you are a girl, and they can do things that you are not allowed to do." This used to make me so angry because I never could understand what difference it made, but these were the rules.

Our business was behind our home while we were growing up and through my high school years. So my father was always there: my mother served as his secretary. My mother worked very hard. She would take care of the house during the day. She would have to stop her housework to do typing for him, and in the evening she would spend hours and hours at the typewriter plus taking care of us. We were never neglected. She did all the cooking and so on, so my mother worked very hard. My father would run back and forth from the factory to the office, which was in our home, so we saw him all the time. He had breakfast, lunch, and dinner with us.

My father was the "godfather" of the family. His brother never seemed to make it in business. His sister was divorced, and in those days Italian women did not go out to work, so her family was my dad's responsibility. He was a real disciplinarian. He was born in Italy, and he had many old-world ideas which my mother, who was born here, did not have. For example, I was not permitted to go to girl-boy parties, and I was not permitted to date alone until I was twenty years old. . . .

I was very proud of being an Italian, and I loved the Italian customs. However, many times when I would be shopping with my parents, I would be very embarrassed when they would speak Italian. I remember turning to my mother and saying, "Speak English. We are in the United States. I don't want you to speak Italian when we are outside the home." I would be very embarrassed about it. I guess that I always felt between two worlds, because many of my friends didn't come from a foreign family as directly as I did, so that they were in my eyes more American than I was.

I wanted to be very American, but I didn't want to lose my Italian heritage either.

When I was in high school, I wasn't even allowed to go ice skating or roller skating, because boys were there and you just didn't go where boys were. I remember I had to go to the movies with my parents, and even in the movies it was always very funny, because my father always made sure that I sat between him and my mother. At sixteen, when you are still going to the movies with your parents, it can be a little bit embarrassing, but this is the way he wanted it and this is how we did it. I did most things with girls. He never objected to having my friends over, and he never objected to my going to my girlfriends' homes. However, anything that involved boys was strictly out.

I went to a public elementary school. Then in ninth grade I went to Our Lady of Mercy Academy. There were restrictions in school too. They were just as bad as my father in those days, what with the uniform, and "Don't roll up your sleeves!" "Don't wear lipstick!" "Don't smoke!" They always had a student council member on every streetcar to give you demerits if they found you with lipstick while in uniform, because that would be a disgrace to the uniform.

I never was allowed to work, and I wanted to work in the worst way. I remember at the academy, they asked the girls to serve as volunteer ushers at the Syria Mosque [concert hall]. I wanted to do that because I loved the opera and I loved the symphony, and I thought this was a good way to see it for nothing. But I was not permitted to take that job, because no daughter of his was going to work! Even though this was volunteer work, it was work away from home among strangers.

I was not permitted to go to my prom, and that really crushed me. I wanted to go so badly that I developed a fever over it, and I was in bed for three days. I remember when I was so sick my dad came in and said to me, "If you get better," and I thought he was going to say, "you can go to the prom," but he said "If you get better, I'll take you out and buy you a whole outfit — purse, shoes, dress, the whole thing." And of course that is not what I wanted to hear. No, he didn't give in.

I was afraid to think of going against his wishes. I will tell you why I was afraid to. My cousins would sneak behind their parents' back and meet fellows on the side, and they were caught. I remember a friend of the family saw one girl with a boy and told the parents, and I always laughed, because any problem that arose with the children, it was like the "Big Five" would meet. I remember walking in and finding my father, my mother, my uncle, and my two aunts sitting in the living room and my cousin standing in the center of the living room. It was like the Inquisition: "What were you doing? Where were you? Where did you meet him? Why did you go behind our backs?" They were all so involved in this discipline, and I think that so frightened me that I did not dare go against their wishes.

My father wanted all of us to have a college education. He was very impressed with the fact that a person had a college education, and I suppose that was because he did not have one, so that from when we were children, he would say, "When you go to college, when you go to college." So I grew up knowing I was going to go to college. However, when it came to deciding on a profession, yes, there was a difference. He was delighted when he heard I wanted to be a teacher, but when he heard that I was minoring in sociology, and that might involve being a social worker, he did not approve at all. No daughter of his was going into the slums and into homes where people don't live right!

I was the first girl and the only girl of all the cousins that went to college. I remember my aunt didn't really approve, and, you know, in those days if you went to college, you were drinking, you were smoking, carousing, and everything else. That was their interpretation of girls that went to college. But my mother and father overlooked all this because they wanted me to have that education.

At that point I wanted to go to a coeducational college, but my dad said, "If you want to go to college, you have to go to Mount Mercy College." I had no choice. It had to be an all-girls school and had to be close to home. I had to commute — I was not permitted to board — and I wanted it so badly that I accepted.

I got a fine liberal arts education at Mount Mercy, but it was a disappointment to me. At the time I was thinking in terms of Maryland University or one of the Big Ten universities, but that was out.

My brothers were going to Carnegie Tech at that time, and they took me to one of their fraternity picnics, and at the picnic two of their fraternity brothers asked me to attend a fraternity dance with them. So I went over to my brothers and I said, "I have just been asked by so-and-so to go to the dinner dance," and my brothers said, "Do you want to go?" I said, "I would love to go"; I could hardly imagine going to a fraternity dance! They said, "Okay, then, you're going with Charlie." I said, "Well, how do you know I want to go with Charlie?" They decided: "You go with Charlie." I said, "I don't know why we're even discussing it. I won't be allowed to go anyway." My oldest brother said, "Let me handle it."

I remember that when we got home, my brother said, "You go to your room and I'll talk to Dad." I heard loud voices in the living room and my dad saying, "No, she will not go," and my brothers saying, "Well, we're going to be there." My brother was dating steadily at the time the girl he finally married. Finally my dad said I could go if my brother and his girlfriend drove me to the dance, and I would meet the boy at the dance, and my brother and his girlfriend would have to bring me back home. The boy was not permitted to pick me up or drive me back. And I said, "No. Under those circumstances I am not going to go." And my brothers said, "Now you are silly, you know. If he doesn't mind doing it this way, why should you? Let me explain to the fellow." For some reason, the fellow agreed to do it that way. Of course, I never saw him again. That was my first date. . . .

You see, my mother was born in this country and had gone to high school here in this country, so that her outlook on life was much different than my father's. But my mother had to go along with my dad. She also came from a family where her father was the dominant figure, so she was used to this kind of life. Although she secretly objected to some of the things he wanted us to do, she would not outwardly defy him.

Many times I would say to my mother, "I'm going to do it anyway." And she would say, "Never do anything behind your father's back, and I'll always tell your father what you are going to do because, heaven forbid, if you should be in an accident . . ." In college I was permitted to go to the Newman Club [Catholic social club] dances with the girls, and I met someone there who invited me to the ROTC Military Ball at Duquesne University. I asked my mother and she asked my dad. I never went directly to my dad; I always went through my mother. She would talk to my dad and then come back with the answer. That time he said it would be all right, but there was a heavy snowstorm and the dance was postponed. When the snow was cleared a few days later, the boy asked me to go to a movie with him and I was allowed to go. When he came to the house, my mother opened the door and she came into my room laughing hysterically. She thought he was the funniest looking thing she had ever seen, and she so disillusioned me that I went to the movie with him, but when he called to tell me the dance was rescheduled, I made up a feeble excuse, and I never went to the Military Ball. . . .

I was still restricted at home. Again, anything I did, I did with girlfriends. I did date, but I felt he always disapproved when I dated and it made me terribly uncomfortable. He would always say to me, even though I was a teacher, "If you go out, drink ginger ale all night, and if you want a highball, you bring the boy in after your date and I'll serve you a highball." And he did. We were always allowed to have wine or a highball at home. He did not want me to drink when I was out on a date, and, you know, again, if I was told not to do something, I didn't do it. I would drink ginger ale, come home, and both my mother and father would be waiting up for me. I had to be in by twelve o'clock. I got an extension to one o'clock when I was twenty-five years old, so you can imagine [laughter]!

I was not allowed to travel with my girlfriends; that was strictly out. Any vacationing had to be with family. I heard about the Fulbright scholarship in Spain. It meant being an exchange teacher for a year in Spain, and I applied for it. I did receive the Fulbright. When I got the letter I was so happy, and my father turned to my mother and said, "I wish she would get married." I must have been twenty-five or twenty-six at the time. I went to Spain, and once I was over there I decided I didn't want to take the whole year, so I transferred to a three-month Fulbright program and then I came back. That was the beginning of my graduate work. I was so fascinated with what I had learned in Spain that I decided to go on to get a master's degree in Spanish.

My work was fine. I became head of the Modern Language Department after about four years at Peters Township. Then I did both teaching and administration. . . .

My mother and father were more concerned about my getting married than I was, but, you see, their idea of getting married was that someone was going to knock on the door and say, "I want to marry your daughter." My dad didn't understand that here in the United States, you date and eventually something happens. He felt that after the second date, if the fellow wasn't talking about marriage I shouldn't be going out with him anymore. As a result, I picked up that kind of a pattern. I would date someone two or three times and drop him and that was the end. I always said I would never marry before I was twenty-five. Of course, I married at thirty-five. I overshot it a little bit, but I'm not sorry.

I dropped my master's program because I was going to get engaged to an Italian boy who didn't want me to go on with my master's degree. Luckily, I realized that he was too domineering, so we broke our engagement. Some of my credits had expired and I had to start my master's program over again.

Actually, I met my husband when I was twenty-five, and I dated him for three months. I remember him saying he never dated a girl for more than three months, and I thought, "No one was going to talk to me like that." So I was just not going to date him anymore, and when he called the next time, I refused him. We met through the University Catholic Club, a club for college graduates.

We were on a picnic and he asked me to dance. During this ten-year interval, occasionally we would meet at one of the university club dances or parties. He would call and ask me to go out, and I would always refuse.

Eventually, ten years later, my husband and I got back together. We started to date again, and that was it. My husband is a mechanical engineer, and he is twelve years older than I am. He is Italian, but that was an accident! I always said that I wasn't going to marry an Italian, because I assumed that all Italian men were as strict as my father, jealous as my father, and possessive as my father, and I wasn't going to get involved with that. But when I met Bob, he was completely different. Actually, he doesn't have much of the Italian culture, because his parents wanted to move away from that. He really isn't as Italian as I am. He is a very easygoing, great guy and is completely different.

When Bob called, my dad said, "I hope you're not going to date him again." Then we started to date, and my dad really liked him and was afraid I was not going to accept his proposal, because Bob had proposed a couple of times and I had said no. When I was at a conference in Washington, D.C., Bob came to my parents and told them that he was interested in getting married but that I wasn't accepting his proposals, so he was planning to surprise me with a ring at Eastertime. My father didn't say anything to me, but he really liked Bob, and when Bob came, my father, who was always there when a boy came to pick me up for a date, took off. He knew that Bob was bringing me a ring, and he did not want to be around. There was still that little bit of jealousy that his daughter, even at the age of thirty-five, might get married!

I said, "I am thirty-five, and I think I should have a small wedding." They said, "No way." I was their only daughter, and this was going to be a big wedding, and it was a big wedding. I was married at St. Bernard's Church. We had over two hundred people at the wedding, and the reception was at the South Hills Country Club. My father said I was to get anything I wanted for this wedding.

The night of the rehearsal, he said, "Are you sure that you have everything you want for this wedding, because I want it to be a perfect day for you." I said, "No, there's one thing I don't have." He said, "What's that?" I said, "Well, I want you to receive Communion on my wedding day." He said, "Now you are really going too far, expecting me to go to Communion." And my mother turned to him and said, "You told her she could have anything she wanted for her wedding day." So he kind of shrugged his shoulders and said, "All right." He went into the confessional and was out in three minutes, and I couldn't understand it, and we said, "How did you do it?" "I just went in and I said, 'Ok, what do you want to know?' And the priest said, 'And how long has it been since your last confession?' And I said, 'Thirty years.' And the priest said, 'Bless you.'" That was the end of the confession [laughter]!

India in the West: New Passages

———▶ ◀———

TODAY, THERE ARE about 1 million Asian Americans originally from India. The first immigrants from South Asia were mostly Sikhs, coming here in the early twentieth century to work in the fields of Washington and California, and their legacies can still be seen in the temples they erected in the Sacramento Valley. Most of the Asian Indians came after the 1965 Immigration Act reopened the gates.

Many had not expected to stay here permanently. Hamida Chopra, for example, came here to join her student husband, thinking their residence in America would be only temporary. But opportunities came, and one year slid into another. Twenty-three years later, they were still here. "America is my home," explained Chopra. Though she has chosen not to become a citizen, she thinks of herself as an American. She is also Indian. She speaks only Urdu in her home and has taught her daughter the language and culture of the ancestral land. She always wears Indian clothing — the *dupatta*, *shalwar*, and *kameez*, for everyday dress, and the *sari* for formal occasions. When Chopra was a newcomer, people looked at her as a "foreigner." "But now these days," she noted, "they look at me and have no curiosity. American society is open, able to absorb differences in cultures and dress. I feel that the definition of what is 'American' has become broader."[1]

Reinventing Herself in America: Shanti

For many immigrant Indian women, however, to be "American" can also collide with what it means to be "Indian." In a paper based on an oral history completed for an Ethnic Studies course at the University of California, Berkeley, in 1997, Gaurav Kalra retells the passages of one such woman — Shanti. An art student in India destined to become no more than a wife there, she immigrated with her husband to America, where she experienced hardships and domestic abuse. She realized that Indian patriarchy had been transplanted to America. Discovering a strength within herself, however, Shanti seized a freedom her adopted country offered and made some courageous choices.*

SOMETIMES WHEN I was alone with my mother, she would tell me stories. I learned many things from my mother's stories. My mother passed away two months ago. It was hard for me. Although she is no longer with me, I will never forget her stories. One day my mother told me a story about my father hunting. My father was hunting with several of his friends far from the home. At the time one of my older sisters was on top of the roof of our house. She was a very small child and was trying to get the attention of a passerby selling mangoes and other fruits. My older sister was leaning over the edge of the house calling to the street vendor. My mom said that my sister fell from the roof at the same moment my father shot a bird off a tree. Both the bird and my older sister fell at that instant and both were dead. I learned not to eat meat on Tuesdays from this story. I also learned there was a price to pay if one broke tradition. My mom would teach or demonstrate many things to me through stories. I don't know what my life would be like as a story. My life is not really a story about breaking tradi-

---

* Some of the names and places have been changed.

tion. My story is about taking care of my kids, surviving. I don't know if there is a connection between an Indian woman surviving in America and breaking tradition. Who knows?

I feel I could write a book about my life. I could write a couple hundred pages today. So much has happened. As a child in India, I would have never imagined life and marriage to be like this. I remember all the movies I used to watch about love and romance and my life has been so different than what I thought it would be. I was born in New Delhi on August 19, 1946. I was the youngest child and I was very spoiled.

My father grew tobacco in a village. He had bought the plantation from other people. He milled tobacco in different forms. When the time of crop came, there would be at least 200 or 300 laborers in the field. My father realized his daughters were really suffering from a lack of education so he sent us to Delhi. We lived there with our mother. I skipped four classes because the tutor at the plantation was very good. The tutor would always make us read English literature. My tutor also told me that the books we were reading were read in the best schools in America.

I wanted so bad to go to America. Much of our cinema came from the United States. Life seemed so glamorous. My favorite American films were the romance movies. I thought men in America treated women very differently than the way men in India treated women. In the American movies, the men would always try to win the heart of a lady. Maybe it was because I was at that age when I started thinking of who my love will be when I am older. The women in these movies had so much control. They had many men to choose from. They were making decisions of which men they would want to marry. No one was making that decision for them. I would spend hours reading these novels and watching films. All this reading did help me in school.

I was so bright. I had skipped many grades and my father and brother were very proud of me. I entered junior high well ahead of my class. I was very lucky to be in school and I was doing very well. I wanted to move to London or America when I got out of college. Many of my teachers came from America or London. They, some even women, spoke of what life was like where they came from. In London or America, all that mattered was if you were intelligent. I could get a good job there, maybe. I didn't exactly know what I was dreaming of when I was in junior high. But something kept me wanting to do well in school. I wanted to leave and see something better.

My father died when I was in my third year in college. He had a heart attack. That was a big shock to me. I was depressed. I didn't finish my finals and I never graduated from college. I don't have a degree. I wasn't thinking in terms of a profession. Most women didn't work. After I was able to deal with my father's death, I went to art school. I always used to love to paint and at that point in my life I wanted to do what made me happy. At school I met an old artist. When I was on my easel making my painting, I noticed the old artist was sketching me. A day later someone from an advertising company came to the class and asked me to model for his textile mills. Within two months, I became one of the most popular models of Delhi. I had big blown-up pictures of me all around the city. Some of the pictures were two stories high. My face was in every major newspaper.

After the death of my father, our family started losing all of our money. Things were very hard. I didn't know where I was going or what I was doing. I agreed to take a few modeling jobs. Then things started to happen quickly and offers were coming in from many companies. I would walk around Delhi and everyone would notice me. I felt like a superstar in the movies. I began to feel glamorous and a part of high society.

The big moment came when I was asked to be in a film. Could you believe it? Movies are very important in India. I had the chance to be a film star. Maybe I could go to Hollywood from the film industry in India. I heard it was possible. My mother was very upset. She would not allow her daughter to ruin herself in a film. I think both my brother and my mother felt they could no longer control me. They were also worried about my ability to find a good husband if I was in a film.

My brother, Sanjay, began looking for a husband for me. My

brother met Hatesh at a party. Hatesh presented himself as coming from a good family and looking for a wife. Sanjay arranged a meeting for Hatesh and me. Hatesh was very good-looking and kind. He looked like an aristocrat and you could tell that many women were trying to marry him. I agreed to marry him. Hatesh was always so kind to me and he treated me like a princess.

I am not sure if I loved him. I am not sure what love is. I don't think love was much of an issue for me. I wanted to be married and I wanted my mom and brother to stop worrying about the responsibility of having to take care of me. I had feelings for Hatesh. I just don't know if I thought too much about those feelings. My major concern was that he come from a good family and he was educated. Hatesh lied on both counts. His family was very poor. Hatesh never went to college.

I was married to Hatesh for only five years when we decided to move to America. We moved to America in 1976. Santosh, my older sister, went to America the year of my marriage and she was very happy there. She asked us to come to the country and live with her. I missed my sister.

My life has gone through so many stages ever since I came to America. I grew up my whole life hearing about America. My mom would tell me that there were not as many wars and as much corruption in America. She would tell me that if you work hard, you can have anything in that country. I thought I would be able to just raise my children in America and my husband would work and take care of us. I was happy to go because I knew my children would get a better education in America.

When we came to America, everyone told us just to let the husband work. But once we came here I left my country. It's not that we just physically left India. As far as I was concerned, we left India, in all respects, and my family was starting a new life in America. I wanted a good life for my children. Two people had to work. My first job was at a preschool in Daly City. I took my kids with me and I didn't have to pay for daycare. I wanted to find a different kind of job.

Then I found a job at McDonald's for four hours a day making under two dollars an hour. I didn't have a car and I would spend a lot of time on the bus. It took me three hours to commute to work each day. I used to watch all the families come into McDonald's each day. I would think about what my kids were doing. I missed my kids. Sometimes I would go into the bathroom and go into a stall and cry. I would begin cleaning the toilet very slowly because I needed time to cry. Once the stall door was closed, I would look at my hands all dirty from cleaning the tables smelling like French fries. I would look at the toilet and see a reflection of myself. A reflection I did not recognize. Who was that Indian woman with the funny brown clothing on and the weird-shaped hat? My husband also took a new type of job.

He got a job in a factory lifting glass. There were many Indians at the factory. Each morning Hatesh expected Indian food prepared for him to take to work. I left early in the morning for work but that did not matter. Each day I would have at least eight *rotis* (Indian bread) for him to take to work. This type of work was not appreciated. It was just expected.

I started going to night school during and after my job at McDonald's. I wanted to make something of myself and I realized that I would be working for a long time in this country. The night school was filled with many types of people. There were many people from many countries. Many could not speak English very well. I learned how to be a graphic artist there.

It was easy for me to go to work because my mother lived down the street at Santosh's house. Chijee was always there to watch my kids.

In this country I had to learn to be American and do everything American. I had to learn what baseball was and I had to learn what parents were expected to do during games. I had to learn how to be active in the school. I had to do this all by myself. I was so busy I did not even have enough time to wonder where my husband was. Did he think that because he helped bring these children into the world that he somehow had no responsibility to take care of them once they were here?

I felt it was unfair that the Indian woman was expected to live in two worlds in this country while the man could still live in one. Why were the women expected to be able to handle all this new American life and still be Indian at home? As a woman, I was expected to learn about this country and how it worked. I was expected to know these things because if I did not know these things, it would be more difficult for my children to survive. My husband acted like he never left India. He also acted like I never left India. I began to learn to live for myself and not solely through my husband. I found solace in my work.

I had been working as a graphic artist, but I quit my job because I was making a lot of money on my side business selling sweatshirts. I spent most of the day painting designs on sweatshirts. That is what I sold in those days. Painting designs on sweatshirts is what made it possible for us to move into the new house in San Mateo. I used to buy the sweatshirts from a wholesale outlet. Then I used to go to fabric stores and get different types of fabric to sew onto the shirts. Then I would paint designs on the shirts. One of my most popular designs was the iris.

I would sell my sweatshirts on weekends at arts and crafts fairs. I really liked working on weekends. I earned a lot of money. But it just wasn't that I was able to earn money that made my business very important to me. In India, I used to paint. In college and for fun. Each sweatshirt I would sell had a painting on it. It was my painting. I did not always like painting the same flower or design over and over again. But with each stroke of paint that I placed on a sweatshirt I began to regain a part of myself. A part that I thought was lost forever.

I was able to watch the kids while I made my sweatshirts. Things were good in those days. I always used to think about all the things I could give my children by working. One of the most important things I wanted my children to have was a good house. A house, my house, is a symbol of all I have worked for in this country. A house means everything to me. When I am old, I want my children to be proud of their mother. That she worked hard enough for them to have a big and nice house. When I have grandchildren, I want them to be able to come to see their grandmother in a house.

Without a house there is no trace of all my work. There is no record of what I wanted to build for my children. I kept on working in these early days of my business because I knew I could save up for a home.

The Christmas that means the most to me is the Christmas when we moved into our new house. It was December of 1986 and my business was going very well. So well in fact that I saved thousands of dollars while we were living in our old house in Daly City. I wanted to bring my children into a better neighborhood. I spent many years looking at houses. Before I would even look at the house, I would go to the nearest school. If I liked the school, then I would consider looking at the house. Most realtors I worked with thought I was crazy. They did not understand how important the education of my children was for me. When I looked at the schools in San Mateo, I was amazed. They were very clean and the teachers were very nice. There were very few Indian families living in San Mateo and I knew all of them.

I opened my own store. At the shop I had to do more than just paint sweatshirts. I had to develop a line of merchandise for my customers. My line was always changing. I now made doll furniture. One quarter of my store was lined with little furniture that could be placed in a doll house. I used to cut the wood and then sand it. I would get paints and I would turn the wood into beautiful doll furniture. I also began painting shoes to match the sweatshirts I had. The shop was very beautiful at the mall.

One night I came home from the mall and I started to sweat like I never had before. Hatesh told me that I was tired and that I should stop working. I told him that I didn't know if I could finish the dresses or not and that if I worked tonight we would have a better day at the mall tomorrow. I had a different pain later on at night when I tried to go to sleep. My bed was soaked with sweat and Hatesh kept saying that nothing was wrong with me. My pain was not going away. I walked along the hallway outside my bedroom to try to get rid of the pain. I went back to bed.

At five-thirty in the morning, I woke up and I had a severe pain in my neck. I started sweating again and was moaning because the pain was so intense. I've had three kids and suffered labor pains but nothing was like my pain that morning. The pain was not in the chest area so I thought that it wasn't a heart attack. My neck and my right arm began to hurt very much. I wanted to go to the hospital.

Hatesh began to get mad at me because I was asking him to take me to the hospital. To my dismay, we did not have health insurance. All these years I had been telling Hatesh that even if he did not like his job that he should keep it in case we ever get sick.

Hatesh called my sister and told her that he had no time to take me to the hospital and so my sister had to drive one hour to come to get me. He did not go with me to the hospital and I was screaming.

I was told I had a severe heart attack and that I would have to be in the hospital for at least a week.

In all of this my husband was not there for me. How unfair, how selfish, his wife was in a hospital. He was going to the race track every day. I made money for the family for all my life and he didn't have time to come see me when I was in the hospital. I was greatly disappointed. I made up my mind — there was one thing on my mind — and that was divorce.

I remember saying to my sister in the hospital that the first thing I am going to do when I get out. I am going to file for divorce. Nothing could change my mind. The issue of divorce had come to my mind many times during our marriage.

For twenty years, I was expected to, without question, make that man roti every morning and night no matter what he did. I no longer considered that man my husband and I had built up hate for all of his actions and words for so many years that I could no longer cook for him. I know this hurt him very much.

As an Indian girl I was disciplined that when you get married that you listen and serve and do not question your husband. Women have no rights. Husband is like god. This god really disappointed me.

My husband always used to hit me. All my kids think they know everything and they always tell me what I should do. They do not even know half of what that man has done to me.

The divorce didn't go through because the courts said I didn't fill out the papers right. I was going to get help from certain groups but I didn't have the energy. I kept living with Hatesh. I still was set on getting a divorce. It was only a matter of time.

Hatesh was very reluctant to move out of the house. He wanted me to sell the house before he would leave. I threatened to call the police. Hatesh eventually moved out. I think it was the best thing for both of us. I did not want to be alone and I needed someone to help me save the house so I began to date.

I met a man, Charles, who would take me to the movies and to dinner. I think Charles is trying to repair this machine. But I do not want to trust it, and I do not want to believe it, it is impossible.

I am trying to believe in Charles and I am attempting to believe in the impossible. I am determined to save the house. It has been nine years since I quit my job as a graphic artist. I am not making enough money with my business. I know it will pick up soon. For now I am going to go back to work as a graphic artist. On the weekends I shall sell the sweatshirts and doll clothes at arts and crafts fairs. Working both jobs will allow me to save the house.

Charles and I are slowly learning to live with one another. I am getting used to watching more sports on television and he is getting used to eating roti at least twice a week. We have learned to compromise.

The first day I went back to work as a graphic artist all of my children called me. They are very proud of me. My daughter told me that I always find a creative solution to deal with any obstacle in my life. I can never accept defeat. I have always had three reasons to keep going in my life: my three children. As I am getting older, I am learning to find myself and my reason for living. Going back to work and continuing my art is allowing me to expand my own horizons. Things may still change in my life. I am ready for those changes. With each change, I develop a deeper understanding of myself and of my strength.

I think back to my first day in night school. There were many people in the room who all spoke different languages. But there was something that brought us together. That was a belief in ourselves and a belief in the opportunity that exists in this country. The entire class lived a life of transition but holding onto those two beliefs was something no one was willing to let go of.

Puerto Ricans: The Island
Is in the Heart

"**W**HY DID YOU COME to New York?" Jesús Colon was often asked. He had left the island when he was a teenager during World War I. In giving his answer, Colon remembered the day at school in Puerto Rico when he was given a "fat history book" of the United States. The eighth grader started looking at the pictures of George Washington and Abraham Lincoln. "Almost by accident," he wrote, "I came to discover a phrase in one of the documents at the end of the book . . . : 'We, the people of the United States. . . .'" Colon was inspired by this statement that included the laborers of Alabama and California, and also himself, his father, and the sugar workers in Puerto Rico.

But then, as a young man, Colon came to realize that "the people," in reality, did not mean people like himself. Though they were citizens, Puerto Ricans were exploited as cheap labor in a colony. They faced a grim future in the sugar-cane fields, with starvation wages. Seeking to escape from such poverty, Colon sailed to New York. But there he found "poor pay, long hours, terrible working conditions, discrimination even in the slums and in the poor paying factories where the bosses very dexterously pitted Italians against Puerto Ricans and Puerto Ricans against American Negroes and the Jews."[1]

Like Colon, tens of thousands of other Puerto Ricans would migrate to the "states." Seven decades after Colon's arrival, there would be two and a half million Puerto Ricans in the United States — nearly half of them in New York City.

Growing Up Puerto Rican in New York: Maria Diaz

Maria Diaz tells her life story in an interview published in a 1980 U.S. Department of Labor report, Pride Against Prejudice. *Reporting but also reflecting on her experiences, Diaz says she cannot "go back" to Puerto Rico, for she was born on the mainland. But she also identifies herself as Puerto Rican and of the culture created in the island's melting pot — a fusion of Spanish, Indian, and African cultures. Would she consider moving to the island? That depends, Diaz answers.*

———————— ◆ ————————

WELFARE WAS OUR means of livelihood from when I was eight years old until I got married. The welfare case worker was around, the investigators, the social workers, all kinds of people would come around the house to ask questions of my mother. Only once in a while would they ask me something. I didn't resent it because I knew that it was going to help us, that we were going to get money, that they would ask questions about the bed, do you need another bed? I remember things like that. At that point they were helpful. They would, at that time, practically give you a full household of things. You would get money for utensils, for laundry, and for other things.

We felt dependent upon them, of course. But it was worse if we didn't have it. My mother was very bitter about it, she resented it. And that was basically why there was a lot of bickering between my mother and father. She nearly killed him one day. She picked up a can of beer and threw it at him, hit him on the head and knocked him out cold, and she had to call the police and everything, and she thought she had killed him. She had reached the end of her rope. She couldn't stand it any more because he had bought beer. "Where the hell did you get money to buy beer, and meanwhile we are starving and waiting on welfare to feed us and you're bringing in beer!"

How did this affect my school? I really don't know. I remember having to tell the teachers that I would be absent on a particular day because I had to go on with my mother to the Welfare Department. And I did feel that the teachers treated us differently. They would require certain things to be brought to school, like Scotch tape or colored chalk or crayons, stuff that I couldn't afford, so the teacher would say, "Well, you can't participate in this group that is going to do this special activity because you don't have the material." My mother was very good about trips, but she couldn't give us money to buy things. She couldn't give us money to buy cards and stuff at the museums, so I remember having one teacher who bought stuff for me. She took us down to the Stock Exchange and to another place where there was a statue of Washington. Anyway I remember the teacher buying me some cards and a little pin because I started to cry. I wanted one, and I couldn't have it, and she said, "Don't worry, Honey, I'll get one for you." And she did.

School was pretty good up until the eighth grade. Trouble really started in the seventh grade. I started to hang around with my "peers" as they call them, and started to drink wine, and I did all kinds of weird things at that age and in that grade. Of course, the students that were older were friends who lived in the same neighborhood. And since I associated all the time with older children, I got introduced to everything that they knew and were doing. And by the eighth grade I was a full-fledged wino, as they say.

I remember seeing older teenagers or men — I'm not sure which — shooting up in the building where my aunt lived. That was a terrifying experience for me. I just stood on the stairway and screamed. I knew it was not a good thing to do 'cause I had heard my father talking about it. He was totally opposed to drugs. That experience of the drugs was unbelievable. It was so gruesome. I think because of that experience — it stayed with me — I never experimented with hard drugs. But, nevertheless, the wine thing had developed, and a lot of kids were doing it.

I had tasted wine at home from my father's wine bottle. And during that time I was smoking. I've been smoking since I was eleven. I was hanging around with boys, too. It was thrilling. It was doing things behind people's backs. But, looking back in retrospect, it was awful because I could've been doing so many other things. . . .

Where did the wine come from? The children would buy the wine for 50 cents a bottle — 35 cents. They would go into the stores themselves and buy it. Usually we got ninth graders to go. Not only did they look older, they were older. Some of the ninth graders were seventeen. They were left back so many times. We were exposed to much older children on our grade level than would be the case in most schools. One of the problems was that if you came from Puerto Rico, and you didn't know how to speak English, even if you were seventeen, you would go into the seventh grade. They would just dump these boys into the slowest section of the grade. So we knew that those were the "dumb" kids.

They weren't dumb, but we thought they were dumb because they didn't know how to speak English. I knew how to speak English because I had been in the school system since kindergarten and because my father spoke English at home. There were children eleven years old mixed with those who were seventeen years old. I think the older children, if you can call a person seventeen years old a child, deliberately took pleasure in corrupting the younger ones. That happened to me and to a lot of other younger kids. They were simply preying on us. They would be fascinated to see an eleven or twelve-year-old kid drunk.

And then you became their tool. This was the kind of thing that happened and continued, and then luckily we moved from that neighborhood. I went into another school where I did not know too many people. So in the ninth grade it was different. And I had good grades in the ninth grade. . . .

I left school at the ninth grade. I had graduated. I went to graduation and that was it. I didn't want to leave school. I was prepared to go back to school in September, but when I went to Mabel Dean Bacon the first week of school, they wouldn't take me because I was pregnant. And I was only fourteen. They didn't tell me to come back after the baby was born. All they said was, "We can't accept you here if you're pregnant. Sorry, you have to get your mother to come in and sign a discharge." And that was that. I stayed home. After that, I had the baby, and then I stayed home for about another four or five months.

And then I went to Seward Park High School. I decided I was going to go back to school. I wasn't going to stay around and do nothing. My mother was going to help with the baby, and so I went to register at Seward Park High School, and I was accepted although I was married, and they knew about the baby. I had a French teacher who thought it was just marvellous that she could call me "Madame" in the class instead of "Mademoiselle." She was just fascinated with that, and it was a wonderful experience. But then during the latter part of the semester the baby started to get sick, and I was missing a lot of classes. It was too much to do both, so I never finished. . . .

As soon as I dropped out of Seward Park, I went into a training program at Mobilization for Youth. It was right across the street from where I lived. I saw all these young people going in there, and they were being trained to do different things. I knew one of them, and I asked her, "What's going on in there?" She said, "Oh, you can go too if you have someone to take care of the baby. And they will teach you how to do a number of things, and they have sewing machines. They have typewriters. They test you in packing and in welding and all kinds of stuff, and then they get you a job." So I thought that was just great, and I went into that program.

Even if I hadn't lived across the street, I think that I would have heard about the program because my sister-in-law was working in an anti-poverty program and she was constantly asking me whether or not I was going to go back to school or whether or not I was going to do something. She's at least ten years older than I am and she had not been working. Then she decided that she wanted to go to work. She started first as a teacher's aide. This was in 1967 and 1968 when the whole paraprofessional thing developed in the city and she was accepted as a teacher's aide. Although she didn't have a high school diploma, she spoke English quite well. So there was no problem about her being a bi-lingual teacher's aide. Then she got a job in an anti-poverty program and she suggested that there were all kinds of special programs for the teenagers and that I should take advantage of them. She encouraged me but she never told me which ones to go to. Obviously she didn't have the information at her fingertips, but she was aware that things existed and she kept telling me that I should go find out.

The program people were very glad to get me, of course. The more Puerto Ricans and blacks they got into the program, the more money they would get. They would give you a test to find out whether you had some kind of basic reading skills and basic adding and subtracting skills, which most students did. . . .

When I finally decided to go to college, it did not seem to be a big decision. It seemed to follow from everything else. I knew the financial thing would be a big hurdle, but I said, "It'll be worth it for me to go to school and lose whatever I'll be losing in terms of money rather than to continue in this kind of job which is really deadend." Although I had gotten my school diploma, I knew that I wouldn't be able to go into an institutionalized social agency to do those kinds of things that I thought had to be done, just because I didn't have a B.A.

When I started college, it was going to lead to a B.A. And from there I would go on to law school. And from there I wasn't quite as sure about where it was going to lead, but I thought I would probably go into free legal services and possibly into some kind of political organization. I just can't wait to go to law school but I get chills down my spine every time I think of taking the LSAT and I have had very little advice about how to get into law school. I graduate from college in the fall and I want to go to law school the following year. That's a long time to think in the future. It means that I won't get through till 1980 if everything goes right.

And I started this all when I was 22 at the end of 1972. I have had this dream for eight years. I don't know of any programs that are going to help me get through law school. I have a certain expectation from friends of mine that are knowledgeable and that I admire very much. They wouldn't cheat me of the opportunity to do certain things if they had the resources in their hands. I don't mean the resources in terms of money, but in terms of contacts and people. So when I get my B.A. degree, I think I will get into law school, but that's another question. I'll worry about that when I come to it. I know that a few years ago the Ford Foundation said they were going to have a big program to increase the number of minorities in professional and graduate schools. I know that those programs exist, but I don't know the specific details of them.

I want to go to a really top flight law school. If I went to schools like Columbia and Harvard, I know I'd be competing with some very able people. And I know they've had the advantage of really first-rate schools from the time they were little. I am concerned not about my capacity to understand, but rather about my capacity to demonstrate that in examinations. But I wouldn't say that it discourages me in any way. To the contrary, it's a challenge.

I have been thinking of going into criminal law, but I'm now thinking more about going into civil law if I get my law degree. I think I could have more effect on things through civil law. It would perhaps open up a political career. That's in the back of my mind. It would be a ladder toward some other thing, but I'm not sure what. If I do go into politics, my whole expectation is not to run on the basis that I'm Puerto Rican, but on the basis of what services I could provide. Puerto Ricans need spokesmen and spokeswomen, but I'm not sure that they need them in New York City.

The whole question of going back to Puerto Rico is very much in the mind of every Puerto Rican in the city. I'm not a native of Puerto Rico, so I don't know what the life style is. I have to see what happens within the next ten years and then make a decision of whether I'm going to go to Puerto Rico. One of the things that would make me decide to go to Puerto Rico is if I don't see that Puerto Ricans in the city make any kind of progress in terms of their economic, political, and social standing. I am looking not for equal opportunity but for equal outcomes. Equal outcome would mean that the percentage of young Puerto Ricans going to college would be the same as for the other groups, that kind of equal outcome. I'm talking about the basic institutions of society — education, youth employment, what kinds of outcomes are going to result out of the opportunity that is offered to these people within the next ten years. That's what I'm going to be looking at because I think that's what is going to determine my decision. If there's some progress, I will stay and work to make sure the progress continues.

I'm not saying that young Puerto Ricans have to become executives of the typical corporation man. If the idea of a nine-to-five job, where you have to dress up all the time, where you have to be formal, is contrary to their idea of self, then they should feel free to reject that career. Some people maintain that the best possibilities are in large corporations or in the professions, but that's not what I'm concerned with. I am concerned with equal outcome. If my son decides that he wants to go to George Washington High School to learn how to repair tvs instead of becoming a doctor, I want him to have as much opportunity to do that as anybody else and I want there to be a market out there waiting for him so that he can do whatever he has learned in high school. That's what I'm talking about. I do not have a pre-conceived notion of where people should go. I think people should be able to make up their own minds. There's potential in everybody.

This is my primary concern. It will determine whether or not America is a place where I feel that I belong. I have noticed that a number of people have a sense of "we" and "they." And when I ask "Who do you mean by 'they'?," sometimes they say the establishment, or white America. I, too, have that sense of the "we" and the "they," but I think I can delineate exactly who the "they" and the "we" are. The "they" are usually those people who succumb to the bureaucratic structure, procedure, mentality. Those are the "they" — where there is a traditional point of view and it is maintained and there is no room for other views. They could be anybody, black, white, green, purple, Puerto Rican, anybody. If that mentality is the rule of the day, those are the "they's." And the "we's" are the other people who have no power to buck the "they's" but constantly try amongst themselves to do whatever they can for each other and buck the system from underneath. My answer is very different from many of my friends. To many of them, "they" are simply white Americans, the "we" are all the rest. I account for the differences in our views partly because of character.

At this point, I have to talk about the Puerto Ricans, because I do know something about my own culture. Part of the problem has been that many Puerto Ricans have always identified themselves with whoever has been ruling them. Spain was the mother country and some people had a ritualistic feeling about Spain. Anything that Spain did was right. Other Puerto Ricans would question this, but they would have to go along with it anyway because they had no power. In spite of that long experience of loyalty to Spain and to Spanish culture, we Puerto Ricans finally developed a culture of our own. We stem out of the Spanish culture, we stem out of the Indian culture, and the Black culture. It's a very cohesive feeling. . . .

If anyone asks me my nationality, I say Puerto Rico. I had no reason to say it otherwise and I don't feel I should say it otherwise. It used to be the census taker would ask you, "Are you black or white?" There was no other category. A lot of Puerto Ricans don't like to be defined as black. But then again, for purposes of getting grants and monies, they can't be defined as white either. We should be defined as Puerto Ricans or coffee-colored or something like that. The truth is that the Puerto Rican population comes in all shades, colors. . . .

My emerging sense of career is not an absolutely clear-cut thing, but there are some specific influences aside from my own personality which account for this emerging sense of career, my willingness to put a lot of time in education. The kinds of things I see happening between groups of people have helped me decide what I want to do. It is the question of getting people together and getting them to unite on something. Some of my friends say that it must be discouraging to have to deal with so much conflict and antagonism but it's not discouraging at all. It's frustrating because you can't get people to see the issues right away. We can't get them to understand the purpose behind what we are saying or what we are trying to accomplish in any given situation. But then again, you know, I am gaining confidence and feel that I can continue because certain things do make sense to me no matter how much people refuse to understand and close themselves off. Eventually there will come a time when they will have no choice but to begin to understand.

I think you can do something for people by being a voice for a more decent community and society.

The 1992 Los Angeles Riot:
Korean-American Dreams
in Flames

B EFORE THE 1965 Immigration Act, Koreans were so small nu-merically that they were a hidden minority. But the new Ko-rean immigration led to the dramatic emergence of Koreans as a very visible group in America. From only 10,000 in 1960, the Korean population jumped to half a million in 1985. In Los Angeles, the home of 150,000 Koreans, a new community sprang up on Olympic Boulevard. Koreatown was a concentration of Korean-owned grocery stores, churches, gas stations, travel agen-cies, barbershops, insurance companies, restaurants, and night-clubs. "One does not feel that one lives in America," a Korean immigrant remarked, "when one lives on Olympic Boulevard." Koreans had come here to make new homes and pursue prosperity, and many of them were realizing their dreams through small busi-nesses.[1]

But then came "Sa-i-gu," "April twenty-nine" — the violence and destruction of the 1992 Los Angeles riot. "Once again, young blacks are taking to the streets to express their outrage at perceived injustice," Newsweek reported, "and once again, whites are fearful that The Fire Next Time will consume them." This conflict was different from the 1965 Watts riot: it was not just between blacks and whites.[2]

The fire this time had consumed the stores and dreams of Korean Americans. "April 29, 1992, the night the store burned down," merchant Young Soon Han recalled, "I didn't even know what was happening. I hadn't been paying much attention to the Rodney King verdict. I didn't think the issue was so serious. But some of the people from the neighborhood came into the store and said, 'Mrs. Han, you'd better run now! People are coming this way, and you will get hurt.' I said, 'Why? I haven't done anything wrong.' But they convinced me I was in danger, so I went home. That night, I kept in contact with the woman who lived in a house behind our store. She finally told me that the store had been burned to the ground."[3]

The governor declared a state of emergency and ordered 6,000 National Guard troops into the city to restore order. When the unrest finally came to an end on May 1, entire areas of Los Angeles resembled a bombed-out city. The human toll was high: 58 deaths, 2,400 injuries, and 12,000 arrests. Over 3,000 businesses had been damaged by fire, vandalism, or looting, and losses totaled $800 million. Most of the businesses damaged or destroyed were Korean-owned. In Koreatown, every building, row after row and block after block, had been reduced to rubble on both sides of the street.

"At first I didn't notice," a Korean shopkeeper said, "but I slowly realized the looters were very poor. This riot happened because of the gap between rich and poor." The tensions and violence were not simply the result of intercultural differences and misunderstandings between Koreans and blacks. The problem was the pervasiveness of poverty within the inner city. "Even if most of the Korean merchants hire one or two employees," explained scholar Edward Chang, "it's not going to make much of an economic impact in South Central L.A."[4]

But thoughtful voices have emerged within the community to confront the racial faultlines of Los Angeles. "Many of us in the second generation," declared community leader Angela Oh on the fifth anniversary of Sa-i-gu, "believe there are a new set of progressive principles which must be adopted in our efforts to go forward as Korean Americans with a new vision. Those principles emphasize concepts of inclusiveness rather than exclusiveness, compassion rather than criticism, and a constant push toward social change for justice, not just for Korean Americans but for all people."[5]

"Not Going to Let the Riots Beat Me":
Sun Soon Kim

In her paper based on an oral history completed in an Asian American Studies course at the University of California, Berkeley, in 1997, Samantha M. Lee gives us an insider's view of "Sa-i-gu." An immigrant from South Korea, Sun Soon Kim worked hard, saved her money, and invested in shops in Korea Town, Los Angeles. Her businesses were reduced to ashes during the 1992 Los Angeles riot. However, she is a strong and spirited woman, as her life story reveals, and she says that she will not let the riots burn her dreams.

———————→ ◂———————

ALL DREAMS AND STORIES have a meaning and a purpose. My existence came from a dream, a dream of a gigantic Koi goldfish found in those Japanese gardens. My mother had a dream that she went to the lake and caught one of these goldfishes and scooped it up into her skirt and brought it home. It is a Korean superstition that Koi goldfish dreams bring good luck. So when mother became pregnant, everyone told her that she would give birth to a boy and that son would have good luck and bring good fortune to the family. But as it turned out, I was born a girl. Girls in Korean society are not treasured as much as boys, since boys are the ones who carry on the family name and take care of the elderly parents. Being a girl, no one told me that I was going to have good luck or good fortune.

I, Sun Soon Kim, was born on May 20, 1949. Before my one-year-old birthday, Korea was in the midst of the Korean War. I don't have any memories of this, but what I do know is from the stories that my great-grandmother and grandmother told me. My family comes from the *yangban* class. During that time, Korea was divided by classes. *Yangban* class was the highest, and many of the kings of Korea were descendants from this class. During the Korean War, many *yangban* families were being killed by the lower classes, and so many had to flee for their lives.

Coming from the *yangban* class, I was pretty sheltered from the suffering and hardships that many Koreans endured during the aftermath of rebuilding South Korea after the devastation of the Korean War. . . . While I was growing up, class distinctions weren't as defined as they were in the previous generations. But there were some unwritten rules, such as, one married someone from the same or higher social status as you, but never someone from a lower social status. I guess I thought that I was more liberal minded than my parents and that my generation was going to challenge those stuffy traditions and patriarchal customs. I was wrong. I tried to rebel, but I was met with resistance.

In college, I wanted to be an artist. My dream was to paint pictures and decorate homes. But my parents crushed that dream. They told me that women were not to be independent and trying to make a living for themselves. If I chose that path, I would be a struggling and starving artist that no one would hire because I was a woman. So they put the pressure on me to discard my ambitions to be an artistic designer and major in home economics, in other words, majoring in finding a husband. College for women was a joke. No one learned anything important. I guess the only respectable profession for women was to be a teacher. But other than that, women were taking courses in sewing, cooking, housekeeping, and how to be a proper housewife, all a bunch of crap. College was mass graduating marriageable girls instead of professional or scholarly women. I guess I had no other choice but to become one of the brainless masses. If I had the support of my parents, things could have been different.

So now I was eligible for the marriage market. I had been educated at Sanghwa University on the proper etiquette on being the proper wife, hostess, and so on. But I had to put my foot down somewhere and say my two bits. There were a lot of arranged marriages still going on. Parents matched prospective singles and arranged marriages according to wealth and social status. There was no way I was going to end up in that fate.

I had a boyfriend, Dae, for about six years, and we decided we were going to get married. This announcement caused a great deal of commotion since my parents had arranged a marriage for me with my neighbor. Yuck! That was like my marrying my brother or something. This guy and I grew up together since we were little, and he was more of a brother than husband material. Another objection my parents had to my marrying my boyfriend was that he came from a lower social class than what I was. I was going to marry down, a major no-no at the time. My parents told me I was going to marry my neighbor — no ands, ifs or buts about it — that was that, case closed.

I had made up my mind that I was going to marry who I wanted and that no one was going to force me into a marriage just based on social status and family alignments. I did the next best thing to avoid this marriage. I got pregnant. Sure that was an extreme, but that was the only choice I had at that time. Being single and pregnant was considered a double sin because that eliminated me for marriage, and my parents had no other choice but to approve the marriage with my boyfriend. They did not want the shame of having a grandchild out of wedlock nor did they want the stigma of raising a loose and immoral daughter. I did not want to hurt them. I know that getting pregnant hurt them a lot. I could see it in their eyes, but it was really important for me to be able to choose and marry whomever I wanted.

My plan was to marry before my tummy grew, but Dae's mother refused to bless the marriage. In Korea, one cannot marry without the approval and blessing of both sides. Instead, I was shamed. This pregnancy idea turned into a disaster. I was so ashamed of being a single unwed mother that I refused to leave the house, and the whole stress of the situation was making me ill. By the time the marriage was blessed, I was too pregnant, too ill, and too sick to be married. I decided to wait until after the birth of my baby to walk down the aisle. I brought shame to the family by getting pregnant, but ultimately, I was shamed the most because I felt the social stigma of being a single unwed mother every time I went outside. My family was supportive and loving during this time, for which to this day I am eternally grateful. One month before the baby was due, I became so ill that I was hospitalized. I was not strong enough and too sick to carry the baby full term, so they had to induce a pre-mature labor and forced birth.

On February 22, 1974, my baby girl was born. At that time, I still wasn't sure if it was worth the whole experience. A month later, the day after I was released from the hospital, I was married to Dae. My daughter, Sammie, was among the invited guests who watched us get married. Her presence at the wedding was met with much resistance because Dae's mother did not want her there because then the guests would know the shameful truth about a baby before marriage. But mother stood her ground and said that Sammie had every right to watch the wedding as anybody. So Sammie watched us get married on her grandmother's lap amongst the gossip.

Almost after a year of marriage, I knew that I had made the biggest mistake of my life. Why did I marry Dae? Why didn't I just listen to my parents and marry my neighbor? Problems started developing after the marriage. Once a woman marries, she pretty much leaves her family to join the family of her husband. First of all, it was up to Dae to support Sammie and me, since it was the man's duty to provide for the family and for the woman to raise the family and keep the house in order. It didn't bother me that we weren't rich or anything. I had left the nest, and now I was on my own. But what really drove me crazy was when Dae decided to quit his job as a magazine editor, one day out of the blue. He had no job lined up, and where was he going to earn money to keep food on the table for Sammie and me? Plus, we were fighting. Honestly, we were in over our heads, too young for the responsibility of adulthood and family. In Dae's mind, he was still a bachelor, not a married family man.

I left him after a year of marriage and went home, big mistake. In those days, divorce was unheard of and unaccepted. No one divorced, no matter how awful the marriage was. So when I came home knocking at my parents' door, they were furious. They told me I was no longer a child and that I had to work things out because I was a married woman and a mother. Father told me that if I was old enough to find a husband to marry and get pregnant, then I was old enough to solve my own problems. I honestly felt that I was being punished for breaking tradition and doing what I wanted to do.

In the end, I remember thinking I should have listened to my parents. Mother told me that if I left and divorced Dae that I was not welcomed at home. I had no other choice but to return back to married life. As a woman, I had no way of supporting a baby and myself. There were no decent jobs available for a single mother without family support, and I had no job and home to go to. So I returned with the intention of giving Dae a divorce and Sammie if he would let me walk out. But destiny had other plans for me. I came to the conclusion that divorce was not an open option for me, so I remained married and tried to work things out.

In September 1977, we immigrated to America. There were significant changes in the United States immigration law so that in 1965, the United States opened its door to family reunification. By 1977, most of Dae's family was already established and settled in California. We were the last of the family to immigrate. So when Dae announced one morning that he was going to America, I had a decision to make, follow him or stay? Since I really had no choice, I packed up my family and bags and off to America I followed. What was in store for me was beyond anything I had ever imagined.

I did not know what to expect. The only images of America that I had seen were from the movies and magazines. I knew that it was more glamorous and so developed, unlike Korea. I never imagined that I would have to work or provide for my family. I did not come here to get rich or find fame; I came here because I wanted my marriage to work and so followed my husband. All of Dae's side of the family told me to let Dae find a job and support the family. But how were we to do that when the relatives turned their backs on us? They had this mentality that since we were the last to arrive, we needed to experience the hardships and poverty that they experienced, and once that was experienced, we would adopt the "American Dream" ideals of hard work, individuality, and "pulling oneself up from one's boot straps."

Since we were on our own and no longer in Korea, survival was the key. Since Dae and I did not have any marketable work skills in America, Dae was taking any kind of job that would put food on the table. In 1980, after two and a half years of trying to let Dae provide for our family, I had enough and took control. I decided to apply for a proof operator position at First Interstate Bank. How I got this job, I honestly do not know, since I did not speak or understand English. I guess the Koi goldfish dream that my mother dreamed about was looking for me and bringing me luck.

Dae's relatives were shocked when I got that job. They did not understand how anyone who had no English skills got hired. I decided that I was going to provide for the family while Dae went to school to learn a trade. This moment in time, I guess I was finally liberated from the strings of Korean traditions and customs that tried to keep me restrained. I was no longer bound to the Korean societal dos and don'ts. Instead, I could do whatever I wanted. This role-reversal, for me, was liberating. Finally, I could make decisions, get a job, and support a family. At the time I was becoming a "breadwinner," Dae was becoming feminized. He was taking care of the kids, Sammie and my son Paul. In a way, I think he resented this role-reversal, but because we were trying to survive, he had no time to really challenge me.

Getting this job was the break I needed. With the little English skills I had, I just faked it and tried to make it through the day. It was hard. I remember there were some days where I had no idea what my supervisors were explaining and asking me to do. I just kind of tried to be one of the flock by copying and doing what everyone else was doing.

We were living with Dae's mother in her studio apartment and wearing hand-me-downs from the relatives. This was hard on the kids because they were so young and always stuck inside the apartment. I felt my kids were prisoners in the apartment since it was too dangerous for them to play outside, and they couldn't run around inside. With the little money I was making, I put a down payment on a small house in a rough part of Oakland. . . .

We were in debt: the house wiped out all of our savings. I borrowed money from the bank and from the Korean rotating credit loan system that I had established with a group of friends. I was barely making it from one paycheck to the next. What made me so mad was that here I was working seven days a week and overtime to put Dae through school, food on the table, and he's having a problem because the bills were in my name first and in his second. I told him that as soon as he made more money than I did, then his name could be on all the bills. Why was he worrying about trivial matters when we were barely making it from one day to the next?

What broke my heart about this were the kids. I could not give them the toys and clothes that they wanted. I looked at my childhood and I was lucky. I was given anything and everything that I ever wanted, but I could not do the same for my kids, even though I wanted to. The kids were obsessed with McDonald's. I did not have the extra money to spend on them, so on payday I would take the kids to McDonald's and buy them hamburgers. It would make them so happy. Twice a month, I would see their happy faces, and excitement over going to McDonald's. But the rest of the month, I would have to worry about making it to the next. Times were tough until Dae finally graduated and got a job at the post office as a supervisor of the mechanics division in the Oakland district. With two incomes coming in, things were getting better.

Now that we were getting by, I decided that it was time to spend some money on the kids. I worked overtime to earn some extra cash to pay for Sammie's piano, violin, ballet, and tennis lessons and for Paul's violin, baseball, tennis, and swimming lessons. I felt that my kids were being deprived of the "American Dream," and so I wanted them to do the same activities that other American children were doing. I felt that I had already lost so much time with the kids by working so much. Finally I was able to make up for that lost time by providing them with all the things they wanted to do and learn. I was working hard for them — for their future, their lives. They were going to get all that they deserved even if it killed me.

After five years at a dead end job of long hours and no opportunity of upward advancement, I decided that I needed a change. With the little money that Dae and I were able to save up, I decided that I was going to open my own shop. I had to think about this long and hard before I made any drastic decisions. It was not an individual decision — it required the opinion of the whole family. I was not doing this for myself; I was doing this for the family. But there were many factors involved, such as the location, the language barrier, what kind of business, and the risk factor. Operating a small business was risky, and with the little capital that was saved, I wanted the highest percentage of success. I heard Koreans talking about the formation of a small Korean community in Los Angeles. I decided to check it out. Around the same time I was thinking about the business, I found out that my cousin was moving to Los Angeles. I couldn't believe how perfect the timing was. Finally, things were starting to look better.

With many discussions, my cousin and I decided we were going to be small business owners. She had brought her three kids here to obtain a better education, while her husband stayed in Korea to oversee and run his company. Together, my cousin and I bought a little shopping center that housed five stores with our life savings. She took three of them because she put in more money than I did, and I took the other two. Between the two of us, we had a market, Korean pastry shop, electronics store, clothing store, and beauty salon.

The location was great, right on Olympic Boulevard in the heart of the Korean community. Being in the Korean community really helped in that it eliminated the language barrier and cultural differences. We also received a lot of support from Korean customers, as well as other ethnic groups. Everything was going great except for the kids. They were running around with the wrong crowd. I discovered that Koreatown was no place to raise kids but a great place to do business. Too many bad influences such as drugs, smoking, alcohol, gangs, and nightclubs, but not enough families. My kids were too young and very impressionable, and I did not want them living at the store either. It seemed so unhealthy, and I did not want them to become business owners like me. I wanted them to get a good education and good paying jobs. Business was picking up and doing well, so once Sammie graduated from the eighth grade, I decided that it was time to move back to the Bay Area. The schools were good, we were near family again, and the kids would be away from all the bad influences of Koreatown.

With my cousin watching over my two stores and sending me the profits, I was able to purchase a bigger house in the Hayward hills. This purchase made me proud because the bigger house represented our economic stability, financial growth, and our achievements in America. We came with nothing except for the clothes on our backs and a couple of suitcases and now we had a house. Finally, I was slowly inching toward the "American Dream" that hard work reaps success. With the steady flow of money coming in, I purchased a small cookie shop in Larkspur in Marin County. All the money that I made was for the kids. Buy the kids whatever they wanted — they were good kids and they deserved it. They were making me proud — they were doing well in school and Paul played the violin for the youth orchestra. For the next few years, life flew by without any problems. I thought I had finally reached the "American Dream."

Then an event happened in 1992 that will forever be in my memory. That was the Los Angeles riot. I had no idea that something like this was about to happen. I guess even having a prior warning would not have helped. How do you deal with something like this? Since I wasn't living in Koreatown I had no idea how much tension was out there. I would hear stories of racial incidents here and there, like the Latasha Harlins incident (a black teenager shot by a Korean shopkeeper in Los Angeles in 1991). But in reality, I had no idea how bad it was or that it was going to explode like it did.

This portion of my life, I just want to forget, like it never hap-

313

pened. I try to make it disappear, but it always finds its way back to me, forever haunting me. No one understands the feelings I have about this, and words probably could not accurately convey what I want to say. The impact of the riots on many Korean merchants runs deeper than imagined. The theorists and scholars really can't explain the impact of the riots. How can they, when they weren't even there to experience it?

What do I remember about that day? Much of it is a blur since I've tried to forget about it. I remember coming home from work in the evening and seeing my kids running out to greet me all excited and flustered. They dragged me upstairs and planted me in front of the television. The images that I saw on all the channels were of people looting, Koreans with guns, and Korean businesses in smoke and on fire. It took a couple of minutes for the images to settle, and when I realized that this was happening for real and that it was going on in Koreatown, I rushed over to the telephone to call my cousin. I tried calling her house and our five stores.

Since no one was responding, I began to panic. I was so worried that I frantically called the airlines hoping to get a flight out, but none of the airlines were flying into Los Angeles. I wanted to fly out there as soon as possible. The children wanted to go with me, but I said no after seeing the images on television, but they insisted, so I booked four seats to Los Angeles for the next day. I spent most of the evening frantically calling Los Angeles. None of the people I knew were home or answering. I needed to know what was going on. I needed answers. I could see businesses that I used to shop at being burned down or looted. I made the kids watch the television in hopes that they would be able to get a glimpse of my shopping center.

What was going on? The images on television were so incoherent, almost like a dream. Was this for real? That night was the longest and darkest night I ever experienced in my life. It was not the anticipation that was killing me, but the not knowing was. The family and I took the first flight to Los Angeles. I did not know what to expect. Koreatown was blocked off, but no one was going to stop me from going to my stores.

"Not Going to Let the Riots Beat Me": Sun Soon Kim

Koreatown looked like it went to war. I guess if I was ever in a war, I know what the end results would look like. I could still see smoke rising from buildings, and Korean merchants trying to salvage any remains of a dream. Since cars couldn't drive through, we parked our car and started to walk. I couldn't believe what I was seeing — like something from the movies. I felt like I was on the movie screen walking through the war zone, and people in the movie theater were watching this.

Words cannot describe the emotions that I was feeling, or the sights that I saw. A block or two before we reached my stores, my cousin ran out to stop me. She was crying and trying to hold me back from seeing the stores. I had to see them. I wanted to see with my own eyes that everything I saw on television the night before was real. My cousin and my husband were trying to hold me back. No one was going to stop me from seeing my stores. I kicked and fought and finally pried myself free and ran and ran. I ran without looking back. I did not care, I just wanted to see. I honestly wasn't prepared for what I was about to see.

In front of me was the remaining rubble of the stores that I had poured my money, sweat, and time into. Everything I had worked so hard to build was crumbled in front of me. I had spent my whole life building a dream that was destroyed in one night. Knowing that I had built this for the kids' future and my future was unbearable. Now we had no future. This realization broke me. I crumbled in the midst of anguish and pain. I cried and wailed tears not for myself, but for all the other merchants whose dreams had also crumbled. I sobbed for myself, my children, my cousin, and fellow immigrants. When my stores were destroyed, a part of me was destroyed. I died, not physically but emotionally. I don't remember much. I think I was just going through the motion of things.

I don't remember leaving Los Angeles. I don't even recall coming home. I know that I was in shock for awhile. I did not talk to anyone, just walked around in a daze and went through the motions of living. Two months after the riots, I knew my kids were worried about me and my physical and mental health. I had a dream one afternoon. In my dream a lion was chasing me. I ran and ran, but the lion caught me and laid on me, suffocating me in its chest. I struggled for awhile, but then I decided that it was pointless. I was going to let this lion suffocate me. But the thought of my kids without a mother and struggling without me gave me the strength and courage I needed; I was going to beat it. At that point I fought and fought. I finally got the lion off of me, and I ran and ran without looking back. I was scared that if I looked back, the lion would catch me again, and I would indeed suffocate to death. The lion to me represented the Los Angeles riots, and when the riots exploded, my version of the "American Dream" was destroyed. Even though a part of me died that day, I decided that it was not going to kill me. I was going to fight and fight hard for what I believed in. I was not going to let the riots beat me. It may have, but now I was fighting back.

It's been five years since the riots. There have been some significant changes in my life. Six months after the riots, I suffered a major heart attack where I could not be on my feet longer than a couple of hours a day. I had to sell my cookie shop in Larkspur, but with that money, my husband decided that he wanted to open his own small business. Both of my kids are in college now and are struggling with the financial changes in our household. But they are doing well in school and making me proud. The riots had a big impact on my life, but I still do not understand why it happened. I still have questions that can't be answered, but now I'm not searching anymore. I'm letting the past go and trying to go on with my life.

Blacks in the Cities:
No Time to Wait

T HE CIVIL RIGHTS MOVEMENT successfully led to legislation
that prohibited racial discrimination and protected the voting
rights of African Americans. But it was not able to address their
problems of poverty and unemployment. The grim reality of job-
lessness in the inner cities generated despair and rage. "You know
the average young person out here don't have a job, man, they
don't have anything to do," a black in Harlem explained angrily
in the early 1960s. "You go down to the employment agency and
you can't get a job. They have you waiting all day, but you can't
get a job." Young urban blacks knew the playing field was not
level. "Those who are required to live in congested and rat-infested
homes," scholar Kenneth Clark noted in *Dark Ghetto*, "are aware that
others are not so dehumanized. Young people in the ghetto are
aware that other young people have been taught to read, that they
have been prepared for college, and can compete successfully for
white-collar, managerial, and executive jobs." One of these alien-
ated blacks predicted in 1962: "When the time comes, it is going
to be too late. Everything will explode because the people they live
under tension now; they going to a point where they can't stand
it no more." This point was dramatically reached in Los Angeles
during the long hot summer of 1965.[1]

"The fire bombs of Watts blasted the civil rights movement into
a new phase," declared Martin Luther King. Ultimately, the struggle to realize the American Dream had to advance beyond anti-

317

discrimination laws and confront what King called the "airtight cage of poverty." The underlying economic basis of racial inequality was a far more elusive and formidable foe than the lynch mobs and police attack dogs. "Jobs are harder and costlier to create than voting rolls," King explained. "The eradication of slums housing millions is complex far beyond integrating buses and lunch counters." This harsh reality of urban squalor and despair was reflected in the jagged mirrors of every northern ghetto. "I see a young Negro boy," King wrote in 1963. "He is sitting on a stoop in front of a vermin-infested apartment house in Harlem. The stench of garbage is in the halls. The drunks, the jobless, the junkies are shadow figures of his everyday world."[2]

Contrary to the claims of pundits like Charles Murray as well as politicians like Ronald Reagan, black families were being pushed onto welfare rolls by unemployment, not simply pulled there by welfare benefits. John Godfrey explained what happened to his family: "By now my wife was pregnant. And I was unemployed. . . . So push came to shove. We went down to welfare. I needed medical protection for her and the baby. It was a sobering experience. I felt — I don't know how to put it into words — I was totally disgusted with myself. I felt I had failed myself, because I was unable to take care of myself and my family."[3]

Soaring unemployment for black men was accompanied by rising welfare enrollments for black women with children. The majority of black welfare mothers were young — under thirty years old. Black women were especially disadvantaged in the labor market and more dependent on welfare because of their lower levels of education and fewer job skills.[4]

Survival for many black women, even for those with husbands, has been difficult on welfare. They have been trapped in a "catch-22" situation. They would like to get off welfare but find themselves forced by low wages to remain dependent on government subsidy. "None of my jobs ever paid more than minimum wage," said Alice Grady. "As soon as I can get a babysitter, I intend to go back to work. But it won't be easy. There is a bus stop right out front, but according to where your job is, you'd probably need two or three buses to get to work. You'd have to leave early in the morning, and you'd be leaving your children because they're not supposed to be at school until eight or nine o'clock. Then you'd have to find a babysitter for them in the evening until you got home. . . . But I'm hoping to get off welfare and get me a good job. Right now they're helping me, but it's just making ends meet. You don't have anything left. . . . Right now my husband is looking for a job. . . . We vote. This year we couldn't because we were homeless. You know, the homeless can't vote. You have to have an address. It's just rough on welfare. It's just not enough. What can I do for school clothes for the kids? When my husband gets a job, we'll be cut back on welfare." A world of barriers surrounds women like Alice Grady, keeping them impoverished and blocking their avenues of exit. At several different points, they have been frustrated by a cycle of poverty generated by low wages and reinforced by inadequate child care, poor public transportation, lack of affordable housing, and political disfranchisement.[5]

Moreover, the employment situation of both black women and men has been devastated by recent major changes in the economy. The movement of plants and offices to the suburbs during the last three decades has isolated many urban blacks from many places of employment. Meanwhile, blacks have also been suffering from the effects of the "deindustrialization of America." Due to the relocation of production in low-wage countries like Malaysia and Mexico, some 22 million American workers lost their jobs between 1969 and 1976. "The decline in blue-collar employment hit black men especially hard," sociologist Andrew Hacker reported.[6]

Staring at the boarded-up factories, many young blacks have been unable to get even their first jobs — work experience essential for acquiring skills as well as self-esteem. One of them, Darryl Swafford, grew up around Gary. Unemployed and dependent on food stamps, he had the same dream as most Americans: "I always had that goal, working in the mill. Have a home, a big car. But now there's no mill and I'm down. Just trying to make it, trying to survive." Many of the jobs available to young blacks have been in the fast-food services like Burger King and McDonald's. But these jobs pay very low wages and lead nowhere. "They treat you like a child on those minimum-wage jobs," complained Danny Coleman, who had worked in a fast-food restaurant. "And there is no way you can make it on that kind of salary. It is just a dead end."[7]

South Central Los Angeles has come to symbolize the plight of poor blacks trapped in inner cities. "South Central Los Angeles is a Third World country," declared Krashaun Scott, a former member of the Los Angeles Crips gang. "There's a South Central in every city, in every state." Describing the desperate conditions in his community, he continued: "What we got is inadequate housing and inferior education. I wish someone would tell me the difference between Guatemala and South Central." This comparison graphically illustrated the squalor and poverty present within one of America's wealthiest and most modern cities. Like a Third World country, South Central Los Angeles is also extremely volatile. A gang member known as Bone explained that the recent violence was "not a riot — it was a class struggle. When Rodney King asked, 'Can we get along?' it ain't just about Rodney King. He was the lighter and it blew up."[8]

The 1992 Los Angeles riot reflected a long history of a black exodus — the migration of Southern blacks to the cities of the North and the West that had begun in the early twentieth century. One of their songs conveyed their determination to pursue the American Dream with impatient hope:

Some are coming on the passenger [train],
Some are coming on the freight,
Others will be found walking,
For none have time to wait.[9]

The "Disappearance" of Work: Hard Times for Jimmy Morse

The sociologist William Julius Wilson has analyzed astutely what happens to blacks in the inner city in his scholarly study When Work Disappears. *But what does it feel like to become economically superfluous? In 1983, Jimmy Morse voluntarily retired rather than risk an imminent layoff. He was forty-seven years old and had thirty years' seniority at US Steel's Gary Works. Morse was one of over ten thousand who had lost their jobs at that plant. His story is based on a 1986 interview published in Leslie Dunbar,* The Common Interest: How Our Social Welfare Policies Don't Work and What We Can Do About Them. *Here he reflects on a lifetime of work and tells what he does to keep from going "stone crazy."*

———————→ ◄———————

MY MOTHER AND FATHER separated when I was about three months old. My father left us in Mississippi and came to Gary. School days there was limited to me, like maybe two months out of the year. I came to Gary so I could help my mother and help my own self.

When I got here, my father asked me, did I want to continue to go to school or go to work. I said I prefer goin' to work. If I had went to school, I would'a been somethin' like a couple years behind the other kids. I chose to go to work, because that's what I left home for. I worked in the canteen at the Gary Works. I got paid once a week with pure cash money in a little brown envelope. After taxes, I had $26 for forty hours' work.

When I got eighteen in 1953, I went in the mill as a laborer like everyone else. I worked hard for thirty years. The last two or three years the bottom was fallin' out of everything. They was lookin' hard at anybody with more than ten years' seniority. They

321

was settin' us up to be fired. Like you didn't have no certain job. The man tell you do certain things that you know you not supposed to do: you go and do it or else. If you tell him, "Hey man, I'm not gon' do it" — that's it! That's it right there! You got fired.

Only thing you could do is say, "Well, I'm gon' do it, but I'm workin' under protest. I will file a grievance." He'll tell you, "Gon' file a grievance." Anytime a man can tell you, "Go get your union man," that means you ain't got nothin' to back you up. The union's hands was tied. No more callin' on the phone talkin', "I can't make it to work." When things was nice, you could call up with two hours' notice. But that had never concerned me. I didn't have nothin' to do with that part. Now if you laid off, if your baby swallowed an open safety pin, wife slipped on some grease in the kitchen, you yourself was on the way to work and had a car wreck — whenever you come back to work you better make sure you got all your papers signed by somebody else. Otherwise, they'd fire you.

When they got ready to lay you off, they just put on the bulletin board NOT SCHEDULED NEXT WEEK. Then you go to the unemployment office and start signin' up. You might be signed up two or three months. One time I was out here a year and a half; that was when I was laid off in November 1981. That's when the bottom fell out of everything. I did get $141 a month unemployment [insurance] and $162 TA [Trade Adjustment Act Assistance].

Only thing saved me from rock bottom is, I been blessed by the Almighty to have my thirty years. Jes' think 'bout the peoples that was tryin' to do somethin' for they self, holdin' they jobs — younger peoples with only fifteen, seventeen years' seniority. They got nothin' comin'. I was jes' blessed that I was as old as I was and had stayed on the job. When the bottom fell outta everythin' like it is right now, I just accident had my thirty years.

When I came out of the mill on my retirement, I thanked the Lord that I got out before I got fired. I had to take what the company offered — take it or leave it. After I signed the papers, I stopped off at Mr. Lucky's Lounge. I bought about $42 worth of drinks. I said: "Hey! This is my retirement. Drink, boys, till it run out. Don't take nothin' wid ya now. Just drink!"

Since 1981, I been takin' the bitter with the sweet. What I do to keep from goin' stone crazy? I fish. When the mills started goin' bad in 1980, I went to the store and bought me some fishin' equipment. If I have good luck some days, I come back and sell the fish. The only thing I want is enough money to go back fishin' tomorrow. I might have a fish two feet long and tell somebody to give me two dollars. He got eight or twelve dollars worth of fish. He's happy and I'm sho' nuff happy, because the next mornin' at five I'm gon' fishin'. When the winter months come, what am I doin'? I'm sittin' up watchin' television. I have a $190 to $215 light bill and I gets $552.63 a month for my thirty years' service. Now, you get the light bill outta there. You get the water bill outta there. Buy some food outta that plus $131 we get in food stamps. You're about $40 short.

That $552.63 is no money considerin' the way that they charge you for everything. It's five of us here — wife, myself, and three boys. The one who is twenty-two is still here with me, because there's no jobs. The eighteen-year-old is in his last year in high school. Them basketball trophies over there belong to him. I enjoy watchin' him play basketball at Roosevelt High School. That helps me look toward another day, otherwise I might flip over, the way things are goin'. [His third son is fourteen.]

I'm glad that you can wear long hair now, because I don't even have to get it cut. I can go a year if I want to. My wife does her own hair and my eighteen-year-old son cuts his. I don't have money to do nothin' like I used to do. I can't afford to put clothes in the dry cleaners. I had to sell my 1974 Ford the other day for little or nothin'. You can't hardly do too much without a car.

I love to drink sociably. I don't go out in the street and fall down. I don't drink to forget all these troubles. I do the same amount of drinkin' that I did when I was workin'. I hope that I never come up with a problem that I jes' got to drink to forget it. I wouldn't want to get in that state where I jes' gotta go and get me a bottle.

Where I'm goin' then? I ain't goin' nowhere! I drink when I go fishin'. I take a bottle with me, if I got enough money, and wets my tongue. I don't try to drink no fifth in no thirty-five or forty minutes. I ain't interested in that. That don't concern me. My biggest hangup right now is the cigarettes. I'll light one cigarette with another cigarette.

I tried to find work. You get in your car and you drive in your area — we'll say twenty miles in radius — you drive to all these corporate employment offices. They got chain-link fences around them with a guard standin' there. The office is closed. If anybody can tell me right now where I could pick up an application lookin' for a job and they're hirin', I will be there. Instead of hirin', they're layin' off the people they got.

I can't move to another city either. I'm a family man. I'm not a drifter. I got kids here in school. I can't jes' reach and grab everything and go to another city. It doesn't make sense. You take your kids to another place, they got to get familiar with everything. They'll be two years back. My boy comin' out of school this year wants to do somethin' for himself. What is he got forward to look to? Not a thing, because it's nothin' gonna change here in the United States in the next twenty-five to thirty years. Who gon' send him to college? You can't get nothin' from the government. What's my son gonna do when he come outta school? He can't borrow nary a penny from the government.

I'm fifty-one years old now. I won't try to go to Chicago and let the man hire me makin' $3.75 an hour and I got to get back and forward to that job. I will not go to Chicago to put no application in at nobody's office. That's jes' too doggone far [thirty-five miles]. If I went to Chicago and got a job, I'd be payin' nothin' but highway. At the end of the year I wouldn't accomplish $400. That's alright for young men like my sons. I'll tell them, any day the sun shines, go and try to get you a job. I'm fifty-one years old. I think I did enough in my younger days. Only thing now, I jes' think I need some help. I need the head man [President Reagan] to quit jazzin' around. If the head man would open up then everybody could breathe a little. But he got everything tight and steady pullin'. People gettin' laid off every day.

If the mills was to open up again, I'd be the first one to get me an application. Oh yeah! But I'm not goin' nowhere from Gary. And I'm not goin' to be standin' up on no corner waitin' for some subcontractor that I ain't never seed before, come by and say: "Hey! I need five men. We gon' pour a basement today." I'm not gettin' in that line. That's for younger men. I look like a fool, jumpin' out there in the line. Let the man that ain't gettin' nothin' do somethin' for himself. I'm gettin' this little $552. Why would I cut off somebody that ain't gettin' nothin'?

I don't see very much hope for the future for me or my sons. I don't feel real sorry for myself. It hurts like heck, but I'm tryin' to get used to this. My forty-seven years was too young for a man to come out of the mills when he wants to work. I always wanted to keep me a car to ride in. I always wanted to be able to go to the store and buy what I wanted to eat and have ten or twelve dollars in my pocket when payday come. Or else I could go to a friend and say: "Hey man, let me have sixty dollars. We get paid next Wednesday." I can't go to nobody that I been knowin' ever since I been in Gary thirty-five years and say: "Hey man! Let me have seven dollars so I can go to the store and get a carton of cigarettes." I ain't got no friend that I can go to now and can't nobody get nothin' from me, because he can't help me and I can't help him.

I know I ain't gonna work no more in the mills, because it ain't no such thing as that anymore. Ain't but four or five departments workin' out there. You could play football on the parkin' lot. The country is in badder shape now than it ever been in my life. What is a depression if we not in one now?

I ain't caught nothin' but wax since Reagan been in there. I know President Carter signed for this foreign steel that's comin' in that made us start workin' down to two shifts and four to six hours a day when you supposed to be workin' eight. Foreign steel was takin' our man-hours away from us. And it ain't no racial thing either. That blue-eyed soul brother is catchin' jes' as much hell as I'm catchin'. The government is breakin' his back, jes' like it's done broke mine. Either you already got it or you ain't gon' get it. That's all!

I'm jes' livin' here in the United States. I got no power to voice myself or nothin'. We don't make steel for our own self anymore. Everything come over here. They got people overseas workin' for twelve and fourteen cents an hour. We might be over here makin' ten or twelve dollars an hour. Reagan, the boss man, gon' catch hisself right out in the middle of the ocean. He won't be able to take the stuff back and he can't bring it here, because can't nobody buy it. Ain't no jobs. I'd have a brand-new car sittin' out there in my driveway if I was workin'.

The people that would be buying brand-new cars to keep this country goin' is the ones that's laid off. The people that would be buyin' clothes to keep the cotton fields goin', the people that could be buyin' things, using things, them the ones that ain't got a buck. I can't see how Reagan figures he's pullin' the country up so fast. I haven't paid federal taxes in four years, but I used to pay as much as $2,500 a year. The government has lost all them taxes.

I don't think about gettin' in an elevator, riding way up to the thirty-fifth floor, get off, step on the landin', and jump. I don't think that way. That don't even cross my mind. I don't think about spinnin' my revolver around, lining up all the peoples in my house and cut down on them, then cut down on myself. I don't think like that. They'll have to get nineteen Mr. Presidents before I do that.

A Chance to Act Affirmatively:
Bryan K. Fair

Affirmative action is at the storm center of ferocious acrimony. So much of the debate, however, has been polemical and deceptive. Americans have been hoodwinked into voting for measures like California's Proposition 209 in 1996. Presented in the disguise of a "civil rights initiative," this proposition did not use the term "affirmative action" but "preferential treatment" instead. The vote was 55 percent in favor. But in Houston the following year, voters were asked to ban "affirmative action," and 55 percent opposed. Actually, most Americans support the continuation of affirmative action programs, at least in some form. A New York Times poll conducted in December 1997 revealed that only 25 percent of those interviewed said the programs should be discontinued, while 43 percent said they should be changed and 24 percent said they should be left as they are.[1]

Shrouded in the debates and the statistics, however, is the way affirmative action works and the difference it can make in the lives of real individuals. The following excerpt is from Bryan Fair's Notes of a Racial Caste Baby: Color Blindness and the End of Affirmative Action, *published in 1997. He is an associate professor of law and assistant academic vice president at the University of Alabama. In describing his experiences of how he escaped from the inner city of Columbus, Ohio, entered Duke University in 1978, then studied law at UCLA, Fair humanizes policies seeking to open equality of opportunity for minorities. He rebuts conservatives like Ward Connerly and Newt Gingrich by simply telling a personal story about his chance to act affirmatively.*

I AM THE EIGHTH of ten children of a single mother, born in a black ghetto in Columbus, Ohio, in 1960. Since my siblings are close in age — the youngest within fifteen years of the oldest — we lived at home at the same time for a significant period. My mother sometimes had two jobs, but still, her wages were low, she received no job benefits, and none of our fathers helped her. We certainly did need welfare; I can't imagine what we would have done without it. Even with it, my family went weeks without regular meals at home. Each month we ran out of food and ate sugar or mayonnaise sandwiches until they too ran out. Sometimes, in order to get something to eat, I had to steal.

Even though each of our houses was old and small, rent in the ghetto was high. We occupied every square foot of space: bedrooms, basement, and attic. We never had our own bedrooms and frequently shared our beds. I shared one with two younger brothers, and the tensions among us ran high. We drew imaginary lines in the bed that were not to be crossed. And when they were, battles broke out until my mother or one of my older siblings threatened punishment. Our house was poorly insulated and infested with roaches and rats. I remember sitting on the couch at night, afraid to put my feet on the floor for fear a rat or mouse might scurry across them. Our campaign against roaches was futile: they were the permanent residents, and we were the transients, moving every couple of years in search of cheaper rent or when we fell behind in our payments to the landlord.

Sometimes during the frigid, below-zero Ohio winters, my family had no gas heat. We never knew ahead of time that our utilities would be disconnected. Instead, we found out when we got home and the temperature inside was not much different from that outside. To stay warm, we huddled under blankets and slept in our clothes. To bathe, we either took icy showers or boiled pots of water on our electric single-burner hotplate. A few times my mother could not pay the electric bill either. I thought we were the poorest people in Columbus. We were not.

When I was seven, I started hustling jobs, and for the next eleven years, after school and on weekends, I ran errands, shoveled snow, cut grass, cleared trash, cleaned bathrooms, swept floors, cooked, stocked groceries, sold candy, and cleaned animal cages. My survival depended on those jobs. They enabled me to buy food, a few clothes, and school supplies and to help my mother pay bills.

I attended elementary school regularly and earned A's and B's in most classes. But when I participated in a voluntary busing program during junior high that moved black kids from the ghetto into predominantly white schools, the work seemed much harder and my grades fell. I couldn't read well, and I had to struggle to finish my homework. Now I was only a C student. When I started high school, one of my teachers told me that although I had an appealing personality, I didn't know very much. To help, he gave me history and literature books to read. Without constantly looking up in the dictionary the many words whose pronunciation and meaning I didn't know, I couldn't make sense of them. I was scared and angry, and I felt trapped.

Many blacks in Columbus and elsewhere in the United States are born into conditions like those I have described, and most remain there. I escaped. I am now a lawyer, a professor of constitutional law, a university administrator, and a published author. I am not poor or dependent on welfare. Neither are any of my siblings. I support myself and help support my mother. How did this happen? One important factor was remedial affirmative action. It helped me move from the ghetto into more rigorous schools and increasingly nurturing environments. So no one can tell me that affirmative action does not work. It did for me, as it has for many other Americans.

One of my reasons for telling this story is to make clear that remedial affirmative action is not the same as the whites-only, racial caste–producing legislation that has often prevailed throughout America's history. My life experiences have convinced me that remedial affirmative action and hard work, plus the support and direction of many people, are what — even though the odds were decidedly against me — enabled me to escape from that Ohio ghetto. Without the educational opportunities, I would have been imprisoned by circumstances and conditions beyond my control. . . .

During my final year of high school, I visited my counselor, Mr. Webb, to discuss colleges. I was interested in four schools: Harvard, Duke, Howard, and Vanderbilt. Harvard was my first choice because, well, because it was Harvard and because Aaron had gone there two years earlier. Howard enjoyed the reputation as the best black college in the country, and each year a number of East High graduates enrolled there. I learned about Duke and Vanderbilt when college recruiters dropped by East after visiting several prestigious private schools in Columbus. When recruiters from around the country made their rounds to Columbus Academy, St. Charles, and Columbus School for Girls, a few also stopped at East. One of our counselors would then round up a few "top" students to meet them.

The Duke recruiter, David Belton, was the most impressive of all of them. Young and dynamic, he represented one of the best private universities in the country. And he looked like me! Reared in Charlotte, North Carolina, by parents who were teachers in mostly black schools, David had attended Duke's rival, the University of North Carolina at Chapel Hill, where he had been the head cheerleader. Despite his Tarheel ties, David's enthusiasm for Duke was contagious, and he also made me feel that I had much to offer the school. You could tell from talking with him that he was interested in more than increasing the numbers of blacks at Duke, that he would be a mentor and friend as well.

Mr. Webb, however, told me that I should prepare to go to one of the local schools, such as Capital University, a private university in Columbus. He didn't think I would do well at a school like Harvard or Duke. I listened politely to his defeatism, trying not to show my disdain. He didn't know how much I hated Columbus, that I wanted more than anything to leave. But he didn't live in black Columbus, so he probably had no idea how I felt. The next time I saw Mr. Webb was to tell him I was leaving Columbus, for Duke.

Like many public and private colleges throughout the country until the early 1960s, Duke did not admit blacks, no matter how smart, how athletic, how wealthy, or how well connected they were. Charles Hamilton Houston and Thurgood Marshall had convinced the Supreme Court that such practices by public schools were unconstitutional. But because it was a private school and thus not affected by the Court's decree, Duke did not abandon this practice until 1963. Since then it has sought to enroll larger numbers of black students. To do so, it has continued to take race into account, but now no applicant is excluded solely on the basis of race.

I was a special admit student at Duke, one of the new students — black as well as white — from around the country that would bring greater diversity to the class of 1982. I had had almost all A's in high school and graduated fifth in a class of more than 250 kids. I had been a member of the honor society and president of the student council and debate team, and I had received numerous awards in high school. Even so, my SAT test scores were far below Duke's median. I had not studied for the test nor been able to take any of the expensive cram courses. Instead, I just signed up and took it one Saturday morning. I scored 850, almost 300 points below the median score for Duke.

David Belton was my champion throughout the Duke admissions process. Despite my scores, he persuaded the committee to take a chance on me: affirmative action at work. But I was not admitted to Duke solely on the basis of my race, and I don't think any white student was excluded solely because of race. Duke did not have a policy that no whites could enroll; it did not engage in "reverse discrimination." Rather, it adopted a diversity admissions policy to ensure that its student body would include some blacks, as well as some whites, from diverse, sometimes underprivileged, backgrounds.

To assist students like me whom it considered at risk, Duke offered a six-week summer transitional program (STP) designed to bridge the gap between high school and college. About fifty students, both black and white, including a number of athletes, were invited to take courses in English and precalculus. This program was another part of Duke's remedial affirmative action strategy, the idea being that by bringing students like me to campus early and allowing us to sample college life, we were less likely to drop out or fail.

The director of STP was Cynthia Hale, a black graduate student in the divinity school. After classes each day, the staff planned other activities to help us adjust to campus life. We had study hall and meetings with counselors regarding study skills. Cynthia was smart and inspiring, with a warm, inviting smile. She believed in all of us and made it clear that she expected us to succeed. She never made any of us feel stigmatized or inferior. We all loved her.

About three weeks into the program, I ran out of money. I had used some of my school savings to help Dee [his mother] pay a bill. But she hadn't repaid me yet, so I had to explain to Cynthia why I would be late in paying my fees. I was embarrassed, frustrated, and ready to quit. When I awoke the next morning, there was an envelope under my door containing enough money to pay my fee. Since no note was enclosed, I was never certain who had put it there.

STP was helpful in many ways. Some of us formed a support group and together explored the campus and the surrounding community. I also had a glimpse of how hard my college courses would be, but I knew that I could do the work. When STP ended, I returned to Columbus for a few days. These six weeks away from Columbus — only the third time I'd ever been out of Ohio — was the longest I had ever been away from my family and friends, and I had missed them terribly.

Many family and friends wanted to see me before I returned to Duke. In particular, one of my grandfather's sisters, Aunt Faye, asked me to drop by. At age eighty-five, she was my oldest living relative and lived in a retirement home. I had visited her many times with Harry and Gert, and at Christmastime we exchanged small gifts. She told me how proud she was that I was going off to college, the first member of my family to do so. Faye then gave me an envelope containing $200 — a fortune! She had been putting it aside for me. Her sacrifice moved me deeply, and her money made an enormous difference during my first days at college. That day I promised myself that I, too, would help my nephews and nieces in some way when they entered college.

One of my East classmates, Jay Tatum, also was going to Duke. We had played pee-wee football together when I was ten. During high school we took most of the same classes and participated in similar extracurricular activities. His parents were divorced. His dad, who had been our football coach, had given us keys to his house, and we came and went at all times of the day and night. Jay's mother, who had been my swimming coach when I was eight, planned to drive us to Duke, which meant that I did not have to spend any of the money that Faye had given me on transportation. Before we left, Jay's stepfather sat me down to explain how hard it was to be successful when one is from a large poor family. He told me that by going away and staying away, I had a great opportunity to leave my past life behind and to help my family later. Much earlier, I had concluded that I had to leave Columbus in order to change my life, and now he confirmed it. Many of my friends' parents lived by the African proverb that "it takes an entire village to raise a child." I could not have escaped black Columbus without them.

I spent my last day at home packing my few belongings in an inexpensive trunk and army surplus duffle bag. The East High School English Department had presented me, as the top student in English, with a new dictionary. Tony gave me a volume of poetry. Theresa and Sheila, my oldest sisters, bought me three new outfits. Dee, who was working at a local bakery, prepared a care package of cookies and pastries. I left at daybreak.

Jay and I moved into Gilbert-Adams Hall on Duke's East Campus two days before classes began. One of the principal benefits of attending Duke was that for only the second time in my life I would be with predominantly white students, this time from throughout the United States and numerous foreign countries. Fewer than 5 percent of the students at Duke were black. I met white kids who came from some of the richest families in the United States. Although very few of the black kids seemed wealthy, many were middle class. I also met a few whites from modest backgrounds whose families worked on small farms or in factories in the South. Some of the white students had never gone to school with blacks and had never had a black friend. And some of the black students had always gone to all-black schools like East.

Duke matched groups of new students with an advanced student counselor to ease the first-year transition. Jay and I were placed in a group with four other guys, including one from England and one from Iran. Merhdad Nemazee's family had fled his country when the shah's government collapsed, and Jay and I became close friends with him. Our group met monthly for meals to talk about academic problems, but because the six of us lived in the same dorm we saw one another almost every day. Duke was a struggle for all of us.

It was not long before I realized once again that I was not as well trained as many of my classmates. I took calculus, economics, English composition, and history. The classes were much harder than I ever imagined they could be. The pace was swift in every one. I had more homework than I could do and always felt a couple of days behind.

When I received an F on my first history paper, I was devastated. The professor's field was the French Revolution, and he seemed mean and arrogant. He called me to his office and made me read my paper to him. I don't know if he did that because I was black or because I had written such a bad paper. In any case, I was nervous, angry, and humiliated. The more he criticized my organization and writing, the angrier I became. He must have felt sorry for me because before I left his office, he softened and made a few helpful suggestions for better organization and writing. I redoubled my efforts and earned a B in that course.

My experiences in other classes were similar. Everything I had learned from Mrs. Barienbrock seemed inadequate to meet the requirements of my English composition instructor, Jeff Thomas. Because he didn't like my ideas or their presentation, I spent most of his class rewriting assignments. In calculus, L. P. Smith might as well have been speaking Russian; I was lost by the end of the first day. Even though I had earned A's in all my math courses at East and had taken precalculus during STP, neither had prepared me for calculus. Smith taught more to the blackboard than to his students. When someone asked a question, he answered by going through the same steps that had confused us initially. I got a D.

A Chance to Act Affirmatively: Bryan K. Fair

My economics course was taught by a Canadian and his graduate assistant. I disagreed with most of their lectures because I didn't see the market as neutral. As far as I was concerned, supply and demand were weighted variables, influenced in part by racial discrimination. Neither Adam Smith nor John Galbraith said enough about America's history of racial bias to change my mind. So after struggling through five economics courses, I changed my major to history.

As a history major, I read about slavery and began to examine the origins of racism in the United States. I studied the Civil War, the promise of the Reconstruction laws, and the failure of Populism. I read about Jim Crow segregation and the subsequent campaign to end it in the public schools and in all public accommodations. Ray Gavins, Larry Goodwyn, and Dick Watson introduced me to the writings of Frederick Douglass, W. E. B. Du Bois, Carter G. Woodson, and John Hope Franklin. As I learned more and more about my own culture and history, I realized how much had been missing from my early education. Most of all, I gained a sense of this country's fixation with racial classifications and its long record of racial privileges for whites and color-based subordination of blacks and other minorities. The more I read, the better I understood the emergence of racial caste in the United States.

Some critics of affirmative action point to decisions by schools like Duke to admit people like me with test scores substantially below the school's standard. They allege such a mismatch is harmful to people like me, presumably meaning that my test scores preclude my competing against other students at Duke and that when students like me fail, we lose the little confidence and self-esteem with which we began.

I disagree. First, Duke gave me a great opportunity, one that did not hurt me in any way. Indeed, all the harm that I suffered came well before Duke, during my years of educational deprivation in ghetto schools that lacked rigor and were run by teachers who had no idea how to improve their students' skills. Even though I went to school every day, I was educated as if high school were the end of the line. Then Duke gave me a chance for more. I learned that its high standards were not beyond my capacity but, rather, only beyond my training.

Second, the white students at Duke displayed a wide range of achievement as well. Not all of them had high test scores, and some of them seemed no better off than me. Some had been admitted to Duke under different special admissions programs — for athletes, children of alumni, large donors, or economically disadvantaged whites. Others had been sponsored by the Methodist Church. Those using the mismatch argument should therefore include these other admits in their attack, but they don't.

Third, the mismatch idea turns history on its head and, if pursued to its logical end, would lead to an even more harmful educational caste system. That is, critics of educational affirmative action should ask why blacks and other minorities frequently lag behind whites on standardized tests. Could it be the result of past educational deprivation? Is the only possible explanation genetic inferiority? Given that most African Americans in this country are barely a generation from illiteracy — a condition in most cases imposed on them — we should be shocked when we do not see a gap.

Beyond education and a degree, Duke gave me a chance to form adult friendships with whites. At Johnson Park, few of my close friends were white. We lived in different places; interracial dating was discouraged; and I rarely spent time away from school with whites. But at Duke, blacks and whites lived in the same dorm, used the same showers, and ate their meals in the same cafeteria. We studied together, sat in class together, and socialized together. The only time I was not with mostly white students was when the Black Student Alliance had a meeting or a party.

I lived in the same room for three years, next to the resident adviser's. Every dorm had upper-division students who worked as counselors in exchange for room and board. One of them was Tom Jeffries. Tom was the son of a Methodist minister, and his mother was a local activist for autistic persons — one of Tom's brothers was a high-functioning autistic adult.

I first met Tom when he applied for the student trustee position on Duke's board of trustees. I chaired the selection committee, and he impressed me more than any other candidate. All his comments were about service — to the students, the university, and the larger Durham community. He wasn't arrogant or self-absorbed, as were many of the other applicants. Unfortunately, Tom seemed very shy, and many on the committee thought he would never be heard. Nonetheless, he was my first choice. After another student was selected, I called Tom to tell him how much I appreciated his ideas and that I hoped he would stay involved in campus life.

Within a year, he was my resident adviser and neighbor. Tom's boyish looks left many parents wondering how someone so young looking could have so much responsibility. But once he spoke, his graceful ways disarmed even the most skeptical. His door was always open, literally and metaphorically, inviting us in. At least once a month, Tom's parents dropped by for a visit and to bring him snack foods. When I met them, I saw how Tom had learned his care for others. His parents were almost like missionaries. They not only served a church but also worked to improve race relations in the state.

Tom was a diligent student, studying every day late into the night. Sometimes we worked together and talked about world issues, about the death penalty, abortion, school desegregation, and affirmative action. Tom had a keen sense of fairness and a deep concern for the poor. He wanted to become a doctor in order to provide medical services for those who could not obtain quality care, but his MCAT scores were too low for the best medical schools. Several schools advised him that he should take more science courses and then take the test again. Although Tom was disappointed, he never wavered in his goal. Before he finished this additional work, he applied to the Peace Corps and was accepted for work in Zaire. I shared his elation with some ambivalence, however, as I was not ready for one of my closest friends to graduate. During my final year, after he had gone, I missed him.

Through a few friends like Tom, I learned while at Duke that not all whites despised blacks, that some wanted to live in integrated communities, and that some abhorred racial discrimination. Tom was one of the few people that I met at Duke with whom I could talk about racial discrimination without making either of us feel guilty or under attack. At Duke, I learned that some whites were committed to racial justice, and coming from black Columbus, that was an important lesson.

During my last year at Duke, I served as a resident adviser in an all-freshmen, three-hundred-person dorm. Two of the seven RAs were black, and more than 90 percent of the students were white. Within a few days, I had students at my door complaining about their courses, especially English composition and Jeff Thomas. I spent long nights talking with these new students about self-confidence and self-esteem. Most of them were uncertain, insecure, and traumatized by bad teaching. They appreciated that I was a Thomas survivor.

When some students rushed fraternities and sororities, I saw how important those groups were to the social opportunities at Duke. Part of my job was to counsel those students who were rejected, which was hardest when one roommate was accepted and the other was not. I explained to the students why I had never pledged a fraternity, how exclusive and arbitrary many of them were, and why they shouldn't participate in such divisive groups. I encouraged them to join other clubs that were open to all, without discrimination. But my advice helped comfort only a small number of students.

None of my students failed to notice I was black. For some it meant a new experience, the first time in their lives that they had had a black person supervising them. For others it was no big deal, as they had gone to schools with a few blacks. For some of the black students, I was someone to talk to about racism at Duke. Like Tom Jeffries, I tried to keep my door open to all my students.

My college experiences also showed me that white students "belonged" at Duke in ways that blacks did not. I don't know whether the white students at Duke were aware of the racial privileges they enjoyed there. Most of them probably never heard anyone say that they were at Duke only because of their race, had anyone ask if

they were athletes or comment on how well they spoke. I suspect that few were stopped by the campus police and asked to
produce identification or explain what they were doing on campus
or that few were followed when they shopped in local stores. In
the classroom, few white students were treated as authorities on
race or spokespersons for all whites. Few had to worry that they
would be rejected from social activities or clubs because of their
race. Indeed a significant privilege of whiteness is not having to
think about being white.

Nobody at Duke was color blind. My classmates always noted
my race, as did my professors and the administrators. I noted theirs,
too. The black workers at Duke served the food and manicured the
grounds, and the white workers held virtually all the administrative
jobs. In each job I held on campus, I was the only one or one of
very few blacks working in a similar capacity. Duke had both black
clubs and white clubs. I was a member of the Black Student Alliance
and one of a handful of black students elected to the student government.

After intimate — though mostly clandestine — associations with
white women at Duke, most made it clear to me that their parents
would not approve of our relationship. The content of my character
was beside the point; my color had its own character, which was
not based on my integrity or my acts but, rather, on the belief that
my color made me less. Just like my ancestors in Ohio, I was still
not white enough.

In addition to everything else I learned at Duke, I became even
more aware of how being black made me different — still American, but black. I discovered that my racial classification had given
me a different history of cumulative disadvantage in obtaining social, political, and economic opportunities in the United States,
based in great part on racial privileges for whites. Blacks could not
live among whites, vote on the same basis as whites did, or attend
elite schools as whites did. They could not play in the same public
parks, swim in the same pools, or obtain service in the same public
accommodations. No matter where I went or what I accomplished
in the United States, I would always be black: a black Duke student,

a black law student, a black lawyer, a black law professor, perhaps even a black law dean or a black university president. Being black was fine. But I learned that despite my racial and cultural pride, when many whites and even some blacks used the term *black*, it was as a negative modifier of my personhood and all my achievements. All my accomplishments stood to be diminished by the taint of my race.

I both loved Duke and hated it. I loved the educational opportunity I had there, and I made lifelong friends during those years. But I hated the feeling that some people on and off campus despised me before I even uttered a word. Some acted as though I had violated a sacred custom: I had not kept my place. I wanted so much to be American and black, and I hoped that whites would learn to celebrate my blackness and not see it as a blemish. I desperately sought signs from whites that they were committed to integration and racial equality. I hated that I saw so few.

Every African American must struggle through what Du Bois described as his or her "twoness" — "an American, a black; two souls, two thoughts, two unreconciled strivings; two warring ideals in one dark body, whose dogged strength alone keeps it from being torn asunder." How can I love a country that denies me equal citizenship? How can I live among people whose wealth was derived in part from my exclusion? How can I help whites understand that I am not a problem and that my blood is not tainted? The challenge for whites is to accept that America has never had a race problem; rather, it has had a white supremacy problem. White supremacy has made color-blind relationships among Americans impossible.

Ever since I realized I would not be a running back for the Dallas Cowboys, I have wanted to become a lawyer. I did not know many lawyers in Columbus, but several were active in local politics and were often in the news. Dee had a friend who was a lawyer who sometimes gave her money. Lawyers all appeared comfortable economically. Also, many of the people in Congress were lawyers, and I wanted to be a national leader. So I thought that going to

law school would enable me to help others. I had grown up with
Perry Mason, The Fugitive, and similar dramas about law. Books like
Harper Lee's To Kill a Mockingbird, John Howard Griffin's Black Like
Me, and Ann Fairbairn's Five Smooth Stones made me want to fight
racial discrimination, and what I learned at Duke made me even
more determined to study law. How, I wondered, could a nation
supposedly founded on principles of freedom, equality, and fairness have our history of discrimination?

I applied to ten law schools during my final year at Duke, long
shots like Stanford, Georgetown, UCLA, and Berkeley, but also to
Ohio State, Washington at St. Louis, USC, Oregon, Howard, and
UC Davis. All the schools had special admissions programs, and all
were interested in enrolling some black students. Every application
requested data about race. The process was decidedly not color
blind.

My first choice was Stanford, in part because my second Duke
roommate, Ken Barrett, had gone there. I had earned good grades
at Duke, especially in history. My senior thesis received an honorable mention from the department; I had been student body president, served as a dormitory resident adviser, and had worked
throughout college. My LSAT score was high, but not spectacularly
so. Although I took the test twice and raised my score, I still fell
below the median at Stanford, which rejected me. Fortunately, I
was admitted to half a dozen schools, including UCLA.

I was accepted at UCLA through an affirmative action program in
which 40 percent of the entering class were admitted as "diversity"
students. The admissions committee examined those files looking
for special factors or characteristics beyond grades and test scores,
such as determination, life experience, economic or cultural disadvantage, language difficulty, community service, advanced degrees, race, gender, and disability. Many, but not all, the minority
students in the UCLA law school are admitted as diversity students,
and some whites are as well.

UCLA started its diversity program in response to the Bakke decision, in which the Supreme Court held that even though fixed racial
quotas were unconstitutional, race could be one of several factors

that schools could use in admissions decisions. The Court referred to the undergraduate admissions program at Harvard as an example of a constitutional program. Harvard admitted a farm boy from Idaho, a poor child from West Virginia, a Latina from East Los Angeles, and a black kid from the Chicago projects. Although it did not ignore grades and test scores, they were only two factors among many others. The Court emphasized that under the Harvard plan, every applicant was treated the same; no one — including me — was excluded solely on the basis of race. After *Bakke*, schools throughout the country instituted modified diversity programs.

The manner in which UCLA administered its diversity program created an unintended hierarchy among students, with some non-diversity admits and some diversity admits clashing over who belonged at the school. Most diversity students had a compelling personal story of hardships overcome. The more tragic the story, the more likely it was that a diversity applicant would be admitted. The admissions staff did not take time to ask nondiversity admits about their stories: if his or her scores were high enough, a non-diversity applicant's life story was irrelevant. Some white students were so insensitive as to tell minority students they didn't belong at UCLA, that they had taken the place of a better-qualified white student. Some professors and administrators pointed to the high attrition rates of some minority students or the lower bar passage rates as evidence that diversity was a bad policy.

The result was predictable: some minority students felt insecure and stigmatized. But those feelings were not created by the diversity policy; rather, they were caused by the many whites who did not support the policy, whites who really believed that diversity admits did not deserve a scarce resource like a law degree. Most of the minority students, however, bided their time, graduated, and passed the California bar examination. But many of them remember how some whites at UCLA treated them, and they don't have much goodwill for the school now.

It would have been better if UCLA had reviewed all its applications under the diversity standard that Justice Lewis Powell championed in *Bakke*, with every applicant having to demonstrate not only academic achievement and promise but also unusual human experiences and qualities. I know that some of the nondiversity students had compelling stories, too, but they were not made part of the admissions decision. Every student at UCLA should have been a diversity admit, for then there would have been no labels dividing the students; all would have been only UCLA law students.

With the 1995 vote by the University of California's board of regents to end racial considerations in admissions, UCLA's diversity program has been jeopardized. It is not surprising that the regents didn't mention the university's preferences for veterans and children of alumni or donors or influential people like the regents themselves. Why has the discussion of preferential admissions in California and elsewhere focused primarily on race? The simple answer is power. The regents' vote symbolizes the subordinate status of many racial minorities, who do not have the political or economic power to prevent their being excluded from schools they help finance through taxes. Ironically, at the same time that regents were voting to end affirmative action for students of color, some of them were making telephone calls on behalf of the children of their friends to help them be admitted.

The vote to end race as a factor in admission constituted a major setback for race relations in this country, portending a return to a time when very few minority students were enrolled at any of the University of California campuses. In fact, this decision will take California back to educational tracking, with even more minorities attending California's second- or third-tier colleges. Everyone in California knows that the public colleges of choice are the UC campuses, not the community colleges or the California State universities, the reason being that the UC campuses have the state's best educational resources. How unfair to reserve those campuses for an elite segment of California's or the nation's population.

Pete Wilson, the current governor of California and former presidential candidate, can stand before the television cameras and use words like *fairness* and *equal opportunity*, but he should know that if test scores become the only criterion for admission at a UC campus, only Asians, a smaller number of whites, and a still smaller number of Latinos and other minorities will qualify. There is nothing fair about educational caste in a country with our history of educational discrimination, and there is nothing fair about telling most blacks and other minorities they cannot attend the best public colleges in the state. If blacks, Latinos, and Native Americans cannot attend the UC schools, they will not have the same employment opportunities as those who can. They will not be able to live in decent housing, and most will remain in America's racial caste system. And that is a recipe for disaster.

I benefited tremendously from attending law school at UCLA. Up to that time, my world had been significantly bipolar — black and white. But while I was at UCLA, I met for the first time substantial numbers of Latinos, Mexicans, Asian Pacific Islanders, Japanese, Chinese, and Koreans. Race matters for other nonwhites as well. When I served as chair of the Black Law Students Association (BLSA), it sponsored programs for the law school and served as an advocacy group for black students. Other minority student groups had similar organizations. We acknowledged our different racial identities and talked about racial subordination and the law as an instrument of that subordination. We also shared food, music, religion, and other cultural traditions. Some of us tried to celebrate our diversity; we did not pretend to be color blind.

Within that diversity throughout Los Angeles, I lived first as a black student, then as a black associate at a corporate law firm, and later as one of six black members of the UCLA law faculty. At the law school and in my law practice, my colleagues did not subscribe to color-blind rhetoric. I knew that some of my professors had reputations for helping minority students succeed in school and get jobs, whereas others vehemently opposed remedial affirmative action. Some of the lawyers I worked with at my firm reached out to me and taught me how to serve clients effectively; others seemed to hold me to a higher standard of performance than they did the other new associates. For them, my mistakes only confirmed their belief that I was not competent. None of my professional colleagues was color blind.

EPILOGUE

Creating a Community
of a Larger Memory

Of every hue and caste am I, of every rank and religion,
A farmer, mechanic, artist, gentleman, sailor, quaker,
Prisoner, fancy-man, rowdy, lawyer, physician, priest.
I resist any thing better than my own diversity.

WALT WHITMAN[1]

IN THE TWENTY-FIRST CENTURY, there will be no white major-ity in the United States. Ours will be a different "city upon a hill" than the one envisioned by John Winthrop. Ours will be a different "manifest destiny" than the one embraced by Thomas Jefferson and Frederick Jackson Turner. At the edge of this tremen-dous transformation is California, where within a few years whites will become a minority — just like blacks, Indians, Hispanics, and Asians. Across America by 2050, we will all be minorities.

As we approach this multicultural millennium, the "culture wars" over whether our diversity is leading to "the closing of the American mind" and "the disuniting of America" has stirred me to reflect on my own experiences. C. Wright Mills described the "sociological imagination" as the study of the intersection between history and biography.[2] Throughout this book, individuals from the past to the present have shared stories that demonstrate the dynamic shuttles between self and society in the epic of multicul-tural America. For the conclusion of this history with "voices," I, too, have a story to tell — another of Whitman's "varied carols" of America.

345

When I was a teenager, I was not academically inclined. In fact, I was a surfer, but I was given an opportunity that led me to leave Hawaii and its beaches. During my senior year at Iolani High School, I took a course in religion from Dr. Shunji Nishi. I remember being impressed that he had a Ph.D. There were other Asian-American doctors, but they were M.D.s. Here was a doctor of philosophy. I remember telling my mother about Dr. Nishi and asking her: "Mom, what's a Ph.D.?" And my mother, who only had an eighth-grade education, answered: "I don't know, but he must be very smart." I began to see Dr. Nishi as a role model, thinking that I, too, could someday have a Ph.D.

Dr. Nishi required all of his students to read *The Screwtape Letters*, by C. S. Lewis. These were letters sent by the chief devil, Screwtape, to his assistant, Wormwood, giving instructions on how to trick Christians into sin. For our weekly assignment, we had to read a letter and then write our own missive. We were to imagine ourselves as Screwtape and write essays that began: "Dear Wormwood." On my papers, Dr. Nishi wrote marginal comments like, "How do you know this is true?" "Interesting," and sometimes, "Insightful." In this way, a relationship developed between the two of us, through my letter-essays and his marginal comments.

During the second semester of my senior year, Dr. Nishi stopped me as I was walking across campus and said, "Ronald, I think you should go away to college." He told me about the College of Wooster, in Ohio, and asked if I would be interested in attending this fine school. I told him that I was unsure about going so far away, and that I had already been accepted to the University of Hawaii. Dr. Nishi said he would send Wooster a letter about me, and I quickly forgot about this conversation. Several weeks later, however, I received a letter from the dean of the College of Wooster, informing me that I had been accepted but then asking me to please fill out the application form. Looking back, I realize that this was an early version of affirmative action. I do not think the dean had even seen my transcript or SATs (which were not very high), but he probably thought I had potential and should be given a special opportunity. Perhaps he also hoped my presence at Wooster would help to diversify the student body culturally and thus enrich the educational experiences of all students.

When I arrived at Wooster, I noticed that there were only a handful of black and Asian students. Often my fellow white students would ask me: "How long have you been in this country?" "Where did you learn to speak English?" They did not see me as an "American." I did not look American and did not have an American name. They saw me as a foreigner. But my grandfather had sailed east to America in 1886, before the arrival of many European immigrant groups. Looking back at this experience, I realized that it was not the fault of the Wooster students that they did not see me as an American. After all, what had they learned in courses called "U.S. History" about Asian Americans?

After I graduated from Wooster in 1961, I entered the Ph.D. program in history at Berkeley. I was admitted on the basis of my academic record because affirmative action was not even a term yet. The Berkeley experience changed my life even further. Inspired by the moral vision of Martin Luther King, many Berkeley students had joined the civil rights movement. They, too, had "a dream" of an America that would live up to its high principle of equality. "Black and white together," they believed, "we shall overcome someday."

In 1964, they began holding civil rights rallies on the steps of Sproul Hall. They wanted to protest and bear witness against segregation and racial violence in Mississippi and Alabama; they also wanted to organize demonstrations against employment inequalities in the Bay Area. When the regents banned these rallies, the students rebelled in the Free Speech Movement, led by Mario Savio. The confrontation between the FSM and the regents culminated when the charismatic Savio told five thousand protesting students that the time had come when the institution had become so odious that we had to put our bodies in the wheels and gears of the machine and make it stop. Hundreds of them then marched into Sproul Hall, the university's administration building, and engaged in a massive sit-in. The police stormed the building, making arrests with clubs and handcuffs. Spontaneously, thousands of students went out on strike, and hundreds of teaching assistants including myself refused to meet with classes. The strike educated the faculty: it made them realize that they could not remain bystanders in this struggle. They had to stand with the students in affirming the view that the university had to protect freedom of speech and also had a responsibility to society. Facing student and faculty opposition, the regents were forced to designate Sproul Hall Plaza a free speech area.

This experience at Berkeley and my moral outrage at the murder of the three civil rights workers in Mississippi and the deaths of black children in the Birmingham bombings led me to focus my dissertation on the Southern defense of slavery. I wanted to study the history of racism in America in order to understand William Faulkner's insight: the past is not even past. How do we free ourselves from our past, I wondered, if we do not even know this past? Professor Charles Sellers was my thesis adviser. A civil rights activist scholar, he was the author of *The Southerner as American*. I also had the privilege of studying with several other leading scholars: Henry May, Kenneth Stampp, Leon Litwack, and Winthrop Jordan. Henry Nash Smith gave me training in literary criticism and an appreciation of literary texts as historical documents.

While I was writing my dissertation in 1965, Watts exploded. "The fire next time" had come to Los Angeles; riveted to their television screens for days, Americans across the country saw searing images — entire blocks engulfed in flames, snipers shooting at the police, chaotic looting, and angry crowds shouting, "Burn, baby, burn." "A riot," Martin Luther King observed, "is the language of the unheard."[3] The message of Watts underlined the urgent need for universities to address the reality of the racial crisis.

Two years later, UCLA hired me to teach its first black history course. When I walked into class for the first time that fall, I found hundreds of eager and excited students packed into a large lecture room. They looked curiously at their professor, and I could feel them thinking, "Funny, he doesn't look black." Gradually, I earned their confidence in me as a teacher; I even became a faculty adviser to the Black Student Union. As I looked at my students in this class,

I saw not only whites and blacks but also Asians and Mexicans. One of them approached me after class one day and said: "We're Chicanos, you know." That was the first time I had heard that nomenclature. "Now I do know," I replied.

This diversity inspired me to help initiate a new course: History 183, "Racial Attitudes in America: A Comparative Perspective" — a study of race reaching beyond the black-white binary to include also Native Americans, Mexicans, and Asians. For the first time in my life, I was studying the history of Asian Americans. As I developed and presented lectures for this course, I learned a valuable lesson: we need to rethink the very way we think about history. Turning away from approaches that were either Eurocentric or ethnic-group specific, I was pursuing a comparative study of our racial and ethnic diversity. In this re-visioning of our past, I began to conceptualize a field of scholarship that would later become known as multicultural studies.

Meanwhile, I was swept into the student struggle for a more culturally diverse curriculum at UCLA. In 1970, I became the chairperson of the history department's ad hoc ethnic studies committee. At a meeting of the history faculty that spring, I presented our report: it urged the department to offer courses and make appointments in Asian-American, Chicano, and Native-American history. With hundreds of student supporters gathered outside of the meeting, the faculty reluctantly voted to accept what the students called the "Takaki recommendations."

That summer, after the students left campus, the history faculty rescinded their approval of the recommendations. Then the chairperson informed me that I would be given an "accelerated" review for tenure. This turned out to be the mechanism for firing me that fall. For months, students protested against this action, but were stymied and frustrated by the department's power to hide its decision behind the "confidentiality" of a "personnel matter."

During the political ferment of the previous spring semester, I knew I had been jeopardizing my career by campaigning for ethnic studies, but I thought my teaching and scholarship would be sufficiently strong for me to be granted tenure. My first book, A Pro-

Slavery Crusade: The Agitation to Reopen the African Slave Trade, had been accepted for publication by the respected Free Press, and I had been awarded a fellowship from the National Endowment for the Humanities to complete a second book on nineteenth-century black novelists. Naively, I had believed I would be judged objectively on the basis of my merit as a teacher and scholar, and had underestimated the power and determination of my senior colleagues to remove me as a threat to the traditional curriculum. My dismissal was distressing, for I had a wife and three very young children to support. I was also worried that I would have no future as a scholar.

Fortunately, another path opened for me. The Ethnic Studies Department at Berkeley had been instituted in response to the 1969 Third World student strike, and they invited me to join this new program. The recommendation for my appointment was submitted to the administration and reviewed by university faculty committees. Coming to a very different decision than the one that had been reached at UCLA, Berkeley determined that my scholarship merited an appointment as an associate professor with tenure. In all likelihood, the decision was also based on an additional consideration — the awareness that Asian Americans were underrepresented in the social sciences and humanities and that my appointment would help to address this shortcoming. This occurred in 1972, after affirmative action had become a policy.

Seventeen years later, my work as a teacher and curriculum transformer at Berkeley reached a high point when the faculty approved a proposal for a multicultural graduation requirement — the "American Cultures Requirement." The impulse for this requirement had been initiated by the Berkeley students in 1987. That fall, a powerful transformation had occurred: minorities constituted 51 percent of the undergraduate student body. The America of the twenty-first century had arrived on our campus. Beginning in the early eighties, under Chancellor Ira Heyman's leadership, the university had committed itself to the pledge of "excellence and diversity." In terms of admissions, this meant affirmative action. Only qualified students would be admitted, but race would be an additional consideration.

This new diversity led to a rethinking of "excellence" in the curriculum. Under the leadership of the Associated Students of the University of California vice president Beth Bernstein and her assistant Mark Min, students began to discuss the idea of a required course for understanding America's racial diversity. The idea gathered support rapidly, and led to a student-sponsored symposium, "The Educated Californian of the Twenty-first Century." There were more than two thousand people in attendance, and out of this event came a proposal for a multicultural requirement. Student support was widespread: organizations of students of color as well as the fraternities and sororities enthusiastically endorsed the proposal. Students were asking the faculty to educate them about the reality of the peoples of the United States. Like the students of the FSM days, students expressed themselves through rallies and sit-ins.

Like the faculty of the time of the FSM, faculty again had to ask themselves: what is the mission of the university and what is its responsibility to society? The debate was intense and often acrimonious. Critics of the proposal castigated it as "political correctness," warning that the courses would constitute propaganda and indoctrination. Some of them also arrogantly reaffirmed the superiority of "western civilization." On the other side, supporters reminded their colleagues that these courses would be taught by Berkeley faculty, teachers with Ph.D.s and appointments approved by faculty personnel committees. Noting that "civilizations," including "western," have never been monolithic and pure, isolated from one another, they pointed out that American society is a vivid illustration of this crisscrossing of different cultures.

During the debate, most Berkeley faculty acted as intelligent and fair-minded people should. They listened to the arguments and evaluated the evidence. Individuals who had not previously thought about the issue now studied it. Many who had initially opposed the proposal began to rethink their views. Many of its supporters thought more carefully about the proposal and realized the need to include the study of European immigrant groups, especially from countries like Ireland, Italy, Poland, and Russia.

After a two-year debate, the Berkeley faculty voted affirmatively to establish a graduation requirement designed to broaden and deepen the understanding of racial and ethnic diversity in the United States. Its purpose was intellectual — to pursue a more inclusive and hence more accurate study of American society. The courses that fulfill this requirement would analyze comparatively different groups of Americans with roots reaching to Europe, Africa, Asia, and also North and South America. Students would examine our ethnic diversity as well as the ties that bind us as one people. The new requirement was implemented in 1991, and today, Berkeley offers more than 150 American Cultures courses taught by faculty in over 20 departments, from ethnic studies and history to music and literature and public health to business administration. Universities and colleges across the country have been seeking to emulate the "Berkeley model of multiculturalism."

Like the teachers at Berkeley and other schools, Americans in general have choices to make about how we define ourselves as Americans. These choices are not only intellectual but also social and political. Denying our multicultural past, we can fight our diversity by heeding jeremiads about the "disuniting of America" and by erecting borders that insulate "us" against "them," the "other." In erudite Eurocentric tomes, we can view our ethnic conflicts as "the clash of civilizations," and also denounce the study of our diversity as "the closing of the American mind." In nervous nativist backlashes against Asian and Latino immigrants, we can aggressively reaffirm Thomas Jefferson's vision of a homogeneous white America. We can cheer militant calls to take back "our" country, "our" culture, and "our" cities. In attacks on affirmative action, we can deny the reality that racial minorities still lack a level playing field in "the pursuit of happiness" through education and employment. We can cut welfare and even food stamps, punishing the poor for being poor, while we reduce taxes for the wealthy. We can accelerate America's expansion into the globalizing economy without concern or compassion for people victimized by the "disappearance" of work. We can vote for politicians who, like the aristocratic planters of seventeenth-century Virginia, unscrupulously exploit our economic anxieties and xenophobic paranoia for their own narrow political purposes. In short, we can resist our diversity and allow it to divide us and possibly even destroy us as a nation.

But as Americans we have a history that, if viewed in "a different mirror," can guide us toward an alternative future. Challenging the traditional master narrative of American history, this "democratic history" teaches us that "the blood of the whole world" flows through us. As Herman Melville observed, "we are not a narrow tribe." Though Americans represent a multiplicity of geographical origins, we can recognize our common membership in a "vast, surging, hopeful army of workers" — the "giddy multitude" of Bacon's Rebellion, which has become more multiethnic across the centuries. We can embrace Lincoln's vision of America as a nation "dedicated" to the "proposition" of equality — a principle conceived by founding fathers like Jefferson but consecrated by black as well as white Union soldiers in the bloody crucible of the Civil War. We can act affirmatively in carrying forward our nation's "unfinished work." With the end of the Cold War, we can shift resources from defense to a domestic Marshall Plan for the economic rebuilding of our cities, the reemployment of American workers, the creation of a national health care system, and the revitalization of our schools. We can still have "a dream." Ours can be a great refusal to allow this yearning for equality to be "deferred," and then "explode" or "dry up like a raisin in the sun." We can "let America be America," to use the poetic phrase of Langston Hughes.[4] In the sharing of our varied stories, we can create a community of "a larger memory."

Notes

Prologue

The "Varied Carols" of America

1. Abraham Lincoln, "Address delivered at the dedication of the cemetery at Gettysburg," November 19, 1863, reprinted in appendix of Garry Wills, *Lincoln at Gettysburg* (New York, 1992), p. 263.
2. Walt Whitman, *Leaves of Grass* (New York, 1958), p. 9; Herman Melville, *Redburn* (Chicago, 1969), p. 169.

Part One

The Ties That Bind

1. Minoru Takaki, conversation with the author, July 1985.
2. Theo. H. Davies and Company to C. McClennan, July 2, 1890, Laupahoehoe Plantation Records, microfilm, University of Hawaii Library; H. Hackfield and Company to G. N. Wilcox, May 5, 1980, Grove Farm Plantation Records, Grove Farm Plantation, Kauai.
3. George H. Fairfield, in Republic of Hawaii, *Report of the Labor Commission on Strikes and Arbitration* (Honolulu, 1895), p. 36.
4. "The Five O'clock Whistle," in the *Kohala Midget*, April 27, 1910.
5. "Plantation Work Begins, Silently, in the Early Morn," *Honolulu Star Bulletin*, January 13, 1934.
6. Ethnic Studies Oral History Project, *Uchinanchu* (Honolulu, 1981), p. 360.
7. *The Higher Wage Question*, reprinted in Bureau of Labor Statistics, *Report of the Commissioner of Labor on Hawaii* (Washington, D.C., 1910), p. 76.
8. Takashi Tsutsumi, *History of Hawaii Laborers' Movement* (Honolulu, 1922), pp. 194–98, in University of Hawaii Archives.
9. Ethnic Studies Oral History Project, *Waialua and Haleiwa* (Honolulu, 1977), vol. 9, p. 223.

Notes

10. Manager of the Hawaiian Agricultural Company to Bureau of Labor, Hawaiian Sugar Planters' Association, April 5, 1919, Hawaiian Agricultural Company Records, University of Hawaii Library; Ethnic Studies Oral History Project, *Waialua and Haleiwa*, p. 11.
11. Curtis Aller, "The Evolution of Hawaiian Labor Relations," unpublished Ph.D. thesis, Harvard University, 1958, p. 39.
12. Hawaii Laborers' Association, *Facts about the Strike* (Honolulu, 1920), p. 1.
13. James Grossman, *Land of Hope: Chicago, Black Southerners, and the Great Migration* (Chicago, 1989), p. 192.
14. Robert L. Wright (ed.), *Irish Emigrant Ballads and Songs* (Bowling Green, Ohio, 1975), p. 539; Carl Wittke, *The Irish in America* (Baton Rouge, 1956), p. 3.
15. Kazuo Ito, *Issei* (Seattle, 1973), pp. 317, 343.
16. Manuel Gamio, *Mexican Immigration to the United States* (Chicago, 1930), pp. 84–85.
17. David R. Roediger, *The Wages of Whiteness* (London, 1991), pp. 136–37.
18. Frederick Law Olmsted, *The Slave States before the Civil War* (New York, 1859), p. 76.
19. Roediger, *Wages of Whiteness*, p. 137; Leon Litwack, *North of Slavery* (Chicago, 1965), p. 163.
20. Litwack, *North of Slavery*, p. 163.
21. William Shanks, "Chinese Skilled Labor," *Scribner's Monthly* vol. 2 (September 1871), pp. 495–96.
22. Walt Whitman, *Leaves of Grass* (New York, 1958), p. 284.
23. Carl Becker, *The Declaration of Independence* (New York, 1961), pp. 180–81.
24. Becker, *Declaration of Independence*, pp. 171–72.
25. Phillis Wheatley, *The Poems of Phillis Wheatley* (Chapel Hill, 1966), p. 34.
26. David Donald, *Lincoln* (London, 1995), pp. 429–31, 455, 462, 466, 471.
27. Frederick Douglass, in Herbert Aptheker (ed.), *A Documentary History of the Negro People in the United States* (New York, 1951), vol. 1, p. 496; James H. Cone, *Martin & Malcolm & America* (New York, 1991), p. 5.
28. Donald, *Lincoln*, p. 527.
29. Yan Phou Lee, "The Chinese Must Stay," *North American Review*, vol. 148, no. 389 (April 1889), p. 476.
30. Tomas Almaguer, "Racial Domination and Class Conflict in Capitalist

Notes

Agriculture: The Oxnard Sugar Beet Workers' Strike of 1903," *Labor History*, vol. 25, no. 3 (summer 1984), pp. 334, 347.

31. "Let America Be America Again," *International Workers Order*, 1938.
32. Malcolm X, *The Autobiography of Malcolm X* (New York, 1965), p. 71.
33. Louis I. Dublin and Samuel C. Kohs, *American Jews in World War II* (n.p., 1947), pp. 186–87.
34. Quoted in Gunnar Myrdal, *An American Dilemma* (New York, 1944), p. 1007.
35. Mario Garcia, *Mexican Americans: Leadership, Ideology & Identity, 1930–1960* (New Haven, 1989), p. 166; Raul Morin, *Among the Valiant: Mexican Americans in WWII* (Alhambra, Calif., 1966), pp. 111–14.
36. Alison Bernstein, *American Indians and World War Two* (Norman, Okla., 1991), p. 42; Evon Z. Vogt, *Navaho Veterans* (Cambridge, 1951), p. 64.
37. Andrew Lind, *Hawaii's Japanese* (Princeton, 1946), pp. 161–62.
38. Chester Tanaka, *Go for Broke* (Richmond, Calif., 1982), p. 171.
39. Martin Luther King, Jr., "I Have a Dream," reprinted in Francis L. Broderick and August Meier (eds.), *Negro Protest Thought in the Twentieth Century* (New York, 1965), pp. 400–405.
40. Leslie Marmon Silko, *Ceremony* (New York, 1978), p. 2.
41. "Social Document of Pany Lowe," Survey of Race Relations, Hoover Institution Archives; Harriet A. Jacobs, *Incidents in the Life of a Slave Girl* (Cambridge, 1987), p. xiii; Minnie Miller, "Autobiography," private manuscript, copy from Richard Balkin.
42. David J. Weber (ed.), *Foreigners in the Native Land* (Albuquerque, 1973), p. vi.
43. Tomo Shoji, presentation, Ohana Cultural Center, Oakland, Calif., March 4, 1988; Lisa Lowe, *Immigrant Acts* (Durham, 1996), pp. 60–83.
44. Benedict Anderson, *Imagined Communities* (New York, 1991).

Part Two

Introduction

1. Perry Miller, *Errand into the Wilderness* (New York, 1964), pp. 1–15.
2. Francis Jennings, *The Invasion of America* (New York, 1976), p. 312.
3. John Winthrop, *Winthrop Papers*, vol. 2 (1623–1630), Massachusetts Historical Society (1931), p. 139.
4. Charles M. Segal and David C. Stineback (eds.), *Puritans, Indians & Manifest Destiny* (New York, 1977), pp. 136–37, 111, 182.

Notes

5. Edward Johnson, *Wonder-working Providence* (New York, 1910), pp. 71, 169, 211, 247–48.
6. David R. Ford, "Mary Rowlandson's Captivity Narrative: A Paradigm of Puritan Representations of Native Americans?" Ethnic Studies 299 paper, Fall 1996, University of California, Berkeley.
7. Winthrop Jordan, *White Over Black* (Chapel Hill, 1968), p. 73.
8. Edmund Morgan, *American Slavery, American Freedom* (New York, 1975), pp. 241–42.
9. T. H. Breen, "A Changing Labor Force and Race Relations in Virginia," *Journal of Social History*, vol. 7 (fall 1973), p. 11.
10. Morgan, *American Slavery, American Freedom*, pp. 404, 306.
11. John Woolman, *Considerations on the Keeping of Negroes*, reprinted in Leslie H. Fishel, Jr., and Benjamin Quarles, *The Black American: A Documentary History* (Glenview, Ill., 1970), pp. 30–32.

A Horror Remembered

1. John Hope Franklin, *From Slavery to Freedom* (New York, 1967), p. 59.

Part Three

Introduction

1. Alexis de Tocqueville, *Democracy in America*, 2 vols. (New York, 1945), vol. 2, pp. 23, 239, 137.
2. Douglas C. North, *The Economic Growth of the United States* (New York, 1966), p. 129.
3. Jefferson to Monroe, November 24, 1801, in Paul L. Ford (ed.), *The Works of Thomas Jefferson*, 10 vols. (New York, 1892–99), vol. 9, p. 317.
4. Fawn Brodie, *Thomas Jefferson* (New York, 1974), p. 96; Jefferson to Edward Coles, August 25, 1814, in Ford, *Works*, vol. 11, p. 416; Jefferson to Francis Eppes, July 30, 1787, in Julian Boyd (ed.), *The Papers of Thomas Jefferson*, 18 vols. (Princeton, 1950–65), vol. 10, p. 653.
5. Thomas Jefferson, *Notes on the State of Virginia* (New York, 1964), pp. 138–39.
6. Jefferson to John Holmes, April 22, 1820, and to Jared Sparks, February 24, 1824, in Ford, *Works*, vol. 12, pp. 334–39, and vol. 13, p. 159.
7. David Donald, *Lincoln* (London, 1995), p. 199.

Notes

8. Ibid., pp. 201, 202.
9. Ibid., pp. 176, 189.
10. Ibid., pp. 221, 343–45, 355, 367–68, 416–18.
11. Ibid., p. 430.
12. Abraham Lincoln, "First Inaugural Address," in The Annals of America, vol. 9 (Chicago, 1968), p. 255; Lincoln to James C. Conkling, August 26, 1863, in Annals, vol. 9, p. 439.
13. Lincoln, "Gettysburg Address," reprinted in Garry Wills, Lincoln at Gettysburg: The Words That Remade America (New York, 1992), p. 263.
14. Walt Whitman, in Horace Traubel, With Walt Whitman, vol. 2 (New York, 1915), pp. 34–35.

The Significance of the Frontier in American History

1. William Cronon, Changes in the Land (New York, 1983), p. 162.
2. Jefferson to Jackson, February 16, 1803, in Andrew Lipscomb and Albert Bergh (eds.), Writings of Thomas Jefferson, 20 vols. (Washington, D.C., 1904), vol. 10, pp. 357–59.
3. Ross to Jackson, March 12, 1834, in Gary E. Moulton (ed.), The Papers of Chief John Ross, vol. 1 (Norman, Okla., 1985), p. 277.
4. Grant Foreman, Indian Removal (Norman, Okla., 1972), pp. 286–88.
5. George Hicks to John Ross, November 4, 1838, in Moulton (ed.), Papers of Ross, vol. 1, p. 687.
6. Foreman, Indian Removal, pp. 309, 296; Thurman Wilkins, Cherokee Tragedy (New York, 1970), p. 314.
7. Gloria Levitas, Frank Vivelo, and Jacqueline Vivelo (eds.), American Indian Prose and Poetry (New York, 1974), p. 180; Wilkins, Cherokee Tragedy, p. 314.
8. James Mooney, The Ghost-Dance Religion and the Sioux Outbreak of 1890 (Washington, D.C., 1896), p. 26.
9. Wayne Moquin (ed.), Great Documents in American Indian History (New York, 1973), p. 307.

From Sunup to Sundown

1. Kenneth Stampp, The Peculiar Institution (New York, 1956), p. 44; Frederick Law Olmsted, The Slave States (New York, 1959), pp. 176–77.
2. Solomon Northrup, Twelve Years a Slave (Buffalo, 1853), pp. 166–68.
3. Stampp, Peculiar Institution, p. 87; U. B. Phillips, Life and Labor in the Old South (Boston, 1929), p. 276.
4. Raymond and Alice Bauer, "Day to Day Resistance to Slavery," Journal

Notes

of *Negro History*, vol. 27 (1942), pp. 388–419; Stampp, *Peculiar Institution*, pp. 88, 90.

5. Sarah Logue to "Jarm," February 20, 1860, and J. W. Loguen to Mrs. Sarah Logue, reprinted in *Boston Liberator*, April 27, 1860.
6. Stampp, *Peculiar Institution*, p. 132; Phillips, *Life and Labor in the Old South*, p. 209; Nat Turner and T. R. Gray, *The Confessions of Nat Turner*, in Herbert Aptheker, *Nat Turner's Rebellion* (New York, 1968), appendix, pp. 136, 138, 130–31.
7. Stampp, *Peculiar Institution*, pp. 100, 127; Eugene Genovese, *Roll, Jordan, Roll: The World the Slaveholders Made* (New York, 1974), pp. 300, 318, 602.
8. Leon Litwack, *Been in the Storm So Long* (New York, 1979), pp. 6, 21.
9. Ibid., p. 19.
10. Ibid., p. 59.

"Don't Give a Nigger an Inch"

1. Frederick Douglass, *Life and Times of Frederick Douglass* (New York, 1962), pp. 28–29, 440–52.

Fleeing English Tyranny

1. Robert L. Wright (ed.), *Irish Emigrant Ballads and Songs* (Bowling Green, Ohio, 1975), p. 37.
2. Lawrence J. McCaffrey, *The Irish Diaspora in America* (Washington, D.C., 1984), pp. 71–72; Wright (ed.), *Irish Emigrant Ballads*, p. 126.
3. Oliver MacDonagh, "The Irish Famine Emigration to the United States," *Perspectives in American History*, vol. 10 (1976), pp. 403, 410–11.
4. Stephan Thernstrom, *Poverty and Progress* (Cambridge, 1964), p. 27; Michael Buckley, *Diary of a Tour in America* (Dublin, 1886), p. 142; Kerby Miller, *Emigrants and Exiles* (New York, 1985), p. 318; McCaffrey, *Irish Diaspora*, p. 71.
5. Carl Wittke, *The Irish in America* (Baton Rouge, La., 1956), pp. 32–33; Buckley, *Tour in America*, p. 164; Wright (ed.), *Irish Emigrant Ballads*, p. 533.
6. Hasia Diner, *Erin's Daughters in America* (Baltimore, 1983), pp. 30–31.
7. Elizabeth Gurley Flynn, *I Speak My Own Piece* (New York, 1955), p. 24.
8. Miller, *Emigrants and Exiles*, p. 505; Philip S. Foner (ed.), *The Factory Girls* (Urbana, Ill., 1977), pp. 6–7.

360

9. Arnold Schrier, *Ireland and the American Emigration* (New York, 1970), p. 24; Carol Groneman, "Working-Class Immigrant Women in Mid-Nineteenth-Century New York: The Irish Woman's Experience," *Journal of Urban History*, vol. 4, no. 3 (May 1978), p. 269.
10. Schrier, *Ireland and the American Emigration*, p. 38; Kerby Miller, "Assimilation and Alienation: Irish Emigrants' Responses to Industrial America, 1871–1921," in P. J. Drudy (ed.), *The Irish in America* (New York, 1985), p. 97.

Strangers from a Different Shore

1. Aaron H. Palmer, *Memoir, geographical, political, and commercial . . .* , March 8, 1848, U.S. Congress, Senate, 30th Cong., 1st sess., Senate misc. no. 80, pp. 1, 52, 60, 61.
2. Huie Kin, *Reminiscences* (Peiping, 1932), pp. 25, 28; A. W. Loomis, "The Old East in the New West," *Overland Monthly* (October 1868), p. 364.
3. A. W. Loomis, "Holiday in the Chinese Quarter," *Overland Monthly* (February 1869), pp. 148, 151.
4. Otis Gibson, *The Chinese in America* (Cincinnati, 1877), pp. 15–16; A. W. Loomis, "The Old East in the New West," p. 364; "Conversation with a Chinese Waiter," Survey of Race Relations, Hoover Institution Archives.
5. Him Mark Lai et al., *The Chinese in America* (San Francisco, 1980), p. 51.
6. Chu-chia to Lung On, July 1889, wife to Lung On, undated; Lung On to Liang Kwang-jin, March 2, 1905; Liang Kwang-jin to Lung On, March 4, 1905.

Part Four

Introduction

1. Frederick Jackson Turner, "The Significance of the Frontier in American History," in *The Early Writings of Frederick Jackson Turner* (Madison, Wis., 1938), pp. 185–228.
2. Gunnar Myrdal, *An American Dilemma* (New York, 1944; rev. ed. 1962), pp. 1004, 1021.
3. "The Hidden Heroes," *New York Times*, December 7, 1991.
4. Lyndon B. Johnson, Commencement Address at Howard University,

Notes

June 4, 1965, reprinted in Clayborne Carson et al. (eds.), *The Eyes on the Prize Reader* (New York, 1991), pp. 611–13.
5. Douglas Massey and Nancy Denton, *American Apartheid* (Cambridge, 1993).
6. Bill Clinton, "One America in the 21st Century," June 14, 1997 (Washington, D.C., 1997).

Beyond the Pale

1. Mary Antin, *The Promised Land* (New York, 1980), pp. 5, 22.
2. Sydelle Kramer and Jenny Masur (eds.), *Jewish Grandmothers* (Boston, 1976), p. 64; Golda Meier, in Maxine Schwartz Seller (ed.), *Immigrant Women* (Philadelphia, 1981), p. 37.
3. Abraham Cahan, *The Rise of David Levinsky* (New York, 1960), pp. 59–60; Anzia Yezierska, *Children of Loneliness* (New York, 1923), p. 152.
4. Susan Glenn, *Daughters of the Shtetl* (Ithaca, N.Y., 1990), pp. 54, 137–38; Deborah Dash Moore, *At Home in America* (New York, 1981), p. 29; Milton Meltzer, *Taking Root* (New York, 1976), p. 65.
5. Glenn, *Daughters of the Shtetl*, pp. 90, 94, 64; Irving Howe, *World of Our Fathers* (New York, 1983), p. 81.
6. Glenn, *Daughters of the Shtetl*, p. 103; Yezierska, *Children of Loneliness*, p. 158.
7. Glenn, *Daughters of the Shtetl*, p. 139.
8. Irving Howe and Kenneth Libo (eds.), *How We Lived* (New York, 1979), p. 185; Meltzer, *Taking Root*, pp. 231–33.
9. Howe, *World of Our Fathers*, pp. 302, 306.

Betrayed by Their Country

1. Gary Okihiro and Julie Sly, "The Press, Japanese Americans, and the Concentration Camps," *Phylon*, vol. 44, no. 1 (1983), pp. 66–69.
2. John Tateishi, *And Justice for All* (New York, 1984), pp. 76, 104; Commission on Wartime Relocation and Internment of Civilians, *Personal Justice Denied* (Washington, D.C., 1982), pp. 160, 172.

Fighting on the "Frontier" of the Pacific War

1. Allen Nevins, "How We Felt About the War," in Jack Goodman (ed.), *While You Were Gone: A Report on Wartime Life in the United States* (New York, 1946), p. 13.
2. Craig M. Cameron, *American Samurai: Myth, Imagination, and the Conduct of*

Notes

Battle in the First Marine Division, 1941–1951 (New York, 1994), pp. 98, 127.
3. John Dower, War Without Mercy (New York, 1986), p. 152; Cameron, American Samurai, p. 117.
4. Milton A. Hill, "The Lessons of Bataan," Science Digest, December 1942, p. 54.
5. James M. Merrill, A Sailor's Admiral: A Biography of William F. Halsey (New York, 1976), p. 111.
6. William Bradford Huie, The Hero of Iwo Jima and Other Stories (New York, 1959), pp. 26–27.
7. Ibid., pp. 34–40.
8. Ibid., p. 64.

Transplanted in Chicago

1. Harriet Pawlowska (ed.), Merrily We Sing: One Hundred Five Polish Folk Songs (Detroit, 1961), pp. 154–55.

El Norte

1. David J. Weber (ed.), Foreigners in Their Native Land (Albuquerque, N. Mex., 1973), p. 199.
2. Ricardo Romo, East Los Angeles (Austin, Tex., 1983), p. 48.
3. Albert Camarillo, Chicanos in a Changing Society (Cambridge, 1979), p. 146; Manuel Gamio, The Mexican Immigrant (Chicago, 1931), p. 15.
4. Paul Taylor, "Songs of the Mexican Migration," in J. Frank Dobie (ed.), Puro Mexicano (Austin, Tex., 1935), pp. 222–24.
5. Gamio, Mexican Immigrant, pp. 69–70.
6. Abraham Hoffman, Unwanted Americans in the Great Depression (Tucson, Ariz., 1974), p. 10; Mark Reisler, By the Sweat of Their Brow (Westport, Conn., 1976), p. 87.
7. Devra Weber, "Mexican Women on Strike," in Alelaida R. Del Castillo (ed.), Between Borders (Encino, Calif., 1990), p. 183.
8. Gamio, Mexican Immigrant, p. 56.
9. Laura H. Parker, "Migratory Children," National Conference of Social Work Proceedings (1927), p. 304; California Commission on Immigration and Housing, Annual Report (1927), p. 18.

Beyond Ellis Island

1. Victor Von Borosini, "Home-Going Italians," Survey, September 28, 1912, p. 792.

Notes

2. John Higham, *Strangers in the Land* (New York, 1966), pp. 66, 183.
3. Jacobus tenBroek, Edward N. Barnart, and Floyd Matson, *Prejudice, War and the Constitution* (Berkeley, 1970), pp. 83–84; Commission on Wartime Relocation and Internment of Civilians, *Personal Justice Denied* (Washington, 1982), pp. 101, 68, 70, 96–97.

Reinventing Herself in America

1. Hamida Chopra, interview with the author, September 12, 1988.

Puerto Ricans

1. Jesús Colon, *A Puerto Rican in New York* (New York, 1961), pp. 22–25, 197, 198, 200.

The 1992 Los Angeles Riot

1. "The Pioneers," *Newsweek*, May 26, 1975, p. 10; Bong-youn Choy, *Koreans in America* (Chicago, 1979), p. 249.
2. "Beyond Black and White," *Newsweek*, May 18, 1992, p. 28.
3. Elaine Kim and Eui-Young Yu, *East to America* (New York, 1996), p. 246.
4. "Sa-I-Gu," PBS broadcast, 1994; Edward Chang, *Asianweek*, June 19, 1992.
5. Frank Wu, "A Long Time Coming: Two Key Appointments Go to APAs," *Asianweek*, June 20, 1997. In his major speech on race given in California on June 14, President Bill Clinton announced that he had appointed Oh to the seven-member advisory board for "One America in the Twenty-first Century: The President's Initiative on Race."

Blacks in the Cities

1. Kenneth B. Clark, *Dark Ghetto: Dilemmas of Social Power* (New York, 1965), pp. 1, 12, 10.
2. James H. Cone, *Martin & Malcolm & America: A Dream or a Nightmare* (Maryknoll, N.Y., 1991), p. 223; Martin Luther King, Jr., *Why We Can't Wait* (New York, 1964), pp. 80, ix; Martin Luther King, Jr., *Where Do We Go From Here: Chaos or Community?* (New York, 1967), p. 6.
3. Donald J. Bogue, *The Population of the United States* (New York, 1985), pp. 584, 11, 45; *Social Security Bulletin, Annual Statistical Supplement*, 1983, p. 248; Leslie Dunbar, *The Common Interest: How Our Social Welfare Policies Don't Work and What We Can Do About Them* (New York, 1988), p. 103.
4. *Social Security Bulletin*, vol. 45, no. 4 (April 1982), p. 8; U.S. Department

Notes

of Health and Human Services, *Aid to Families with Dependent Children:
1979 Recipient Characteristics Study*, pp. 3, 17; Carol B. Stack, *All Our Kin:
Strategies for Survival in a Black Community* (New York, 1975), p. 51; William Julius Wilson and Kathryn N. Neckerman, "Poverty and Family
Structure: The Widening Gap between Evidence and Public Policy
Issues," in Sheldon H. Danziger and Daniel H. Weinberg (eds.), *Fighting Poverty: What Works and What Doesn't* (Cambridge, p. 235; Bogue,
Population, p. 603; *Social Security Bulletin*, vol. 45, no. 4 (April 1982),
p. 5; United States Commission on Civil Rights, *Unemployment and Underemployment Among Blacks, Hispanics, and Women* (Washington, 1982),
p. 51; Bogue, *Population*, p. 166; William Julius Wilson, *The Truly Disadvantaged: The Inner City, the Underclass, and Public Policy* (Chicago, 1987),
pp. 72–92.

5. Dunbar, *Common Interest*, pp. 165–67.
6. John Reid, "Black America in the 1980s," *Population Bulletin*, vol. 37,
no. 4 (December 1982), p. 7; Barry Bluestone and Bennett Harrison,
*The Deindustrialization of America: Plant Closings, Community Abandonment, and
the Dismantling of Basic Industry* (New York, 1982), p. 270; Andrew
Hacker, *Two Nations: Black and White, Separate, Hostile, Unequal* (New York,
1992), p. 101; Wilson, *Truly Disadvantaged*, pp. 12, 90–91.
7. Darryl Swafford, quoted in Jacob Lamar, "Today's Native Sons," *Time*,
December 1, 1986, p. 28; Danny Coleman, quoted in Lamar, "Today's Native Sons," p. 29.
8. Gregory Lewis, "L.A. Riot Area Likened to Third World Nation," *San
Francisco Examiner*, May 31, 1992; April Lynch, "Southland's Hopes
Turn to Ashes: Promise Eroded by Recession, Ethnic Tensions," *San
Francisco Chronicle*, May 22, 1992.
9. Song in *Chicago Defender*, May 28, 1917, quoted in Allan Spear, *Black
Chicago* (Chicago, 1967), p. 135.

A Chance to Act Affirmatively

1. "In Poll, Americans Reject Means But Not Ends of Racial Diversity,"
New York Times, December 14, 1997.

Epilogue
Creating a Community of a Larger Memory

1. Walt Whitman, *Leaves of Grass* (New York, 1958), p. 38.

365

2. C. Wright Mills, *The Sociological Imagination* (New York, 1976).
3. Martin Luther King, quoted in Willie L. Brown, "Riots Echo Decades-Old Anguish of Dispossessed," *San Francisco Examiner*, May 3, 1992.
4. Langston Hughes, "Lennox Avenue Mural," in Langston Hughes, *The Langston Hughes Reader* (New York, 1958), p. 123; Langston Hughes, "Let America Be America Again," *International Workers Order*, 1938.

Sources

Part Two

"A Horror Remembered: Olaudah Equiano's Passage to America," from Olaudah Equiano, *The Interesting Narrative and Other Writings*, edited by Vincent Carretta (New York: Penguin, 1995), first published in Great Britain, 1789, pp. 55–61.

Part Three

"The Coming of the Wasichus: Black Elk's Boyhood Memories," from *Black Elk Speaks: Being the Life Story of a Holy Man of the Oglala Sioux*, as told through John G. Neihardt (Lincoln, Neb.: University of Nebraska Press, 1961), originally published in 1932 by William Morrow and Company, pp. 7–19.

"The End of the Frontier for a Winnebago," from Paul Radin, *The Autobiography of a Winnebago Indian, University of California Publications in American Archeology and Ethnology*, vol. 16, no. 7, April 15, 1920, pp. 3–33.

"'Don't Give a Nigger an Inch': Frederick Douglass Learns to Read," from Frederick Douglass, *Life and Times of Frederick Douglass* (from the 1892 edition), pp. 70–87.

"'The Best Mistress and Master in the World': Millie Evans," from B. A. Botkin (ed.), *Lay My Burden Down: A Folk History of Slavery* (Chicago: Univ. of Chicago Press, 1945), pp. 61–65.

"'Git This Nigger to the Cotton Patch': Jenny Proctor's Complaint," from B. A. Botkin (ed.), *Lay My Burden Down: A Folk History of Slavery* (Chicago: Univ. of Chicago Press, 1945), pp. 89–93.

"After Slavery: A Personal Account of a New Bondage," from Hamilton Holt (ed.), *The Life Stories of Undistinguished Americans, as Told by Themselves* (New York: James Pott and Co., 1906), pp. 183–99.

Sources

Sources

"Finding Her Voice for Militant Labor: Elizabeth Gurley Flynn," from I Speak My Own Piece: Autobiography of "The Rebel Girl," Elizabeth Gurley Brown (New York: Masses & Mainstream, 1955), pp. 30–44.

"'How Can I Call This My Home?': Lee Chew," from Hamilton Holt (ed.), The Life Stories of Undistinguished Americans, as Told by Themselves (New York: James Pott and Co., 1906), pp. 281–299.

"'Like Country Pretty Much': Kee Low," from "Life History of Kee Low," interviewed by C. H. Burnett, August 4, 1924, folder 179, box 27, Survey of Race Relations, Hoover Institution.

"'A Chance to Take Care of Myself': A Chinese-American Daughter," from "Story of a Chinese Girl Student," in Orientals and Their Cultural Adjustment, Social Science Institution, Fisk University, Nashville, Tennessee, 1946, pp. 14–22.

Part Four

"A Sweatshop Girl: Sadie Frowne," from "The Life Story of a Polish Sweatshop Girl," Hamilton Holt (ed.), The Life Stories of Undistinguished Americans, as Told by Themselves (New York: James Pott and Co., 1906), pp. 34–46.

"Dear Editor: Letters from Jewish America — Problems and Advice," from Isaac Metzker (ed.), A Bintel Brief: Sixty Years of Letters from the Lower East Side to the Jewish Daily Forward (Garden City, N.Y.: Doubleday and Company, 1971), pp. 68–70, 81–83, 129–31, 153–55, 158–61, 173–75, 189–90.

"A Birthright Denied: Monica Sone," from Monica Sone, Nisei Daughter (Boston: Little, Brown and Company, 1953), pp. 158, 166–78.

"A Birthright Renounced: Joseph Kurihara," from Joseph Kurihara, autobiography, typescript, in Japanese Evacuation and Relocation Study, call number: 67/14c, box no. A17.05, pp. 1–52, Bancroft Library, University of California, Berkeley.

"The Indian Hero of Iwo Jima: Letters from Ira Hayes," from William Bradford Huie, The Hero of Iwo Jima and Other Stories (New York: Signet, New American Library, 1959), excerpts from 14–18, 24–25, 30, 37–38, 40, 42, 44–45, 55–56.

"Bilingual Education in Polonia," from a Polish immigrant woman's story, Immigration History Research Center, University of Minnesota.

"A Stepchild of America: Thomas Napierkowski," from Thomas Napierkowski, "Stepchild of America: Growing Up Polish," in Michael Novak

Sources

(ed.), *Growing Up Slavic in America* (Bayville, N.Y.: EMPAC Publication, 1976, pp. 9–20.

"Searching for a Door to America: Jesús Garza," from Manuel Gamio (ed.), *The Mexican Immigrant: His Life Story* (Chicago: Univ. of Chicago Press, 1931), pp. 14–21.

"A Song of El Norte: Camelia Palafox," by Jose Palafox, University of California, Berkeley, 1997.

"Twice a Minority: María Jiménez Joins the Army," from Marilyn P. Davis, *Mexican Dreams/American Dreams: An Oral History of Mexican Immigration to the United States* (New York: Henry Holt and Company, 1990), pp. 354–60.

"Growing Up Between Two Worlds: Joanna Dorio," from Corinne Azen Krause, *Grandmothers, Mothers, and Daughters: Oral Histories of Three Generations of Ethnic American Women* (Boston: Twayne, 1991), pp. 33–40.

"Reinventing Herself in America: Shanti," by Gaurav Kalra, University of California, Berkeley, 1997.

"Growing up Puerto Rican in New York: Maria Diaz," in Dean Morse (ed.), *Pride Against Prejudice: Work in the Lives of Older Black and Young Puerto Rican Workers* (New York: U.S. Dept. of Labor, 1980), pp. 191–215.

"'Not Going to Let the Riots Beat Me': Sun Soon Kim," by Samantha M. Lee, University of California, Berkeley, 1997.

"The 'Disappearance' of Work: Hard Times for Jimmy Morse," from Leslie W. Dunbar, *The Common Interest: How Our Social-Welfare Policies Don't Work, and What We Can Do About Them* (New York: Pantheon, 1988), pp. 90–94.

"A Chance to Act Affirmatively: Bryan K. Fair," from Bryan K. Fair, *Notes of a Racial Caste Baby: Color Blindness and the End of Affirmative Action* (New York: New York University Press, 1997), pp. xv–xvii, 47–60.

An Additional Memory:
Acknowledgments

MEMORY ALSO helps us to be grateful. Caroline Kieu Lihn Valverde, my research assistant, searched the Internet for the bibliography and also photocopied thousands of pages of documents. Kent Haldan helped me find the Joseph Kurihara papers in the Bancroft Library. José Palafox, Samantha M. Lee, and Gaurav Kalra as well as other students in Ethnic Studies 195 and Asian American Studies 120 enthusiastically joined me in the pursuit of "democratic history." Helen Lara Cea and Jason Ferreira generously gave bibliographical assistance. David Ford helped me re-read Mary Rowlandson and shared his discovery of her subversive subtext. Jennifer Josephy, the editor of all of my Little, Brown books, gave me timely encouragement to continue with the project. Her thoughtful editorial criticisms opened the way to important rethinkings. Rick Balkin was more than my agent: he was also a blunt and honest critic of my drafts. My neighbor and intellectual friend Debby Rogin gave me something to consider that helped me to refocus the beginning of this book. For the draft for Part One, my colleague of thirty-one years, Larry Friedman, engaged me in a useful discussion on the formation of ethnic multiplicity. Through her demanding editing, Carol Takaki gave my essays greater coherence and clarity. More important, our lively discussions and sometimes intense debates deepened our understanding of our national "proposition," to use Lincoln's language, as a powerful tie binding us together in "a larger memory."

About the Author

Ronald Takaki is professor of Ethnic Studies at the University of California, Berkeley, where he has been teaching for over two decades. The grandson of Japanese immigrant plantation laborers in Hawaii, he has a Ph.D. in American history from Berkeley. The Berkeley faculty has honored Takaki with a Distinguished Teaching Award, and the Society of American Historians has elected him to be a fellow. He designed and then directed Berkeley's Ethnic Studies Ph.D. Program, the first of its kind in the nation. He was instrumental in the institution of Berkeley's American Cultures graduation requirement for understanding our society's racial and ethnic diversity. Takaki has lectured in Japan, Russia, Armenia, and South Africa. Takaki's approach in his scholarship is truly comparative and multicultural. His *Iron Cages: Race and Culture in Nineteenth-Century America* has been critically acclaimed, and his prizewinning *A Different Mirror: A History of Multicultural America* has been hailed by *Publishers Weekly* as "a brilliant revisionist history of America that is likely to become a classic of multicultural studies."

CPSIA information can be obtained at www.ICGtesting.com
Printed in the USA
BVOW010135110912

300125BV00002B/2/A

9 780316 831697